PUNISHMENT
AND REHABILITATION

Basic Problems in Philosophy Series

A. I. Melden and Stanley Munsat
University of California, Irvine
General Editors

The Problem of Abortion
Joel Feinberg, Rockefeller University

Ethical Relativism
John Ladd, Brown University

Human Rights
A. I. Melden

Egoism and Altruism
Ronald D. Milo, University of Arizona

Guilt and Shame
Herbert Morris, University of California, Los Angeles

The Analytic-Synthetic Distinction
Stanley Munsat

Civil Disobedience and Violence
Jeffrie G. Murphy, University of Arizona

Punishment and Rehabilitation
Jeffrie G. Murphy

Immortality
Terence Penelhum, University of Calgary

Morality and the Law
Richard A. Wasserstrom, University of California, Los Angeles

War and Morality
Richard A. Wasserstrom

PUNISHMENT AND REHABILITATION

edited by

JEFFRIE G. MURPHY

University of Arizona

Wadsworth Publishing Company, Inc.
Belmont, California

Design: Gary A. Head

Cover: Russ K. Leong

Production supervised by: Beverly A. Johnson

ISBN 0-534-00335-4

L. C. Cat. Card No. 73-83718

Printed in the United States of America

    3 4 5 6 7 8 9 10—77 76 75 74

To keep the price of this book as low as possible, we have
used an economical means of typesetting. We welcome your
comments.

Series Foreword

The Basic Problems in Philosophy Series is designed to meet the need of students and teachers of philosophy, mainly but not exclusively at the undergraduate level, for collections of essays devoted to some fairly specific philosophical problems.

In recent years there have been numerous paperback collections on a variety of philosophical topics. Those teachers who wish to refer their students to a set of essays on a specific philosophical problem have usually been frustrated, however, since most of these collections range over a wide set of issues and problems. The present series attempts to remedy this situation by presenting together, within each volume, key writings on a single philosophical issue.

Given the magnitude of the literature, there can be no thought of completeness. Rather, the materials included are those that, in the judgment of the editor, must be mastered first by the student who wishes to acquaint himself with relevant issues and their ramifications. To this end, historical as well as contemporary writings are included.

Each volume in the series contains an introduction by the editor to set the stage for the arguments contained in the essays and a bibliography to help the student who wishes to pursue the topic at a more advanced level.

A. I. Melden
S. Munsat

Contents

Introduction

The topic of punishment fascinates men, learned and un-
learned alike, to a degree that is rare for any topic that
may even in part be called "philosophical." The fiction of
crime and punishment, whether that of Dostoevski or Collins
or Agatha Christie, is perennially popular; and public debate on punitive topics (e.g., the legalization of mariju-
na, the abolition of the death penalty, preventive detention, etc.) is closely followed by the media. Important
and far-reaching developments in tax and real estate law
stimulate no comparable popular interest—this in spite of
the fact that most of us pay taxes and own or rent homes
and comparatively few of us will ever experience a serious
threat of criminal punishment, much less the actual infliction of such punishment.
  The intense interest, then, is perhaps perplexing, and
many fanciful explanations for it have been given. Some
psychiatrists say that our fascination with punishment is a
vicarious satisfaction of certain unconscious mental states
—e.g., the desire to inflict punishment (or at least hurt)
on others or the fear that we ourselves may come to suffer
a kind of punishment. Philosophers of an existentialist
persuasion may claim that we see (and envy) the criminal as
a paradigm of a completely free person—autonomous from the
chains of social obligation. Others who are inclined to be
somewhat more flattering to human nature may explain our
interest in punishment on conscious grounds that are perfectly rational: the prudential fear that we may become victims of crime and the moral desire to reduce suffering and
injustice in the world by means that do not themselves contribute unnecessarily to suffering and injustice. And theo-
logians see, in punishment, an earthly example of the cosmic drama of sin and redemption.

1

No doubt there is some truth in all of these claims—
at least as explanations of why crime and punishment capture the popular imagination. But a different question is
why the topic captures the *philosophical* imagination. Why
has this topic, unlike other popular issues (e.g., sex),
produced a genuinely astounding volume of writings from
philosophers at least from the time of Plato on down
through articles in the most recent philosophical journals?
I think that there are several explanations for this; and
it is worth mentioning them at the outset. I shall focus
on six that are, though related, reasonably distinct.

1. *The Intersection of Law and Morals*. In the criminal law, we find a body of evolved and codified thought directed toward issues at the heart of morality—excuse and
justification, responsibility, duty and obligation, good
and evil, right and wrong. As a result, frequently a study
of the legal use of a certain concept, *excuse*, say, will illuminate the moral use of that concept. Such a study of a
legal concept is never final in moral analysis and it does
not always even illuminate. But it sometimes does; and
moral philosophers need all the help they can get, from
whatever quarter.
     Just as a study of the law can sometimes illuminate
moral thinking, so too can moral thinking illuminate legal
matters. How, for example, is anyone ever to come to terms
with constitutional concepts like "cruel and unusual punishment" or "due process of law" without an ability to think,
in morally sophisticated ways, about the nature of suffering and injustice? And of course it goes without saying
that all existing systems of criminal law are at numerous
points vulnerable to a variety of moral criticisms. A moral man cares about what happens to people (what they are
stopped from doing, when they are hurt, etc.) and the criminal law is an example of an institution which functions by
directly making things happen to people—for better or for
worse. The moral man wants it to be for better.

2. *The Moral Centrality of the Topic of Punishment*.
The concept of punishment stands at the core of moral thinking; and, as a result, its analysis necessarily affects
(and in turn is affected by) a great many other moral concepts: blame, praise, reward, responsibility, mercy, forgiveness, justice, charity, obligation, and rights—just to
name some. Also its analysis affects, and is affected by,
the analysis of what might be called the *moral feelings*:

resentment, indignation, remorse, guilt, shame, for example. It is not a topic that one can discuss without making clear one's commitments on most of the other major issues of moral philosophy. And, in turn, one's major moral commitments will entail consequences for one's attitude toward punishment—witness the division, in the theory of punishment, between utilitarians (with their moral stress on the avoidance of suffering) and Kantians (with their moral stress on the avoidance of injustice). I am not sure that there is any topic in moral philosophy that does not ramify in this way. Punishment, however, is a very clear and dramatic example of one that does.

   3. *Metaphysical Involvement.* Another reason why the topic of punishment, and the family of moral concepts surrounding it, are of philosophical interest is their obvious involvement with issues of metaphysics. For it is impossible to discuss, for example, the nature of a just system of responsibility and excuse without coming to terms with the mind-body problem, the problem of free will and determinism, and issues in the analysis of human action. It is also very difficult to generate and make exciting certain metaphysical issues (free will and determinism is a good example here) without noting the moral and legal perplexities from which these issues tend to grow. In examining what men think about punishment one also learns what they think about the nature of persons—what it is to be a person and what sort of status a person is to enjoy. From *Oedipus Rex* we learn, not just the Greek view on punishment, but also and necessarily something of their view on human beings and their place in the universe.

   4. *Political Philosophy.* It could be persuasively argued that the central problem of political philosophy is in coming to terms with the nature and justification of coercion. Punishment is state coercion in its most obvious (and perhaps most brutal) form. And thus any political philosophy which addresses itself to the core of its discipline must come to terms with the issue of punishment in order either to praise it with Kant and Hegel, tolerate it with Bentham and Mill, or oppose it with Marx and Kropotkin. It is not to be avoided.

   5. *Philosophy and Empirical Science.* Another exciting aspect of the topic of punishment is the way in which,

unlike a great many topics in philosophy, it intersects and is relevant to discoveries in empirical science. Philosophical theories are not themselves empirical; and philosophers are not in general occupationally qualified to assess the confirmation of empirical claims. Philosophical theories can, however, presuppose certain empirical claims for their truth or intelligibility. Thus philosophers cannot always safely ignore empirical work, since such work may undercut the presuppositions of their own theories. They have an obligation, therefore, to keep themselves informed of relevant work in the scientific community.

Theories of punishment represent a clear example of philosophical theories with empirical presuppositions. The utilitarian deterrence theory, for example, presupposes that men rationally calculate consequences before engaging in crime. One who seeks to evaluate this theory cannot simply ignore the claim often made by psychiatrists that criminality is rarely deliberative but is usually impulsive. And could the retributive theory of punishment, with its stress on doing the just thing, remain intact if the Marxist analysis of criminality as growing out of poverty and unjust exploitation were accepted as true? Philosophy here has something to learn from science.

But science has something to learn from philosophy as well. Psychiatrists and social scientists are frequently arguing for reform in the criminal law, even the abandonment of punishment entirely, on grounds that lie outside their scientific competence—e.g., B. F. Skinner's claim that the concepts of autonomy, dignity, and responsibility have been refuted by science, or Karl Menninger's claim that justice is unscientific. The philosopher has an important job in pointing out these confusions, in making sure that empirical scientists are accepted as authorities only on claims that are empirical and not on their amateur philosophical speculations.

6. *Practical Urgency*. Here the philosophical and the popular interest intersect. Many philosophers want their work to be socially useful, and the issues of punishment and responsibility seem to provide an area in which philosophical work can have practical social utility. Everybody wants to do something about the criminal law. Law and order hard-liners want to make it even more terrifying. Some want to eliminate it for a variety of reasons all the way from the Christian's "we are all guilty" to the psychiatrist's "nobody is guilty." The most interesting new challenge comes from behavioral science. From all sides we are

bombarded with a variety of scientific challenges to criminal responsibility: criminals are mentally ill; criminals
suffer from brain pathology; criminals have chromosome abnormalities; criminals are labeled deviants for certain social purposes; criminals are simply people who need their
patterns of reinforcement changed. Very often these claims
are coupled with the claims that determinism has at last
been established; that the concepts of responsibility, freedom, and dignity have been shown to be superstitions; and
that we can at last move away from punishment into a land
of benevolent scientific therapy where deviants will simply
be rewired or programmed in order to make them socially acceptable.

The present anthology is addressed to this issue of
practical urgency—an urgency underlined by the obvious
fact that no sensible person could wholly approve of the
present practices of criminal punishment that exist in our
society. As recent prison riots have brought to light,
most American prisons are inhuman pestholes that breed
crime rather than reduce it. Animal brutalities from
guards and fellow-prisoners (e.g., homosexual rapes) are
the order of the day. Young persons, guilty perhaps of
nothing more serious than marijuana possession, may be
placed into a context where they are brutalized before they
return to society—alienated and become expert in sophisticated criminal techniques they have learned from older
fellow-prisoners. Only the extremely shortsighted could
advocate more of the same as a solution to the growing problem of crime in our society; but alas, as usual, there is
no poverty of shortsighted people in positions of influence
and power.

For this reason, books like Dr. Karl Menninger's widely read *The Crime of Punishment* (New York, 1968)—a brief
preliminary study for which is contained in this collection
—are in many ways welcome contributions to the "law and
order" debate in American society. Menninger, an eminent
psychiatrist, dramatically points up the failures and in-
humanities of our present penal practices and persuasively
advocates drastic reform. And for this much, all reasonable and decent men should surely be grateful to him. However, he goes beyond such negative criticism and advocates
an alternative method of handling the crime problem; and
his alternative method is, to say the very least, highly
controversial.

Like a great many psychiatrists and social scientists,
Menninger tends to regard criminal behavior as symptomatic
of personality disorder. Thus he proposes that we drop
our present practice of punishing criminals in prisons and

indeed that we drop the whole complex business of the criminal law and criminal procedure. In his view, this wastes
time and money, is inhuman, and fails to perform the important task of eliminating crime; for punishment, he claims,
neither deters nor reforms men. Retribution, the only other possible justification left, can be rejected since it
rests, according to Menninger, on an outdated and unscientific conception of personal responsibility or free will.

Since criminal behavior is really a kind of sickness,
then, we should respond to such behavior therapeutically.
Criminal behavior is to be *cured*, not punished. Instead of
perpetuating the inhuman practice of confining people in
prisons, we should treat and rehabilitate them in hospitals.
When necessary, for their own good and ours, we may even
employ preventive and indefinite detention. Since this
confinement will be for therapy, and not for punishment, it
will not be objectionable but will rather be a benefit to
all concerned.

The above sounds wonderful, but it may be too good to
be true. We should certainly humanize our present penal
institutions and provide greatly increased opportunities
for at least voluntary therapy. But should we abandon the
criminal process entirely? Would it genuinely benefit even
the criminal if we did so? At least in the criminal law a
prisoner has some procedural protections contained in our
Bill of Rights. But there is no therapeutic bill of rights
—e.g., no developed concept of "cruel and unusual *therapy*"
which might be used to block such things as electric shocks,
lobotomies and more sophisticated forms of psychosurgery,
and certain drugs. Defective as the criminal process is,
would it be obviously better to move toward what Nicholas
Kittrie has called the "therapeutic state" in which psychiatrists have increased political power and discretionary
control over the lives of citizens? (This has happened in
Soviet Russia, and the increasing number of political dissi-
dents there classified as "mentally ill" is disquieting.)
Several of the essays in this collection—including my own
—build a case for being skeptical about therapy as a comprehensive response to crime. Attica was a disgrace to
America, certainly, but it would have been no less a disgrace had it been called a hospital rather than a prison.

The readings begin with a legal case: *People v. Levy*.
In this case, Levy (a "sexual psychopath") is told that his
appeal against indefinite confinement in San Quentin is
"without merit" since he is there, not to be punished, but
to be cured and as a protective measure for society. This
case should allow the reader to appreciate, in a dramatic

way, the practical importance of the issue.[1] If he imag-
ines himself in the position of Levy, he will perhaps be
able to see that a therapeutic outlook, where loss of liberty is involved, is at least not an unmixed blessing.

In the first essay, Stanley I. Benn provides a comprehensive overview of punishment as a philosophical problem.
He analyzes the concept of punishment, discusses various
classical theories of its justification, considers questions of personal responsibility for conduct, and closes
with a brief examination of a therapeutic response to crime.
This essay can best be viewed as providing a general introduction to the readings that follow.

The next five selections are concerned with the justification of punishment. The selection from Kant is a classical defense of a *retributive* theory. According to this
theory, punishment is justified primarily by backward-
looking considerations—i.e., the criminal, having engaged
in wrongful conduct in the past, *deserves* his punishment.
It would be unjust for him not to receive it. In receiving
it, he pays a kind of *debt* to his fellow citizens—to those
other members of the community who, unlike him, have made
the sacrifice of obedience that is required for any just
legal system to work. Since all men benefit from the operation of a just legal system, and since such systems require general obedience to work, it is only fair or just
that each man so benefiting make the sacrifice (obedience
or self-restraint) required and thereby do his part.[2]
Those who do not must pay in some other way (receive punishment) because it would not be fair to those who have been
obedient if the criminal were allowed to profit from his

---

[1] It should also let the reader appreciate how easy (and
dangerous) it is to be led astray from an important moral
issue by a mere change in terminology. Involuntary therapy, even if not called "punishment," is *prima facie* objectionable for the same reason punishment is—namely, it is
coercive.

[2] This theory has been elaborated by John Rawls in his
"Legal Obligation and the Duty of Fair Play," in *Law and
Philosophy*, edited by Sidney Hook (New York: New York Uni-
versity Press, 1964). It has been reprinted in my *Civil
Disobedience and Violence* (Belmont: Wadsworth, 1971). For
further discussion of Kant's theory of punishment, see my
Kant: The Philosophy of Right (London: Macmillan, 1970),
and my "Three Mistakes about Retributivism," *Analysis*,
April, 1971.

own wrongdoing. (In this view a certain kind of "profit"—not bearing the burden of self-restraint—is intrinsic to criminal wrongdoing.) Hegel, who elaborated this Kantian retributive theory, argued that the criminal, who as a rational man could see that even he derived benefits from participation in a community of law, could be regarded as *rationally willing* (though not empirically desiring) his own punishment. This being so, he deserves it in the sense that he has a *right* to it. Though the claim that a criminal has a right to be punished seems initially counterintuitive, Herbert Morris in his article attempts to show that the claim contains an important moral insight.

Bentham, in his classic statement of the *utilitarian* theory of punishment, predicates his entire discussion upon the assumption that the retributive theory outlined above is nothing but a combination of obscurantist nonsense and primitive vindictiveness. Punishment, he argues, is to be justified solely by an appeal to forward-looking considerations. The only important questions are the following: Will punishing this man bring about more good than bad consequences for society as a whole? That is, will it deter, incapacitate, or reform? If so, will this result in benefits sufficient to outweigh the misery that punishment will cause? If the answer is *no*, then we should not punish even if, in some obscure sense, the criminal "deserves" it; for this would be productive of no useful consequences. And, in a utilitarian view, consequences are all that matter in morality.[3] But what if the man is *innocent*—i.e., clearly does *not* deserve punishment? It might still produce good consequences if we did punish him, make a scapegoat of him for example to others. That this could be the case is surely a contingent possibility. And yet it seems clearly wrong (unjust) to punish such a man, no matter how good the consequences, and so there may be some virtue in the

---

[3]The move toward a therapeutic response to crime can be seen as, at least in part, an outgrowth of a utilitarian outlook. If one is going to evaluate punishment solely in terms of its social consequences—e.g., its capacity to reduce crime—one might quite reasonably reach the conclusion that therapy would do a better job of bringing these consequences about. Even a retributivist, however, could become sympathetic to a therapeutic approach to crime if he became convinced that criminals were so mentally abnormal that they could not fairly be held responsible. A person with such a belief about criminals would find it difficult to regard them as fully *deserving* their punishment.

retributivist's insistence on desert after all. John Rawls,
in his essay, tries to combine the best features of both a
retributive and a utilitarian outlook—formulating the utilitarian theory so that punishment of the innocent will not
be allowed.

The readings on the justification of punishment conclude with a brief essay by Karl Marx. In the spirit of
Kant, Marx criticizes utilitarian theories because they are
willing to use persons as mere means to the social good.
But by what right, Marx asks, does society punish me for
the deterrence of someone else?[4] (And besides, he suggests,
punishment does not do a very good job of deterring anyway.)
His objection to the Kantian-Hegelian retributive theory,
however, is more complex. This theory, he suggests, is
formally correct. That is, the theory does take human dignity and autonomy into account in the abstract and thus
would be applicable within a properly designed society.
However, to think that it applies to the present state of
society (i.e., a society, in Marx's judgment, where corrupt economic institutions generate unjustified laws, allow
crime-breeding poverty, and encourage all men to be egois-
tic and competitive) is merely to provide a philosophical
halo for the *status quo*. As usual, Marx properly puts us
on our guard to refrain from embracing theories, thinking
they have application, only because we uncritically accept
a variety of false beliefs about the world in which we live
—e.g., the belief that individuals are responsible for crime. On Marx's view, a fundamental change in the social and economic fabric of society
would be required before we could in practice be justified
in punishing even the guilty. And given the proper changes
(e.g., the elimination of poverty and institutions which
encourage selfishness and greed), the very need to punish
might disappear or at least be radically reduced.[5]

---

[4]When put into the broader context of political philosophy,
the justification of punishment is just one instance of
what may be regarded as the basic problem of political philosophy—the problem of *coercion*. What, if anything, gives
the state the right or authority to coerce its citizens?

[5]The most sustained treatment of crime and punishment by a
Marxist is Willem Bonger's *Criminality and Economic Conditions* (Bloomington: Indiana University Press, 1969; an
abridgment of the original 1916 edition). For a more comprehensive and balanced inquiry into the origin of criminality (but one that is not totally out of sympathy with
the Marxist approach), see Edwin M. Schur's *Our Criminal*

The criminal process, of course, involves more than the infliction of punishment. Central to it are also such issues as police practices, the nature of litigation and plea bargaining, rules of admissible evidence, the role of counsel, the nature of a fair trial or hearing, and many more. In his essay, Herbert Packer identifies two competing evaluative emphases or "models" whereby the entire criminal process may be viewed. The "due process model" focuses upon and regards as central the protection of the rights and liberties of the individual in his dealings with the law—e.g., is concerned to protect him against unreasonable search and seizure, self-incrimination, police brutality, and the like. The "crime control model" focuses upon and regards as central the protection of the public against crime. Without too much distortion, we can say that the Warren Court was largely an advocate of the due process model and that the Department of Justice, under President Nixon, is an advocate of the crime control model. No sane man could accept either model to the total exclusion of the other, of course, and so the issue here is one of emphasis. The move toward therapeutic rehabilitation as a total response to crime can, in many ways, be regarded as a humanized outgrowth of the crime control model. The main difficulties with this move, then, are its tendencies to conflict with the due process model. To use a simple example: It is by no means clear that an efficient system of therapeutic crime control is consistent with such due process guarantees as a right to counsel in an adversary legal proceeding or with a right against self-incrimination.

The above readings, then, all provide a general background for a consideration of the specific issue of punishment versus therapeutic rehabilitation as a total response to crime.[6] The articles by Benjamin Karpman, Karl Menning-

---

[5](cont.) *Society: The Social and Legal Sources of Crime in America* (Englewood Cliffs, N.J.: Prentice-Hall, 1969). Samuel Jordan, a prison inmate in Pennsylvania, has provided an interesting Marxist analysis of prison reform in his "Prison Reform: In Whose Interest?," *Criminal Law Bulletin*, November, 1971. See also my "Marxism and Retribution," *Philosophy & Public Affairs*, Spring, 1973.

[6]It is important to remember that the issue around which this collection is based is that of therapy as a *total* response to crime, replacing entirely the criminal process. Those opposing this are not necessarily committed to being opposed to therapy as a partial alternative in some cases (e.g., cases where the person to be treated requests or

er, B. F. Skinner, and Barbara Wootton all seek alternatives to punishment from a variety of viewpoints. Karpman,
a psychiatrist, presents a strong statement of the view
that "criminality is but a symptom of insanity" and should
be treated accordingly. Menninger, as discussed earlier, advocates therapy rather than punishment as a "more scientific" response to crime. Skinner, a behavioral psychologist,
argues that our response to punishment should be purely empirical—i.e., does it work as a conditioning technique?
He is doubtful of its efficacy (in part because it rests on
what is, in his judgment, an outdated and unscientific concept of responsibility) and advocates a search for alternatives. Wootton, a sociologist and lay magistrate in England, advocates a strict liability system of criminal law.
Courts will not be allowed to consider such issues as a
man's motives, intentions (*mens rea*), or sanity. They
shall determine only if the defendant engaged in the behavior he is charged with having engaged in. If he did, then
he will be turned over to a team of psychiatrists and sociologists (who *may* at this point consider motives, intentions, and sanity) to determine the length and kind of
treatment he shall receive. The goals of such a determination are the prevention of crime and his own reform as a
means to the prevention of crime.

These essays are followed by four which attempt to
mount a case against therapeutic rehabilitation as a total
response to crime—again from a variety of perspectives.
Francis Allen's piece is an early and very influential
statement by an eminent lawyer. Thomas Szasz, a psychiatrist, maintains that the rehabilitative ideal is politically dangerous (potentially totalitarian) because the notion of "mental illness" on which it rests is an expression
of evaluative preference (moral, political, ideological)
and is not, as its defenders try to make it appear, a value-
free scientific or medical term. His objections are thus
substantive. In my own two brief essays I present, in addition to substantive objections, certain *procedural* objections to a therapeutic outlook on crime. I suggest that it
invites such practices as preventive and indefinite detention and is difficult (perhaps impossible) to square with

---

[6](cont.) freely consents to the treatment). Those who oppose replacing the criminal process with a system of therapeutic rehabilitation, therefore, should not be thought of
as necessarily being a part of some ignorant crusade against
psychiatry or mental health *simpliciter*. To oppose psychiatric *coercion* is not necessarily to oppose all psychiatry.

a protection of individual liberty and due process. I
also stress the heterogeneous character of all the different
kinds of behavior labeled "criminal" and how this fact
should make us suspicious of theories which attempt to explain all in terms of one common cause.

The collection closes with an essay by Joel Feinberg,
who attempts to defend the ideal of therapeutic rehabilitation against the kinds of objections raised above.

What is the explanation of crime? Does it flow, as
many traditionalists would say, from the free and responsible decisions of wicked men? Is it, as many psychiatrists
would say, a kind of mental illness? Or is it perhaps, as
many Marxist and non-Marxist sociologists would say, a
product of defective socioeconomic institutions, institutions which are themselves so "criminal" that those who
have power in them lack the moral right to demand either
therapy or punishment for those who act against the rules?
Perhaps the correct answer is some combination of all the
above. And this possibility alone should make us quite
wary of any simple and neat solutions to the problem of how
we should deal with criminal behavior. Simple solutions on
this question are almost certain to be simpleminded. If
the essays in this volume help the reader to appreciate the
complexities of these issues and to become more cautious
and thoughtful about them, then the collection will have
been a success.

One final personal note: I have profited greatly from
conversations and correspondence with many people on the
issues of punishment and rehabilitation. In particular I
acknowledge a debt to Herbert Morris, Professor of Philosophy and Law at U.C.L.A., for opening up new philosophical
perspectives on punishment for me that I otherwise would
have missed, and to David Wexler, Professor of Law at the
University of Arizona, from whom I have learned a great
deal.

Jeffrie G. Murphy

PEOPLE v. LEVY

California District Court of Appeals, 1957
151 Cal. App. 2d 460, 311 P. 2d 897

Peters, P.J.—The superior court, pursuant to the
terms of the Sexual Psychopath Act (Welf. & Inst. Code,
§§5500–5521) found Levy to be a sexual psychopath who would
not benefit from further hospitalization and was a menace
to the health and safety of others, and committed him for
an indeterminate period to the Department of Mental Hygiene
for placement for treatment as a sexual psychopath at San
Quentin. Levy appeals, admitting that the lower courts
complied precisely with the provisions of the relevant statutes, but contends that the act is substantially criminal
in nature and is unconstitutional as applied to him. What
appellant really seeks is a reappraisal by this court of
the essential nature of the Sexual Psychopath Act and a reversal of a line of Supreme and appellate court decisions
holding that the act is essentially civil in nature.

The background of this controversy is somewhat complex.
In July of 1954 appellant was charged with the misdemeanor
of annoying and molesting a child under the age of 18 in
violation of section 647a, subdivision (1), of the Penal
Code. He pleaded guilty in the municipal court. He had at
least one prior misdemeanor sex conviction. After a probation hearing, the municipal court adjourned the criminal
proceeding and certified appellant to the superior court,
as provided in section 5501 of the Welfare and Institutions
Code. As provided in the act, the superior court appointed
two psychiatrists to examine appellant. They reported that
he was an alleged sexual psychopath. Pursuant to section
5512 of the Welfare and Institutions Code the court found
appellant to be an alleged sexual psychopath and committed
him to the Mendocino State Hospital for a 90-day observation period. Within the time limited the medical director
at Mendocino reported to the court that after appellant had
been given physical and psychiatric examinations, and kept
under observation, his condition was diagnosed as a case of
"Sociopathic Personality Disturbance, Sexual Deviation
(Homo-sexuality and Pedophilia)." The medical director at
Mendocino also opined that appellant was a sexual-psycho-
path as defined in the statute, was a menace to the health

and safety of others, and would not benefit by treatment in
a state hospital. The report observed that appellant had a
long record of antisocial behavior and was a confirmed homosexual with a predisposition toward child molestation. Appellant was returned to the superior court, and that court
on October 29, 1954, after a hearing, found appellant to be
a sexual psychopath who would not benefit from care or
treatment and remanded him to the municipal court for further proceedings.

In November of 1954 the municipal court, by stipulation
of all concerned, again certified appellant to the superior
court for a hearing to determine whether he was a sexual
psychopath. On November 19, 1954, the superior court, on
the basis of the previous report of the medical director of
Mendocino, again found that appellant was a sexual psychopath, and this time ordered him committed for an indeterminate period to the Department of Mental Hygiene for placement in the Atascadero State Hospital. (Welf. & Inst. Code,
§5518.)

Some 17 months later, in April of 1956, the medical
director at Atascadero diagnosed appellant's condition as
being the same as the diagnosis at Mendocino. He certified
that appellant had not recovered from his psychopathy and
opined that appellant was still a menace to the health and
safety of others. Pursuant to section 5517(c) of the Welfare and Institutions Code he recommended that appellant
"be recommitted to the Department of Mental Hygiene for
placement in an institutional unit for the treatment of
sexual psychopaths in a facility (California State Prison
at San Quentin) of the Department of Corrections." The superior court referred the case to its probation department,
another hearing was had, and on May 11, 1956, appellant was
again found to be a sexual psychopath and a menace to others, and the case was again remanded to the municipal court
for further proceedings as provided in section 5518 of the
Welfare and Institutions Code. The municipal court, after
considering a supplementary probation report, promptly (May
16, 1956) recertified appellant to the superior court.
Shortly thereafter that court, for the fourth time, determined that appellant was a sexual psychopath, concluded
that he would not be benefited by further hospitalization,
found that he was still a menace to the health and safety
of others and that he was predisposed to the commission of
sexual offenses, and committed him "for an indeterminate
period to the Department of Mental Hygiene, for placement
in an Institutional Unit for the treatment of Sexual Psychopaths in a facility of the Department of Corrections, namely: The California State Prison at San Quentin." It is

from this order that this appeal is taken. It should be
mentioned that appellant was represented by counsel during
most of these proceedings.

The first major contention of appellant is that the
act, as applied to a person first convicted of a misdemean-
or and certified to the superior court as a probable sexual
psychopath, and then committed by that court to San Quentin
for an indeterminate period, is unconstitutional for the
reason that it subjects the accused to double jeopardy in
violation of section 13, article I of the California Constitution. This argument is unsound if the proceeding under
the act is essentially civil in nature, because the double
jeopardy clause, of course, is applicable only to two successive criminal proceedings for the same offense.

This is no longer an open question in this state. The
courts, whenever presented with this problem, have held the
act to be civil in nature. . . . In People v. McCracken, 39
Cal. 2d 336, 346 [246 P. 2d 913], it was pointed out that
"It is obvious therefore that the primary purpose of the
Legislature was to protect society against the activities
of sexual psychopaths . . . , and that it was not intended
to make sexual psychopathy a mitigating circumstance. On
the contrary, the sexual psychopath may be removed from society under the Sexual Psychopath Law until he is cured or
until he is no longer considered a menace to the safety of
others. The court may thereafter resume the criminal proceeding and impose the punishment allowed by law since the
confinement as a sexual psychopath is not a substitute for
punishment, the entire statutory procedure being civil in
nature rather than penal." [Review of other cases omitted.]

In the face of these authorities appellant nevertheless argues that although the act may have originally been
conceived by the Legislature as a civil proceeding it has
gradually developed into a criminal proceeding. This argument is predicated upon the fact that some procedural safeguards commonly existing in criminal cases also exist in
cases under the sexual psychopath act. Thus, the person involved is entitled to bail pending determination of his
status; he is entitled to be present at the hearing; if he
has no counsel the court may appoint one for him or order
the public defender to serve; his liberty is, of course, at
stake; and he is entitled to a state paid transcript on appeal. . . . Certainly, if, as appellant admits, the act was
originally civil in substance, the addition of procedural
safeguards which are ordinarily incidental to criminal proceedings could not ordinarily convert the proceeding from a
civil one to a criminal one. It is the substantive effect
of the act and not its procedural aspects that controls its

character.   The above cases all hold that the act is not punitive in character, but civil in nature.   That is the decisive point so far as the contention that jeopardy attaches is concerned.

Of course, even though the act is civil in nature it does involve a deprivation of personal liberty, and so is necessarily subject to constitutional safeguards.   Based on this premise appellant argues that the definition of "sexual psychopath" in section 5500 of the Welfare and Institutions Code as applied to a person originally convicted of a misdemeanor is so vague, uncertain, arbitrary and unreasonable that it violates the due process clauses of the state and federal Constitutions.   That section provides:

"As used in this chapter, 'sexual psychopath' means any person who is affected, in a form predisposing to the commission of sexual offenses, and in a degree constituting him a menace to the health or safety of others, with any of the following conditions:

"(a) Mental disease or disorder.

"(b) Psychopathic personality.

"(c) Marked departures from normal mentality."

The difficulty with this argument is that the courts have already directly or indirectly held that the act does not violate the equal protection and due process clauses. . . .

Before the statute can be properly interpreted its purpose and intent must be ascertained.   In People v. McCracken, 39 Cal. 2d 336, 345 [246 P. 2d 913], the Supreme Court stated: "The sexual psychopath law was passed by the Legislature because experience had shown that persons who came within the classification of sexual psychopaths were unable to benefit from ordinary penal confinement and were in need of medical treatment. . . . The Legislature therefore gave the courts power to commit a person determined to be a sexual psychopath to a medical facility for an indeterminate period of time until the person had been cured or was unable to benefit from further treatment. . . .

". . . It is obvious therefore that the primary purpose of the Legislature was to protect society against the activities of sexual psychopaths."

The United States Supreme Court in Minnesota ex rel. Pearson v. Probate Court, 309 U.S. 270, has already passed on the constitutional questions here involved.   There the Minnesota statute defined (p. 272) "psychopathic personality" as "the existence in any person of such conditions of emotional instability, or impulsiveness of behavior, or lack of customary standards of good judgment, or failure to appreciate the consequences of his acts, or a combination of any such conditions, as to render such person irresponsible for his conduct with respect to sexual matters and thereby dangerous to other persons."

The state court construed this provision as including (p. 273) "those persons who, by an habitual course of misconduct in sexual matters, have evidenced an utter lack of power to control their sexual impulses and who, as a result, are likely to attack or otherwise inflict injury, loss, pain or other evil on the objects of their uncontrolled and uncontrollable desire. It would not be reasonable to apply the provisions of the statute to every person guilty of sexual misconduct nor even to persons having strong sexual propensities. Such a definition would not only make the act impracticable of enforcement and, perhaps, unconstitutional in its application, but would also be an unwarranted departure from the accepted meaning of the words defined."

The Supreme Court of the United States, taking the statute precisely as it had been interpreted by the state court, held it immune from attack. The court held that the three criteria set forth in the statute were sufficiently certain. The court stated (p. 274): "These underlying conditions, calling for evidence of past conduct pointing to probable consequences, are as susceptible of proof as many of the criteria constantly applied in prosecutions for crime." . . .

The Legislature does not have detailed knowledge of psychiatry. In this field the best that it can do is adopt general broad definitions and leave it to the common sense and fairness of the courts to see to it that individual rights are not illegally affected. There are many similar statutes that are as "vague" as the one under consideration. Thus, the definition of "mentally ill persons" in section 5040 of the Welfare and Institutions Code is quite general. Equally general and vague is the definition of persons of sound mind in section 21 of the Penal Code. Section 5250 of the Welfare and Institutions Code purports to define "feebleminded persons" and such definition is not fundamentally different from the one under consideration. Reference should also be mentioned to the broad definitions contained in the compulsory sterilization act—section 6624 of the Welfare and Institutions Code—upheld in Buck v. Bell, 274 U.S. 200. . . .

The last contention of appellant is closely connected with the points already discussed. It is that the statutory procedure which permits a person convicted of a misdemeanor to be transferred from court to court, and from hospital to court to hospital to court as was appellant, is arbitrary and unreasonable, particularly when such procedure

culminates in an indeterminate commitment to San Quentin.
This argument is based on a misconception of the purposes
of the statute.

The main purpose of the act is to protect society
against the activities of sexual psychopaths. The secondary purpose is to rehabilitate the sexual psychopath. . . .
In People v. McCracken at page 346 the Supreme Court properly pointed out that "the sexual psychopath may be removed
from society under the Sexual Psychopath Law until he is
cured or until he is no longer considered a menace to the
safety of others." Thus, the place of commitment and the
possibility of criminal punishment on the misdemeanor
charge does not affect the validity of the objectives of
the act, which are admittedly proper.

The emphasis that appellant places on the fact that
he was originally convicted of a misdemeanor, and now finds
himself in San Quentin, possibly for life, is misplaced.
This argument would be sound only were his confinement punishment. As we have already seen, the purpose of the confinement is to protect society and to try and cure the accused.

The arguments of appellant are without merit. The
order appealed from is affirmed.

PUNISHMENT

Stanley I. Benn

The word "punishment" is used in varying contexts.
The punishment meted out by the state to a criminal or by a

Reprinted with permission of the publisher from *The Ency-
clopedia of Philosophy*, Paul Edwards, Editor-in-Chief, Volume 7, pp. 29–35. Copyright © 1967 by Crowell Collier and
Macmillan Inc. Stanley I. Benn, until recently Lecturer in
Government at the University of Southampton, is now at the
Australian National University, Canberra. He is the author,
with R. S. Peters, of *The Principles of Political Thought*
(title in Great Britain: *Social Principles and the Democratic State*).

parent to his children is not the same as the punishment boxers give or receive. The latter, however, is punishment only in a metaphorical sense, for it lacks several of the features necessary to a standard case of punishment. Characteristically, punishment is unpleasant. It is inflicted on an offender because of an offense he has committed; it is deliberately imposed, not just the natural consequence of a person's action (like a hang-over), and the unpleasantness is essential to it, not an accidental accompaniment to some other treatment (like the pain of the dentist's drill). It is imposed by an agent authorized by the system of rules against which an offense has been committed; a lynching is not a standard case of punishment. Philosophers who have written on punishment have usually had in mind punishment in the standard sense rather than in any extended or metaphorical sense.

The philosopher's interest in punishment is mainly connected with questions of justification. It is, prima facie, wrong to deliberately inflict suffering or deprivation on another person, yet punishment consists in doing precisely this. What conditions, the philosopher asks, would justify it? Or, more generally, what kind of consideration would count toward a justification? For instance, if a person had already committed a crime, that would clearly be relevant to the question of whether he ought to be punished (although it might not be conclusive). What if he were only expected to commit a crime in the future? Or, again, is it relevant to the question of whether this man should be punished to say that punishing him would deter others? And assuming that criminals ought to be punished, how should we set about deciding appropriate penalties?

It is not, of course, the business of the moral or social philosopher to provide a justification for any particular act or system of punishment or even of the institution of punishment in general. Philosophers are not necessarily apologists for their society and age. They are interested in the procedures and modes of argument that we are committed to by our fundamental conceptions of morality and in criteria of criticism and justification rather than in inquiries into whether actual institutions satisfy them.

Philosophers, it is true, have not always made this distinction; they have often worked on the understanding that a philosophical argument could be seriously shaken by showing that it leads to conclusions inconsistent with some widely approved institution or moral rule. Moreover, for many philosophers, if such a rule or institution seemed to imply a principle inconsistent with other moral principles accepted by the society, there must necessarily be some broader principle, which a philosopher could discover and by which the conflict could be resolved. Applied to the case of punishment, this would mean that a philosopher must reconcile the apparently conflicting principles that wrongdoers should be punished and that it is wrong to deliberately make another man suffer. But this is surely a misconception of the nature of philosophy. There is no point, after all, in asking whether and how punishment can be justified if one assumes in advance that it can. For justification a number of contingent facts are required that the philosopher as such is not qualified to provide. His task is to analyze what is being asked for and so to point out what kinds of facts and arguments are admissible to the discussion.

JUSTIFICATION OF PUNISHMENT

The question of justification arises at two levels. One can take for granted the principle that wrongdoers should be punished and ask whether a particular case of punishment was justified. At this level the philosopher is concerned with the criteria in a general system which any particular act of punishment must satisfy. One can, however, question the very idea of punishment as an institution which involves deliberately inflicting pain or deprivation. This raises the philosophical question of how one justifies a set of rules or an institution like a penal system. Corresponding to these two levels of justification are two broadly opposed approaches to punishment, the retributivist and the utilitarian. Each, in fact, has been taken to offer an answer to the problems at both levels, but the persuasive force of retributivism is mainly in its answers to problems of the first type, and of utilitarianism to questions of the second type. Characteristically, the retributivist stresses guilt and desert, looking back to the crime to justify punishment and denying that the consequences of punishment, beneficial or otherwise, have any relevance to justification. The utilitarian, on the other hand, insists that punishment can be justified only if it has beneficent consequences that outweigh the intrinsic evil of inflicting suffering on human beings.

Retributivist Theories

The most thoroughgoing retributivists, exemplified by Kant, maintain that the punishment of crime is right in itself, that it is fitting that the guilty should suffer, and that justice, or the moral order, requires the institution of punishment. This, however, is not to justify punishment but, rather, to deny that it needs any justification. To say that something is right or good in itself means that it does not need to be justified in terms of the value or rightness of anything else. Its intrinsic value is appreciated immediately or intuitively. But since at least some people do doubt that punishment is right, an appeal to intuition is necessarily unsatisfactory. Again, to say "it is fitting" or "justice demands" that the guilty should suffer is only to reaffirm that punishment is right, not to give grounds for thinking so.

Some retributivists, while admitting that punishment is, prima facie, evil, maintain that it is nevertheless better that the wicked should be punished than that they should prosper more than the virtuous and, perhaps, at their expense. In this view, the function of criminal law is to punish wickedness or immorality in order to maintain a kind of cosmic distributive justice. However, it is not self-evident that wickedness should be punished any more than it is self-evident that legal guilt should be. Archbishop Temple, himself a retributivist, declared that he had no "intuition that it is good that the wicked should suffer." Nor is it clear that virtue must be rewarded or that universal justice requires the kind of human rectification that this sort of retributivism envisages. Of course, in a universe in which the wicked prospered, there might be no incentive to virtue, but this is essentially a utilitarian mode of argument. Again, evil motives and a bad character are necessary conditions of wickedness but not of legal guilt and criminal liability. The state's function is to punish breaches of those rules which in the public interest ought to be upheld; it is a matter of indifference in law (but not in morals) that some men who observe the rules do so from the unworthy motive of fear and others break them from laudable motives of principle. Conversely, it is at least doubtful whether the criminal law should provide penalties for offenses against morality except where the public interest is at stake—e.g., whether it should extend to cases of lying other than, say, false pretenses and perjury.

Though immorality is neither a necessary nor a sufficient condition for punishment, the relation between law and morals is nevertheless a close one, and what punishment is to the one, blame is to the other. Both regulate social intercourse, and in any given society the aims and ideals upheld by the law will usually correspond, more or less,

with those upheld by the dominant morality. Moreover, in
the family and the school punishment is often used to reinforce moral condemnation as part of the process of moral
education. Some writers who regard punishment as moral
retribution couple this idea with the argument that the
point of punishment is to be found in what Lord Justice
Denning has called "the emphatic denunciation by the community of a crime." In this view, punishment reinforces
the community's respect for its legal and moral standards,
which criminal acts would tend to undermine if they were
not solemnly denounced. There is, however, no intrinsic
reason why denunciation should take precisely the form of
inflicting suffering on criminals, unless, perhaps, one accepts Ewing's view that punishment has the advantage of impressing both on the criminal and on everyone else that a
breach of law and morals is so serious that society must do
something to prevent it. That, however, is surely to justify punishment by its utility in maintaining respect for the
law. Rashdall refers to "the enormous importance of the
criminal law in promoting the moral education of the public
mind," but Rashdall was a utilitarian who justified punishment by reference to "the production of good effects on
conscious beings."

For Hegel punishment is necessary to annul the wrong
done by the criminal. By this he means something more than
restitution or compensation, neither of which is, strictly
speaking, punishment. It is, rather, that the criminal has
upset the balance of the moral order, which can be restored
only by his being made to suffer. Or, in terms of the dia-
lectic, crime is a negation of right and as such a nullity;
punishment negates the negation, thus reaffirming the right.
But in what sense can punishment be said to restore the balance or annul the wrong, unless it is taken for granted
that criminals deserve to be punished? This is precisely
the point in question.

Utilitarian Theories

The utilitarian position is exemplified in Bentham's
remark that "all punishment is a mischief. . . . If it
ought at all to be admitted, it ought only to be admitted
in as far as it promises to exclude some greater evil."
By reforming the criminal, by deterring him or others from
similar offenses in the future, or by directly preventing
further offenses by imprisonment, deportation, or execution, the good that comes out of punishment may outweigh
(so the utilitarian argues) the intrinsic evil of suffering

deliberately inflicted. Without such effects, or if the suffering inflicted exceeded the suffering avoided, the institution would be unjustified.

The critics of utilitarianism claim that if people generally could be persuaded that an innocent man was guilty, utilitarianism would justify punishing him since as a warning to others he would be just as useful as a genuine offender. Again, offenders might be deterred by threatening to punish their wives and children, particularly, if as is so often the case with political terrorists and resistance fighters, it were difficult to catch the offenders themselves. Or, again, if punishment could be justified as a way of reforming criminals, it would seem better to punish them before, rather than after, they committed their crimes. Retributivists claim that utilitarians are in danger of losing sight of two conditions which are necessary to the very idea of punishment—namely, that an offense should have been committed and that punishment shall be of the offender himself, who alone can be said to deserve it. "Punishment is punishment," wrote F. H. Bradley, "only when it is deserved"; punishment for any other reason is "a crying injustice."

The dilemma of utilitarianism, then, at least in its crude form, is that it justifies punishing innocent people provided that such punishment causes less suffering than might otherwise be caused by the would-be criminals it deters. Some utilitarians argue that in the end the deception would break down, that it could not be used systematically, or that the long-term consequences would be bad for society. But these answers are unsatisfactory because they depend on assumptions of purely contingent consequences. Our revulsion against punishing innocent men seems to go deeper than that. In any case, these answers will not meet the case for punishing hostages, which can certainly be done systematically and requires no deception or secrecy.

Punishment and Principles of Justice

To meet the above criticisms, a crude utilitarianism would have to be supplemented by other moral principles— namely, that differences in treatment must be justified by relevant differences in circumstance or condition, where "relevance" is defined in the light of general rules, and that every human being should be treated with at least a minimum of respect as a source of claims and not as a mere instrument for the promotion of the interests of others. It can be argued that punishment of the innocent or of

hostages is an abuse not because it necessarily makes for
more unhappiness than it prevents but because it treats innocent men in a way that is appropriate only for the guilty
and makes an arbitrary difference in treatment between them
and other innocent men. Moreover, a legal system is designed to guide conduct by laying down rules and attaching
penalties to those who choose to break them. It is acceptable, in the words of J. D. Mabbott, only because "the criminal makes the essential choice; he 'brings it on himself.'"
Otherwise, punishment would not be consistent with the principle of respect for persons. The hostage, on the other
hand, has no chance to settle his own fate; he is used as a
mere lever for manipulating other people's conduct, and his
own interest is subordinate to that of the other members of
society. Punishment of the innocent ignores, in short,
fundamental procedural rules of justice and morality without which utilitarianism would make little sense, for unless everyone is worthy of equal consideration as a source
of claims, whose interest is to count in assessing the utility of a course of action? Whom are we entitled to treat
as simply a tool for advancing other men's interests—as
Aristotle's "slave by nature"—and what would count as a
reason for considering other men before him?

This has bearing, too, on the reasons for accepting as
excuses such defenses as duress, unavoidable accident, or
ignorance of fact—conditions under which an offender can
claim that he could not help doing what he did. Bentham
argued that to punish anyone under such conditions would be
pointless and, therefore, mischievous, because the threat
of penalties could not possibly deter anyone in the future
who was similarly placed. Now, it is true that nothing
would be lost if such people escaped punishment, provided
they could be distinguished from cheats trying to take advantage of such excuses and provided enough offenders without such excuses could be detected to furnish examples for
others. The principle of "strict liability," which exists
in some legal systems for certain offenses, has been defended on the utilitarian ground that it is impossible to
tell a genuine excuse from a pretense. It is questionable,
however, whether a person who would otherwise be treated as
innocent ought to be treated as guilty because someone else
might otherwise escape a merited penalty. Punishing the
man who commits an offense through ignorance or accident,
because it is too difficult to tell whether he really did
it on purpose or because we have to make an example of *someone*, is very like punishing the innocent as a warning to
the guilty. The utilitarian case for these excuses is unsatisfactory inasmuch as it makes them subject to such
qualifications.

A better ground for such excuses is that punishment is morally acceptable only if it is the consequence of an act freely chosen by the criminal, which it would not be under these conditions. A man acting in ignorance or by accident cannot be said to bring his punishment on himself. Punishment, seen as a way of influencing conduct, cannot be justified if there has been no real possibility of choice. Moreover, the punishment of involuntary offenses introduces into men's lives the possibility of disasters which they can neither foresee nor avert.

Utilitarianism, then, must be supplemented by principles of justice if it is not to clash with other moral principles that are usually considered fundamental. It has, however, the merit, as an approach to the justification of punishment, that it provides a clear procedure for determining whether the institution is acceptable in general terms. This the retributivist approach cannot do because it denies the relevance of weighing advantages and disadvantages, which is what we ultimately must do in moral criticism of rules and institutions. Consequently, a retributivist justification of punishment as an institution usually turns out to be a denial of the necessity for justification, a veiled reference to the beneficial results of punishment (a utilitarianism in disguise), or an appeal to religious authority.

When it is a question of justifying a particular case of punishment, however, the retributivist is in a far stronger position. There would be no point in having a general rule if on every occasion that it had to be applied one had to consider whether the advantages in this particular case warranted acting in accordance with it. Moreover, the point of punishment as deterrent would be quite lost were there no general expectation, based on the general operation of the rule, that guilty men would be punished. Assuming, then, that a penal system can be justified in utilitarian terms, any offense is at least prima facie an occasion for a penalty. Equally, without an offense there is no question of a penalty. The retributivist contention that punishment is justified if, and only if, it is deserved is really applicable, therefore, to the justification of particular instances of punishment, the institution as such being taken for granted.

SEVERITY OF PUNISHMENT

The clash between the utilitarian and retributivist approaches to punishment also arises in considering the criteria by which appropriate punishments are assessed.

The retributivist insists that the punishment must fit the crime; the utilitarian relates the penalty to the general aims of the system, to the prevention of further crime, and, perhaps, to the reform of the criminal.

The most extreme form of retributivism is the law of retaliation: "an eye for an eye." This alone, Kant claimed, could provide a just measure of the penalty, since it was the crime itself and nothing else that settled it. However, to try to apply it literally might be monstrously cruel, or, as Kant recognized, it might be absurd. Thieves can be deprived of their property and murderers hanged, but what penalty is appropriate to the dope-peddler, the blackmailer, and the smuggler?

There is not much sense, either, in trying to construct a table of equivalents so that the amount of suffering inflicted by the criminal could be meted out to him in some other form. How can such a table be drawn up? How many years must a blackmailer spend in jail to experience suffering equal to his victim's? Is it possible, in any case, to make comparisons of suffering between persons? Of course, we do assess the gravity of an offense and try to ensure that the punishment for a trivial offense is less severe than for a serious one. But this is possible only because we take for granted an existing scale of penalties and grade new offenses accordingly. Such grading does not imply an intrinsic relation between the crime and the penalty apart from that established by the scale. Some retributivists admit this but claim nevertheless that the penalties prescribed by the law ought to reflect the moral heinousness of the offense. The most serious offenses against morals deserve the most severe penalties. This, however, only shifts the question a step back, for what makes one moral offense more serious than another?

Utilitarians have tended to concentrate on deterrence, turning away from the actual criminal act except as one of a class of actions that might be prevented by punishing the particular instance severely enough (but only just enough) to make the action unattractive to the offender and to possible future offenders. Unfortunately, there are always people who cannot be deterred or reformed. Beyond a certain point the additional suffering one would have to inflict on all offenders to reduce their number might be so great as to exceed the amount of suffering thereby averted. The aim of the utilitarian, then, would presumably be to select the penalty at which the aggregate of suffering caused by crimes actually committed and punishments actually inflicted would be the smallest possible.

The utilitarian approach has often been criticized as justifying severe penalties for trivial offenses and vice versa. To eliminate parking offenses might need heavier penalties than to eliminate blackmail, which would be monstrous. But this criticism misses the point of the utilitarian case. There would, indeed, be no objection to threatening the severest penalty for any offense providing the threat never had to be carried out. Punishment is only an unfortunate consequence of the fact that the threats, which are the true operative elements in the system, are partially ineffective and would be wholly ineffective if they were not carried out when they failed to deter. In fixing penalties, the utilitarian's problem is not, therefore, to minimize the number of offenses, irrespective of the punishment inflicted, but to minimize the total amount of suffering from both sources. If we call parking offenses trivial, we mean that each one causes relatively little suffering; therefore, we are prepared to put up with a large number of them rather than incur the cost of making offenders suffer heavy penalties. Blackmail, on the other hand, causes so much suffering that if heavier penalties would yield even a small reduction in the number of offenses, there might be a net gain even though offenders would suffer more than they did before. In this way a utilitarian might agree with the retributivist that severe penalties ought to be restricted to serious offenses, but he would argue that we call an offense serious precisely because it causes a great deal of suffering. For the retributivist only serious crimes *deserve* severe penalties; for the utilitarian only serious crimes are worth averting at the cost of severe penalties.

The utilitarian approach to this matter does not supply a procedure for sentencing particular criminals (any more than a justification for punishment as an institution would be a case for any particular application of it). Arguing from expected consequences, one might establish a kind of standard penalty for each class of offense. Officials drafting new rules might consider whether a proposed maximum penalty would keep offenses down to manageable proportions, or people concerned about road accidents might argue that heavier penalties for motoring offenses would make drivers more careful. Deciding the sentence in a particular case, however, is clearly a different matter. The maximum penalty is a limiting factor, but questions like the degree of responsibility, provocation, and the offender's previous record are all relevant. However, one might reasonably ask why, as a matter of principle, they should be relevant.

PUNISHMENT AND RESPONSIBILITY

The problem of responsibility arises in relation to punishment as it does in relation to blame in moral theory. The principle, discussed already, that a man ought not to be punished for doing what he cannot help creates difficulties when extended to actions which a man could not help doing because of his own state of mind instead of external or contingent factors, like duress or ignorance of fact. An insane man, as defined, say, by the M'Naghten rules (that is, one who did not know what he was doing or did not know that what he was doing was wrong), cannot be said to choose his act because he cannot know it for what it is. But sometimes a man may know that what he is doing is wrong yet still be unable to stop himself from doing it. He may be subject, for instance, to an irresistible temptation or provocation. But how is that to be understood? A temptation is not irresistible merely because a particular man has yielded to it or even because he might have been expected to yield to it. However, a temptation may be so strong that we might expect any ordinary person to yield to it (even though a few people may in fact resist it), or, as one might say, it might be "more than human nature can stand." In that sense it may be "irresistible."

Some people, of course, find it much more difficult than others to resist temptation. Some, like kleptomaniacs, are "impelled" to act in the sense that deliberation neither plays, nor could play, any part in what they do. Such people might be distinguished from plain wrongdoers by the fact that nothing—not blame, punishment, praise, or rational argument—seems to affect their disposition to break the rules. Or, again, their actions may lack any point, or if they can be said to have any point, it is only in relation to a set of aims and standards of achievement so distorted and eccentric that they are intelligible only to a psychiatrist. The kleptomaniac who steals nylon stockings for which he has no possible use (according to ordinary standards of utility) might properly be said to be unable to help stealing them. Far more difficult is the case of the psychopath, who seems to have no wish to resist temptation or, rather, who knows that some of the things he wants to do are wrong in the sense that other people disapprove of them but on whom this knowledge enforces no internal restraint beyond prompting a degree of caution. Criminals of this type would once have been described as "wicked" but are now often described as incapable of self-control. To say, however, that they are not responsible for their acts creates the odd situation that anyone is liable to punishment who usually resists temptation but sometimes fails, whereas the man who never resists is not liable at all.

The determinist has a short way with these difficulties. Since everyone's actions are the response of his character to a given set of circumstances, how can anyone ever be held responsible for his actions? We do what we must, given what we are, and what we are is the end of a causal chain going back to before we were born. If one knew a person well enough, one might predict that under given conditions he would commit a crime. Is this compatible with saying that he can choose whether to do so, or is his belief in his freedom to choose simply an illusion? Can the result of a genuine choice be predicted?

To say that something is predictable is not, however, the same as saying it is unavoidable. We can forecast a man's actions just because we know the kind of choices that he regularly makes. The more we know of his dispositions and his preferences, the more likely we are to be right. But that does not mean that he never acts voluntarily or that he never makes a real choice but only thinks he does. If all choices are illusions, what would a real choice be like? A man's behavior may be predictable because he can be relied upon to do what is reasonable, but to act with good reason is the very reverse of being subject to an inner compulsion. An essential difference between voluntary and involuntary action is that it makes sense to speak of the motives, aims, and reasons for the former but only of the causes of the latter. It is only when a person's behavior seems pointless or when explanations in terms of aims do not seem sufficient that we look for the kind of cause which would justify saying that he could not help himself. Of course, a complete account of voluntary and rational behavior must refer to causes as necessary conditions for action, but such causes would not constitute a sufficient explanation. An account of the electronic activity in the brain would not provide a sufficient explanation of a move in a game of chess unless the move was so completely and absurdly irrelevant that it had to be accounted for simply as the result of a nervous twitch. In that case, however, it would not really be a move in the game at all, not an action, indeed, but something that happens to the player. The weakness of the determinist position, insofar as it purports to undermine the notion of responsibility, is that it treats such abnormalities as the explanatory model for the normal.

It is arguable, in any case, that the concept of responsibility *requires* that human behavior be causally

accountable rather than the reverse. As Hume pointed out
in *An Enquiry Concerning Human Understanding*,

> [Where actions] . . . proceed not from some *cause*
> in the character and disposition of the person
> who performed them, they can neither redound to
> his honour, if good; nor infamy, if evil. . . .
> The person is not answerable for them; and as
> they proceeded from nothing in him that is dura-
> ble and constant, and leave nothing of that na-
> ture behind them, it is impossible [that] he can,
> upon their account, become the object of punish-
> ment or vengeance.

In Hume's view universal causality is consistent with the
concept of choice and is a necessary condition for responsibility and, therefore, for blame and punishment.

Strictly speaking, all that is necessary for a theory
of punishment is that human conduct should be capable of
being modified by threats. For some people—for instance,
compulsive lawbreakers like kleptomaniacs—that is not the
case. Others, however, commit crimes believing they can
escape punishment; still others, in a spirit of rebellion,
indifference, or, more rarely, of martyrdom, prefer to do
what they want and risk the consequences rather than conform. Why they prefer it—what conditions account for
their being the men they are—is irrelevant. To say "they
prefer it" is to say they might have chosen to do otherwise
but did not, and that is all that is necessary for the concept "responsibility." To ask whether they were free to
prefer otherwise, being what they were, is to ask whether
they could choose to choose, and it is not clear that this
really means anything. The experience of punishment may
provide a reason for choosing differently next time, but to
have a reason for choosing is not to be without a choice
and, therefore, without responsibility.

Extenuation

Though a criminal may be held responsible for his actions, there may nevertheless be circumstances which, so it
is said, diminish responsibility or extenuate guilt. Temptation or provocation, though not irresistible, may have
been very great. The offender may have had a good character, and there may be no reason to expect any future lapse.

In some cases mitigation of sentence on such grounds
can be readily justified in utilitarian terms. Little is

to be gained by punishing the obviously exceptional lapse;
a very small penalty might be enough to dissuade other respectable people who might otherwise be tempted to imitate
it and for whom the shame of being treated as a criminal,
whatever the penalty, is usually deterrent enough.

However, it is not easy to show, at least in utilitarian terms, that mitigation is reasonable in all the instances in which it is commonly thought appropriate. Nor
does everyone agree on what are extenuating circumstances.
It is not self-evident that whoever is sorely (but not ir-
resistibly) tempted should be treated more leniently than
people who have done the same thing but under less temptation. A strong temptation might be withstood if there were
sufficient counterinducement. Leniency might weaken the
resolve of others in the future. Some people treat crimes
of passion leniently; others would say that the temptation
is so commonly felt that if people were not discouraged
from taking the law into their own hands by treating offenses of this kind severely, such offenses would rapidly
multiply. Again, some people would accept a plea of drunk-
enness as an extenuation of an offense, whereas others
would consider it an aggravation.

It is doubtful whether our ideas on this aspect of
punishment depend on utilitarian considerations. Nor is
there any reason to suppose that any system of utilitarian
argument could show them to be consistent and rational. It
was suggested earlier that though the criteria of morality
and law, of blame and punishment, are not identical, they
influence one another. If we blame people less for yielding to strong temptation, we also feel they deserve a less
severe punishment. But this only shifts the question a
step back. Why should temptation mitigate blame?

A possible answer might be that at least some temptations can be pleaded as partial justifications. Thus, a
man who pleads that he killed someone to shorten his suffering or a woman who kills her deformed baby is appealing
to another moral principle to excuse the act. Similarly, a
man who kills his wife's lover might claim that his victim
was violating his rights. These are not complete justifications, as a plea of self-defense would be, but they are
excuses which count, as it were, against the initial presumption of guilt and so incline us to look at the offense
more sympathetically and more leniently, whatever the advantages of severity in terms of deterrence, prevention, or
reform. There is nothing irrational in striking a balance
of desert.

But differences of opinion about a criminal's deserts
often turn not on the way such a balance is struck but on

the extent to which his judges (or their critics) are able
to comprehend his action. Anyone who could imagine himself
tempted in similar circumstances would probably be more
sympathetic than someone who could not and who would therefore see no reason for being indulgent. On the other hand,
anyone who suspected that he himself might yield to such a
temptation and who flinched from the possibility might react to it with very great severity indeed.

PUNISHMENT AND REFORM

There is no reason to suppose, then, that the sentencing practice of the courts will display rational and
consistent principles; furthermore, any attempt to set up
criteria of rational judgment on strictly utilitarian principles is likely to cut across deeply rooted moral convictions. Accordingly, some criminologists and psychiatrists,
like Eliot Slater and Bernard Glueck, and some penal reformers, like Barbara Wootton, have swung away from the
general conceptions of punishment and desert. Instead of
asking what penalty is warranted by the crime, whether the
agent was fully responsible for his action, whether circumstances exonerate him wholly or in part, they prefer to ask
what kind of treatment is most likely to rehabilitate him,
subject, of course, to the example it might set for others.
This comes very close to repudiating altogether the
concept of punishment as a deliberate infliction of suffering, which the criminal deserves, consequent to a voluntary
breach of the law. First, the treatment most likely to rehabilitate him need not be unpleasant (though if it is to
instill a measure of discipline, it very well may be).
And, second, avoiding the question of moral responsibility,
the reformer also avoids the question of what the criminal
deserves, because the reformer's prime concern is with the
treatment he needs. Criminals would no more deserve punishment than the sick deserve medicine. Indeed, for such
writers as Samuel Butler and the American lawyer Clarence
Darrow, criminality is a kind of sickness to be treated
rather than a wrong to be punished.
Attractive as this approach may seem on humanitarian
grounds, it has at least one serious consequence. The concepts of responsibility and desert cannot be discarded
without some loss. For it is not a necessary condition of
medical treatment that a patient must have shown symptoms
of a disease; those exposed to smallpox are vaccinated before they develop a fever. Without the principle that punishment must be deserved, there would be no obstacle to

subjecting people likely to become criminals to corresponding forms of penal prophylaxis. Moreover, if we substitute for punishment the idea of rehabilitative treatment, there is nothing against sentencing a person of bad character to a severe course of treatment for the most trivial offense if his character would be better for it in the end. This would clearly be incompatible with the usually accepted principle that trivial offenses should not carry severe penalties.

Reformism of this kind is open to attack from another quarter. The point has been made by Hegel and Bosanquet, among others, that retributive punishment is a kind of tribute to the moral personality of the criminal. It is precisely as a morally responsible agent, recognized as capable of making reasoned choices and accepting the consequences, that the criminal is punishable. Bosanquet goes so far as to say that punishment is "his right, of which he must not be defrauded." It is to be distinguished, argued Bradley, from the discipline or correction appropriately administered to animals and children. Punishment "is inflicted because of wrong-doing, as desert, the latter is applied as means of improvement." Since rational adults are neither animals nor children, no one has the right to treat them as if they were. It might be similarly argued that lunatics are under tutelage because they are incapable of looking after their own interests and cannot be expected to respect those of other people. The sane criminal, on the contrary, can be made to pay for his antisocial choices in order to demonstrate to him and, through him, to others that crime does not pay, but it diminishes his stature as a rational adult to deny that he is responsible for ordering his own life and to impose upon him ends of another person's choosing.

Nevertheless, retributivists have often been much concerned with moral reformation. They have insisted, however, that this was something the criminal must do for himself. Because it was associated with shame and rejection, punishment could bring the criminal up short and force him to reconsider his life in the light of society's condemnation of his actions. But the remorse which was a necessary condition for self-reformation was entirely dependent on the criminal's recognition that his punishment was deserved. Without that there could be no inward reformation, no reassertion of moral standards, but only a sense of resentment and injustice. Accordingly, punishment can yield the benefits of reform only if it is thought of, above everything else, as retributive—as the appropriate desert of a responsible guilty agent. It is this which distinguishes the

retributive approach to moral reformation from the kind of
utilitarianism which turns its back on desert and responsibility and is concerned only with the needs of rehabilitation.

It is, of course, an open question whether punishment
ever does produce the kind of self-reformation the Hegel-
ians had in mind or whether it does so more often than it
produces a moral decay. Indeed, our knowledge of the facts
of criminal behavior is probably far too scanty and uncertain for us to know how relevant much of the philosophical
discussion of punishment really is. We cannot say for
sure that a penal system is justified because it tends to
reform criminals. Nor do we know, for that matter, whether
the deterrent view of punishment is applicable to all kinds
of crime. Many people commit offenses without seeming to
take any account of consequences before they act, and they
repeat the same offenses again and again in spite of punishment. Perhaps those who do not, would not repeat them
even without punishment. Perhaps there would be no more
cases of certain classes of crime than there are already;
perhaps the only people to commit them are those who also
do not take account of consequences before they act. It
seems likely that some potential offenders are deterred
from evading taxes or from smuggling by the threat of punishment, but is there any certain evidence that the threat
of punishment deters anyone who would otherwise commit rape
or arson? Utilitarians tend to assume that punishment as
an institution can be justified by its beneficial consequences, but the argument depends on certain a priori assumptions about criminal (or would-be criminal) behavior
that may be greatly overintellectualized. However, even
though research should prove the usual utilitarian justifications for punishment groundless, that does not mean that
some other, nonutilitarian justification is better. The
proper procedure may well be to ask, with the utilitarian,
whether the consequences are by and large beneficial; it is
equally possible that punishment as an institution might
fail that test. A theory of punishment that led to the
conclusion that all punishment was wrong need be no more
necessarily mistaken than a theory that led to a similar
conclusion as regards, say, slavery, which, after all, was
accepted as uncritically in Aristotle's day as punishment
is today.

THE RIGHT TO PUNISH

Immanuel Kant

The right to punish contained in the penal law [*das Strafrecht*] is the right that the magistrate has to inflict pain on a subject in consequence of his having committed a crime. It follows that the suzerain of the state cannot himself be punished; we can only remove ourselves from his jurisdiction. A transgression of the public law that makes him who commits it unfit to be a citizen is called either simply a crime (*crimen*) or a public crime (*crimen publicum*). [If, however, we call it a public crime, then we can use the term "crime" generically to include both private and public crimes.] The first (a private crime) is brought before a civil court, and the second (a public crime), before a criminal court. Embezzlement, that is, misappropriation of money or wares entrusted in commerce, and fraud in buying and selling, if perpetrated before the eyes of the party who suffers, are private crimes. On the other hand, counterfeiting money or bills of exchange, theft, robbery, and similar acts are public crimes, because through them the commonwealth and not just a single individual is exposed to danger. These crimes may be divided into those of a base character (*indolis abjectae*) and those of a violent character (*indolis violentae*).

Judicial punishment (*poena forensis*) is entirely distinct from natural punishment (*poena naturalis*). In natural punishment, vice punishes itself, and this fact is not taken into consideration by the legislator. Judicial punishment can never be used merely as a means to promote some other good for the criminal himself or for civil society, but instead it must in all cases be imposed on him only on the ground that he has committed a crime; for a human being can never be manipulated merely as a means to the purposes

From pp. 99–106 of *The Metaphysical Elements of Justice* (*Metaphysische Anfangsgründe der Rechtslehre*, Part I of the 1797 *Metaphysik der Sitten*), translated by John Ladd, Indianapolis, 1965. Copyright 1965 by the Bobbs-Merrill Company. Reprinted with permission of the publisher.

of someone else and can never be confused with the objects
of the Law of things [*Sachenrecht*]. His innate personality
[that is, his right as a person] protects him against such
treatment, even though he may indeed be condemned to lose
his civil personality. He must first be found to be deserving of punishment before any consideration is given to the
utility of this punishment for himself or for his fellow
citizens. The law concerning punishment is a categorical
imperative, and woe to him who rummages around in the wind-
ing paths of a theory of happiness looking for some advantage to be gained by releasing the criminal from punishment or by reducing the amount of it—in keeping with the
Pharisaic motto: "It is better that one man should die than
that the whole people should perish." If legal justice
perishes, then it is no longer worth while for men to remain alive on this earth. If this is so, what should one
think of the proposal to permit a criminal who has been condemned to death to remain alive, if, after consenting to
allow dangerous experiments to be made on him, he happily
survives such experiments and if doctors thereby obtain new
information that benefits the community? Any court of justice would repudiate such a proposal with scorn if it were
suggested by a medical college, for [legal] justice ceases
to be justice if it can be bought for a price.

What kind and what degree of punishment does public
legal justice adopt as its principle and standard? None
other than the principle of equality (illustrated by the
pointer on the scales of justice), that is, the principle
of not treating one side more favorably than the other.
Accordingly, any undeserved evil that you inflict on someone else among the people is one that you do to yourself.
If you vilify him, you vilify yourself; if you steal from
him, you steal from yourself; if you kill him, you kill
yourself. Only the Law of retribution (*jus talionis*) can
determine exactly the kind and degree of punishment; it
must be well understood, however, that this determination
[must be made] in the chambers of a court of justice (and
not in your private judgment). All other standards fluctu-
ate back and forth and, because extraneous considerations
are mixed with them, they cannot be compatible with the
principle of pure and strict legal justice.

Now, it might seem that the existence of class distinctions would not allow for the [application of the] retributive principle of returning like for like. Nevertheless, even though these class distinctions may not make it
possible to apply this principle to the letter, it can
still always remain applicable in its effects if regard is
had to the special sensibilities of the higher classes.

Thus, for example, the imposition of a fine for a verbal
injury has no proportionality to the original injury, for
someone who has a good deal of money can easily afford to
make insults whenever he wishes.   On the other hand, the
humiliation of the pride of such an offender comes much
closer to equaling an injury done to the honor of the person offended; thus the judgment and Law might require the
offender, not only to make a public apology to the offended
person, but also at the same time to kiss his hand, even
though he be socially inferior.   Similarly, if a man of a
higher class has violently attacked an innocent citizen who
is socially inferior to him, he may be condemned, not only
to apologize, but to undergo solitary and painful confinement, because by this means, in addition to the discomfort
suffered, the pride of the offender will be painfully affected, and thus his humiliation will compensate for the
offense as like for like.

But what is meant by the statement: "If you steal from
him, you steal from yourself"?   Inasmuch as someone steals,
he makes the ownership of everyone else insecure, and hence
he robs himself (in accordance with the Law of retribution)
of the security of any possible ownership.   He has nothing
and can also acquire nothing, but he still wants to live,
and this is not possible unless others provide him with
nourishment.   But, because the state will not support him
gratis, he must let the state have his labor at any kind of
work it may wish to use him for (convict labor), and so he
becomes a slave, either for a certain period of time or indefinitely, as the case may be.

If, however, he has committed a murder, he must die.
In this case, there is no substitute that will satisfy the
requirements of legal justice.   There is no sameness of
kind between death and remaining alive even under the most
miserable conditions, and consequently there is also no
equality between the crime and the retribution unless the
criminal is judicially condemned and put to death.   But the
death of the criminal must be kept entirely free of any
maltreatment that would make an abomination of the humanity
residing in the person suffering it.   Even if a civil society were to dissolve itself by common agreement of all its
members (for example, if the people inhabiting an island
decided to separate and disperse themselves around the
world), the last murderer remaining in prison must first be
executed, so that everyone will duly receive what his actions are worth and so that the bloodguilt thereof will not
be fixed on the people because they failed to insist on carrying out the punishment; for if they fail to do so, they
may be regarded as accomplices in this public violation of
legal justice.

Furthermore, it is possible for punishment to be equal in accordance with the strict Law of retribution only if the judge pronounces the death sentence. This is clear because only in this way will the death sentence be pronounced on all criminals in proportion to their inner viciousness (even if the crime involved is not murder, but some other crime against the state that can be expiated only by death). . . .

It may also be pointed out that no one has ever heard of anyone condemned to death on account of murder who complained that he was getting too much [punishment] and therefore was being treated unjustly; everyone would laugh in his face if he were to make such a statement. Indeed, otherwise we would have to assume that, although the treatment accorded the criminal is not unjust according to the law, the legislative authority still is not authorized to decree this kind of punishment and that, if it does so, it comes into contradiction with itself.

Anyone who is a murderer—that is, has committed a murder, commanded one, or taken part in one—must suffer death. This is what [legal] justice as the Idea of the judicial authority wills in accordance with universal laws that are grounded a priori. . . .

In opposition to this view, the Marquis of Beccaria,[1] moved by sympathetic sentimentality and an affectation of humanitarianism, has asserted that all capital punishment is illegitimate. He argues that it could not be contained in the original civil contract, inasmuch as this would imply that every one of the people has agreed to forfeit his life if he murders another (of the people); but such an agreement would be impossible, for no one can dispose of his own life.

No one suffers punishment because he has willed the punishment, but because he has willed a punishable action. If what happens to someone is also willed by him, it cannot be a punishment. Accordingly, it is impossible to will to be punished. To say, "I will to be punished if I murder someone," can mean nothing more than, "I submit myself along with everyone else to those laws which, if there are any criminals among the people, will naturally include penal

---

[1] [Cesare Bonesana, Marquis di Beccaria (1738–1794), Italian publicist. His *Dei delitti e delle pene* (1764) (*On Crimes and Punishments*, trans. Henry Paolucci, "The Library of Liberal Arts," No. 107 [New York: The Liberal Arts Press, 1963]) was widely read and had great influence on the reform of the penal codes of various European states.]

laws." In my role as colegislator making the penal law, I cannot be the same person who, as subject, is punished by the law; for, as a subject who is also a criminal, I cannot have a voice in legislation. (The legislator is holy.) When, therefore, I enact a penal law against myself as a criminal it is the pure juridical legislative reason (*homo noumenon*) in me that submits myself to the penal law as a person capable of committing a crime, that is, as another person (*homo phaenomenon*) along with all the others in the civil union who submit themselves to this law. In other words, it is not the people (considered as individuals) who dictate the death penalty, but the court (public legal justice); that is, someone other than the criminal. The social contract does not include the promise to permit oneself to be punished and thus to dispose of oneself and of one's life, because, if the only ground that authorizes the punishment of an evildoer were a promise that expresses his willingness to be punished, then it would have to be left up to him to find himself liable to punishment, and the criminal would be his own judge. The chief error contained in this sophistry (πρωτονψευδοζ) consists in the confusion of the criminal's own judgment (which one must necessarily attribute to his reason) that he must forfeit his life with a resolution of the Will to take his own life. The result is that the execution of the Law and the adjudication thereof are represented as united in the same person. . . .

PERSONS AND PUNISHMENT

Herbert Morris

> They acted and looked . . . at us, and around in
> our house, in a way that had about it the feeling
> —at least for me—that we were not people. In
> their eyesight we were just things, that was all.
> —*Malcolm X*

> We have no right to treat a man like a dog.—*Governor Maddox of Georgia*

Alfredo Traps in Durrenmatt's tale discovers that he
has brought off, all by himself, a murder involving considerable ingenuity. The mock prosecutor in the tale demands
the death penalty "as reward for a crime that merits admiration, astonishment, and respect." Traps is deeply moved;
indeed, he is exhilarated, and the whole of his life becomes more heroic, and, ironically, more precious. His defense attorney proceeds to argue that Traps was not only
innocent but incapable of guilt, "a victim of the age."
This defense Traps disavows with indignation and anger. He
makes claim to the murder as his and demands the prescribed
punishment—death.

The themes to be found in this macabre tale do not often find their way into philosophical discussions of punishment. These discussions deal with large and significant
questions of whether or not we ever have the right to punish, and if we do, under what conditions, to what degree,
and in what manner. There is a tradition, of course, not

Reprinted from *The Monist*, 52, No. 4 (October 1968),
pp. 475-501, with the permission of the author and The Open
Court Publishing Company, LaSalle, Illinois. Herbert Morris is Professor of Philosophy and Professor of Law at the
University of California, Los Angeles. He is the editor of
Freedom and Responsibility, Stanford, 1961, and the author
of a number of articles that have appeared in philosophical
and legal journals on a variety of topics in moral philosophy, the philosophy of law, and the philosophy of mind.

notable for its present vitality, that is closely linked
with motifs in Durrenmatt's tale of crime and punishment.
Its adherents have urged that justice requires a person be
punished if he is guilty. Sometimes—though rarely—these
philosophers have expressed themselves in terms of the
criminal's *right to be punished*. Reaction to the claim
that there is such a right has been astonishment combined,
perhaps, with a touch of contempt for the perversity of the
suggestion. A strange right that no one would ever wish to
claim! With that flourish the subject is buried and the
right disposed of. In this paper the subject is resurrec-
ted.

My aim is to argue for four propositions concerning
rights that will certainly strike some as not only false
but preposterous: first, that we have a right to punishment; second, that this right derives from a fundamental
human right to be treated as a person; third, that this
fundamental right is a natural, inalienable, and absolute
right; and, fourth, that the denial of this right implies
the denial of all moral rights and duties. Showing the
truth of one, let alone all, of these large and questionable claims is a tall order. The attempt, or, more properly speaking, the first steps in an attempt, follow.

1. When someone claims that there is a right to be
free, we can easily imagine situations in which the right
is infringed and easily imagine situations in which there
is a point to asserting or claiming the right. With the
right to be punished, matters are otherwise. The immediate
reaction to the claim that there is such a right is puzzle-
ment. And the reasons for this are apparent. People do
not normally value pain and suffering. Punishment is associated with pain and suffering. When we think about punishment we naturally think of the strong desire most persons have to avoid it, to accept, for example, acquittal
of a criminal charge with relief and eagerly, if convicted,
to hope for pardon or probation. Adding, of course, to the
paradoxical character of the claim of such a right is difficulty in imagining circumstances in which it would be denied one. When would one rightly demand punishment and
meet with any threat of the claim being denied?

So our first task is to see when the claim of such a
right would have a point. I want to approach this task by
setting out two complex types of institutions both of which
are designed to maintain some degree of social control. In
the one a central concept is punishment for wrongdoing and
in the other the central concepts are control of dangerous
individuals and treatment of disease.

Let us first turn attention to the institutions in which punishment is involved. The institutions I describe will resemble those we ordinarily think of as institutions of punishment; they will have, however, additional features we associate with a system of just punishment.

Let us suppose that men are constituted roughly as they now are, with a rough equivalence in strength and abilities, a capacity to be injured by each other and to make judgments that such injury is undesirable, a limited strength of will, and a capacity to reason and to conform conduct to rules. Applying to the conduct of these men are a group of rules, ones I shall label 'primary,' which closely resemble the core rules of our criminal law, rules that prohibit violence and deception and compliance with which provides benefits for all persons. These benefits consist in noninterference by others with what each person values, such matters as continuance of life and bodily security. The rules define a sphere for each person, then, which is immune from interference by others. Making possible this mutual benefit is the assumption by individuals of a burden. The burden consists in the exercise of self-restraint by individuals over inclinations that would, if satisfied, directly interfere or create a substantial risk of interference with others in proscribed ways. If a person fails to exercise self-restraint even though he might have and gives in to such inclinations, he renounces a burden which others have voluntarily assumed and thus gains an advantage which others, who have restrained themselves, do not possess. This system, then, is one in which the rules establish a mutuality of benefit and burden and in which the benefits of noninterference are conditional upon the assumption of burdens.

Connecting punishment with the violation of these primary rules, and making public the provision for punishment, is both reasonable and just. First, it is only reasonable that those who voluntarily comply with the rules be provided some assurance that they will not be assuming burdens which others are unprepared to assume. Their disposition to comply voluntarily will diminish as they learn that others are with impunity renouncing burdens they are assuming. Second, fairness dictates that a system in which benefits and burdens are equally distributed have a mechanism designed to prevent a maldistribution in the benefits and burdens. Thus, sanctions are attached to noncompliance with the primary rules so as to induce compliance with the primary rules among those who may be disinclined to obey. In this way the likelihood of an unfair distribution is diminished.

Third, it is just to punish those who have violated
the rules and caused the unfair distribution of benefits
and burdens. A person who violates the rules has something
others have—the benefits of the system—but by renouncing
what others have assumed, the burdens of self-restraint, he
has acquired an unfair advantage. Matters are not even
until this advantage is in some way erased. Another way of
putting it is that he owes something to others, for he has
something that does not rightfully belong to him. Justice—
that is, punishing such individuals—restores the equilibrium of benefits and burdens by taking from the individual
what he owes, that is, exacting the debt. It is important
to see that the equilibrium may be restored in another way.
Forgiveness—with its legal analogue of a pardon—while not
the righting of an unfair distribution by making one pay
his debt is, nevertheless, a restoring of the equilibrium
by forgiving the debt. Forgiveness may be viewed, at least
in some types of cases, as a gift after the fact, erasing a
debt, which had the gift been given before the fact, would
not have created a debt. But the practice of pardoning has
to proceed sensitively, for it may endanger, in a way the
practice of justice does not, the maintenance of an equilibrium of benefits and burdens. If all are indiscriminately
pardoned less incentive is provided individuals to restrain
their inclinations, thus increasing the incidence of persons taking what they do not deserve.
    There are also in this system we are considering a
variety of operative principles compliance with which provides some guarantee that the system of punishment does not
itself promote an unfair distribution of benefits and burdens. For one thing, provision is made for a variety of
defenses, each one of which can be said to have as its object diminishing the chances of forcibly depriving a person
of benefits others have if that person has not derived an
unfair advantage. A person has not derived an unfair advantage if he could not have restrained himself or if it is
unreasonable to expect him to behave otherwise than he did.
Sometimes the rules preclude punishment of classes of persons such as children. Sometimes they provide a defense if
on a particular occasion a person lacked the capacity to
conform his conduct to the rules. Thus, someone who in an
epileptic seizure strikes another is excused. Punishment
in these cases would be punishment of the innocent, punishment of those who do not voluntarily renounce a burden others have assumed. Punishment in such cases, then, would
not equalize but rather cause an unfair distribution in
benefits and burdens.

Along with principles providing defenses there are requirements that the rules be prospective and relatively clear so that persons have a fair opportunity to comply with the rules. There are, also, rules governing, among other matters, the burden of proof, who shall bear it and what it shall be, the prohibition on double jeopardy, and the privilege against self-incrimination. Justice requires conviction of the guilty, and requires their punishment, but in setting out to fulfill the demands of justice we may, of course, because we are not omniscient, cause injustice by convicting and punishing the innocent. The resolution arrived at in the system I am describing consists in weighing as the greater evil the punishment of the innocent. The primary function of the system of rules was to provide individuals with a sphere of interest immune from interference. Given this goal, it is determined to be a greater evil for society to interfere unjustifiably with an individual by depriving him of good than for the society to fail to punish those that have unjustifiably interfered.

Finally, because the primary rules are designed to benefit all and because the punishments prescribed for their violation are publicized and the defenses respected, there is some plausibility in the exaggerated claim that in choosing to do an act violative of the rules an individual has chosen to be punished. This way of putting matters brings to our attention the extent to which, when the system is as I have described it, the criminal "has brought the punishment upon himself" in contrast to those cases where it would be misleading to say "he has brought it upon himself," cases, for example, where one does not know the rules or is punished in the absence of fault.

To summarize, then: first, there is a group of rules guiding the behavior of individuals in the community which establish spheres of interest immune from interference by others; second, provision is made for what is generally regarded as a deprivation of some thing of value if the rules are violated; third, the deprivations visited upon any person are justified by that person's having violated the rules; fourth, the deprivation, in this just system of punishment, is linked to rules that fairly distribute benefits and burdens and to procedures that strike some balance between not punishing the guilty and punishing the innocent, a class defined as those who have not voluntarily done acts violative of the law, in which it is evident that the evil of punishing the innocent is regarded as greater than the nonpunishment of the guilty.

At the core of many actual legal systems one finds, of course, rules and procedures of the kind I have sketched.

It is obvious, though, that any ongoing legal system differs in significant respects from what I have presented
here, containing 'pockets of injustice.'

I want now to sketch an extreme version of a set of
institutions of a fundamentally different kind, institutions proceeding on a conception of man which appears to
be basically at odds with that operative within a system
of punishment.

Rules are promulgated in this system that prohibit
certain types of injuries and harms.

In this world we are now to imagine when an individual
harms another his conduct is to be regarded as a symptom of
some pathological condition in the way a running nose is a
symptom of a cold. Actions diverging from some conception
of the normal are viewed as manifestations of a disease in
the way in which we might today regard the arm and leg move-
ments of an epileptic during a seizure. Actions conforming
to what is normal are assimilated to the normal and healthy
functioning of bodily organs. What a person does, then, is
assimilated, on this conception, to what we believe today,
or at least most of us believe today, a person undergoes.
We draw a distinction between the operation of the kidney
and raising an arm on request. This distinction between
mere events or happenings and human actions is erased in
our imagined system.[1]

---

[1]"When a man is suffering from an infectious disease, he is
a danger to the community, and it is necessary to restrict
his liberty of movement. But no one associates any idea of
guilt with such a situation. On the contrary, he is an object of commiseration to his friends. Such steps as science recommends are taken to cure him of his disease, and
he submits as a rule without reluctance to the curtailment
of liberty involved meanwhile. The same method in spirit
ought to be shown in the treatment of what is called
'crime.' "

Bertrand Russell, *Roads to Freedom* (London: George Allen and Unwin Ltd., 1918), p. 135.

"We do not hold people responsible for their reflexes
—for example, for coughing in church. We hold them responsible for their operant behavior—for example, for whispering in church or remaining in church while coughing.
But there are variables which are responsible for whispering as well as coughing, and these may be just as inexorable. When we recognize this, we are likely to drop the
notion of responsibility altogether and with it the doctrine

There is, however, bound to be something strange in this erasing of a recognized distinction, for, as with metaphysical suggestions generally, and I take this to be one, the distinction may be reintroduced but given a different description, for example, 'happenings with X type of causes' and 'happenings with Y type of causes.' Responses of different kinds, today legitimated by our distinction between happenings and actions, may be legitimated by this new manner of description. And so there may be isomorphism between a system recognizing the distinction and one erasing it. Still, when this distinction is erased certain tendencies of thought and responses might naturally arise that would tend to affect unfavorably values respected by a system of punishment.

Let us elaborate on this assimilation of conduct of a certain kind to symptoms of a disease. First, there is something abnormal in both the case of conduct, such as killing another, and a symptom of a disease such as an

---

[1](cont.) of free will as an inner causal agent."

B. F. Skinner, *Science and Human Behavior* (1953), pp. 115–116.

"Basically, criminality is but a symptom of insanity, using the term in its widest generic sense to express unacceptable social behavior based on unconscious motivation flowing from a disturbed instinctive and emotional life, whether this appears in frank psychoses, or in less obvious form in neuroses and unrecognized psychoses. . . . If criminals are products of early environmental influences in the same sense that psychotics and neurotics are, then it should be possible to reach them psychotherapeutically."

Benjamin Karpman, "Criminal Psychodynamics," *Journal of Criminal Law and Criminology*, 47 (1956), p. 9.

"We, the agents of society, must move to end the game of tit-for-tat and blow-for-blow in which the offender has foolishly and futiley engaged himself and us. We are not driven, as he is, to wild and impulsive actions. With knowledge comes power, and with power there is no need for the frightened vengeance of the old penology. In its place should go a quiet, dignified, therapeutic program for the rehabilitation of the disorganized one, if possible, the protection of society during the treatment period, and his guided return to useful citizenship, as soon as this can be effected."

Karl Menninger, "Therapy, Not Punishment," *Harper's Magazine* (August 1959), pp. 63–64.

irregular heart beat. Second, there are causes for this
abnormality in action such that once we know of them we can
explain the abnormality as we now can explain the symptoms
of many physical diseases. The abnormality is looked upon
as a happening with a causal explanation rather than an action for which there were reasons. Third, the causes that
account for the abnormality interfere with the normal functioning of the body, or, in the case of killing, with what
is regarded as a normal functioning of an individual.
Fourth, the abnormality is in some way a part of the individual, necessarily involving his body. A well going dry
might satisfy our three foregoing conditions of disease
symptoms, but it is hardly a disease or the symptom of one.
Finally, and most obscure, the abnormality arises in some
way from within the individual. If Jones is hit with a
mallet by Smith, Jones may reel about and fall on James who
may be injured. But this abnormal conduct of Jones is not
regarded as a symptom of disease. Smith, not Jones, is
suffering from some pathological condition.

With this view of man the institutions of social control respond, not with punishment, but with either preventive detention, in case of 'carriers,' or therapy in the
case of those manifesting pathological symptoms. The logic
of sickness implies the logic of therapy. And therapy and
punishment differ widely in their implications. In bringing out some of these differences I want again to draw attention to the important fact that while the distinctions
we now draw are erased in the therapy world, they may, in
fact, be reintroduced but under different descriptions. To
the extent they are, we really have a punishment system
combined with a therapy system. I am concerned now, however, with what the implications would be were the world
indeed one of therapy and not a disguised world of punishment and therapy, for I want to suggest tendencies of
thought that arise when one is immersed in the ideology of
disease and therapy.

First, punishment is the imposition upon a person who
is believed to be at fault of something commonly believed
to be a deprivation where that deprivation is justified by
the person's guilty behavior. It is associated with resentment, for the guilty are those who have done what they
had no right to do by failing to exercise restraint when
they might have and where others have. Therapy is not a
response to a person who is at fault. We respond to an individual, not because of what he has done, but because of
some condition from which he is suffering. If he is no
longer suffering from the condition, treatment no longer
has a point. Punishment, then, focuses on the past;

therapy on the present. Therapy is normally associated
with compassion for what one undergoes, not resentment for
what one has illegitimately done.

Second, with therapy, unlike punishment, we do not
seek to deprive the person of something acknowledged as a
good, but seek rather to help and to benefit the individual
who is suffering by ministering to his illness in the hope
that the person can be cured. The good we attempt to do is
not a reward for desert. The individual suffering has not
merited by his disease the good we seek to bestow upon him
but has, because he is a creature that has the capacity to
feel pain, a claim upon our sympathies and help.

Third, we saw with punishment that its justification
was related to maintaining and restoring a fair distribution of benefits and burdens. Infliction of the prescribed
punishment carries the implication, then, that one has
'paid one's debt' to society, for the punishment is the
taking from the person of something commonly recognized as
valuable. It is this conception of 'a debt owed' that may
permit, as I suggested earlier, under certain conditions,
the nonpunishment of the guilty, for operative within a
system of punishment may be a concept analogous to forgiveness, namely pardoning. Who it is that we may pardon and
under what conditions—contrition with its elements of
self-punishment no doubt plays a role—I shall not go into
though it is clearly a matter of the greatest practical and
theoretical interest. What is clear is that the conceptions of 'paying a debt' or 'having a debt forgiven' or
pardoning have no place in a system of therapy.

Fourth, with punishment there is an attempt at some
equivalence between the advantage gained by the wrongdoer—
partly based upon the seriousness of the interest invaded,
partly on the state of mind with which the wrongful act was
performed—and the punishment meted out. Thus, we can understand a prohibition on 'cruel and unusual punishments'
so that disproportionate pain and suffering are avoided.
With therapy attempts at proportionality make no sense. It
is perfectly plausible giving someone who kills a pill and
treating for a lifetime within an institution one who has
broken a dish and manifested accident proneness. We have
the concept of 'painful treatment.' We do not have the
concept of 'cruel treatment.' Because treatment is regarded as a benefit, though it may involve pain, it is
natural that less restraint is exercised in bestowing it,
than in inflicting punishment. Further, protests with respect to treatment are likely to be assimilated to the complaints of one whose leg must be amputated in order for him
to live, and, thus, largely disregarded. To be sure, there

is operative in the therapy world some conception of the "cure being worse than the disease," but if the disease is manifested in conduct harmful to others, and if being a normal operating human being is valued highly, there will naturally be considerable pressure to find the cure acceptable.

Fifth, the rules in our system of punishment governing conduct of individuals were rules violation of which involved either direct interference with others or the creation of a substantial risk of such interference. One could imagine adding to this system of primary rules other rules proscribing preparation to do acts violative of the primary rules and even rules proscribing thoughts. Objection to such suggestions would have many sources but a principal one would consist in its involving the infliction of punishment on too great a number of persons who would not, because of a change of mind, have violated the primary rules. Though we are interested in diminishing violations of the primary rules, we are not prepared to punish too many individuals who would never have violated the rules in order to achieve this aim. In a system motivated solely by a preventive and curative ideology there would be less reason to wait until symptoms manifest themselves in socially harmful conduct. It is understandable that we should wish at the earliest possible stage to arrest the development of the disease. In the punishment system, because we are dealing with deprivations, it is understandable that we should forbear from imposing them until we are quite sure of guilt. In the therapy system, dealing as it does with benefits, there is less reason for forbearance from treatment at an early stage.

Sixth, a variety of procedural safeguards we associate with punishment have less significance in a therapy system. To the degree objections to double jeopardy and self-incrimination are based on a wish to decrease the chances of the innocent being convicted and punished, a therapy system, unconcerned with this problem, would disregard such safeguards. When one is out to help people there is also little sense in urging that the burden of proof be on those providing the help. And there is less point to imposing the burden of proving that the conduct was pathological beyond a reasonable doubt. Further, a jury system, which, within a system of justice, serves to make accommodations to the individual situation and to introduce a human element, would play no role or a minor one in a world where expertise is required in making determinations of disease and treatment.

In our system of punishment an attempt was made to maximize each individual's freedom of choice by first of all delimiting by rules certain spheres of conduct immune from interference by others. The punishment associated with these primary rules paid deference to an individual's free choice by connecting punishment to a freely chosen act violative of the rules, thus giving some plausibility to the claim, as we saw, that what a person received by way of punishment he himself had chosen. With the world of disease and therapy all this changes and the individual's free choice ceases to be a determinative factor in how others respond to him. All those principles of our own legal system that minimize the chances of punishment of those who have not chosen to do acts violative of the rules tend to lose their point in the therapy system, for how we respond in a therapy system to a person is not conditioned upon what he has chosen but rather on what symptoms he has manifested or may manifest and what the best therapy for the disease is that is suggested by the symptoms.

Now, it is clear, I think, that were we confronted with the alternatives I have sketched, between a system of just punishment and a thoroughgoing system of treatment, a system, that is, that did not reintroduce concepts appropriate to punishment, we could see the point in claiming that a person has a right to be punished, meaning by this that a person had a right to all those institutions and practices linked to punishment. For these would provide him with, among other things, a far greater ability to predict what would happen to him on the occurrence of certain events than the therapy system. There is the inestimable value to each of us of having the responses of others to us determined over a wide range of our lives by what we choose rather than what they choose. A person has a right to institutions that respect his choices. Our punishment system does; our therapy system does not.

Apart from those aspects of our therapy model which would relate to serious limitations on personal liberty, there are clearly objections of a more profound kind to the mode of thinking I have associated with the therapy model.

First, human beings pride themselves in having capacities that animals do not. A common way, for example, of arousing shame in a child is to compare the child's conduct to that of an animal. In a system where all actions are assimilated to happenings we are assimilated to creatures—indeed, it is more extreme than this—whom we have always thought possessed of less than we. Fundamental to our practice of praise and order of attainment is that one who can do more—one who is capable of more and one who does more—is more worthy of respect and admiration. And we have thought of ourselves as capable where animals are not of making, of creating, among other things, ourselves. The conception of man I have outlined would provide us with a status that today, when our conduct is assimilated to it in moral criticism, we consider properly evocative of shame.

Second, if all human conduct is viewed as something men undergo, thrown into question would be the appropriateness of that extensive range of peculiarly human satisfactions that derive from a sense of achievement. For these satisfactions we shall have to substitute those mild satisfactions attendant upon a healthy well-functioning body. Contentment is our lot if we are fortunate; intense satisfaction at achievement is entirely inappropriate.

Third, in the therapy world nothing is earned and what we receive comes to us through compassion, or through a desire to control us. Resentment is out of place. We can take credit for nothing but must always regard ourselves— if there are selves left to regard once actions disappear— as fortunate recipients of benefits or unfortunate carriers of disease who must be controlled. We know that within our own world human beings who have been so regarded and who come to accept this view of themselves come to look upon themselves as worthless. When what we do is met with resentment, we are indirectly paid something of a compliment.

Fourth, attention should also be drawn to a peculiar evil that may be attendant upon regarding a man's actions as symptoms of disease. The logic of cure will push us toward forms of therapy that inevitably involve changes in the person made against his will. The evil in this would be most apparent in those cases where the agent, whose action is determined to be a manifestation of some disease, does not regard his action in this way. He believes that what he has done is, in fact, 'right' but his conception of 'normality' is not the therapeutically accepted one. When we treat an illness we normally treat a condition that the person is not responsible for. He is 'suffering' from some disease and we treat the condition, relieving the person of something preventing his normal functioning. When we begin treating persons for actions that have been chosen, we do not lift from the person something that is interfering with his normal functioning but we change the person so that he functions in a way regarded as normal by the current therapeutic community. We have to change him and his judgments of value. In doing this we display a lack of respect for the moral status of individuals, that is, a lack of respect for the reasoning and choices of individuals. They are but animals who must be conditioned. I think we can understand

and, indeed, sympathize with a man's preferring death to being forcibly turned into what he is not.

Finally, perhaps most frightening of all would be the derogation in status of all protests to treatment. If someone believes that he has done something right, and if he protests being treated and changed, the protest will itself be regarded as a sign of some pathological condition, for who would not wish to be cured of an affliction? What this leads to are questions of an important kind about the effect of this conception of man upon what we now understand by reasoning. Here what a person takes to be a reasoned defense of an act is treated, as the action was, on the model of a happening of a pathological kind. Not just a person's acts are taken from him but also his attempt at a reasoned justification for the acts. In a system of punishment a person who has committed a crime may argue that what he did was right. We make him pay the price and we respect his right to retain the judgment he has made. A conception of pathology precludes this form of respect.

It might be objected to the foregoing that all I have shown—if that—is that if the only alternatives open to us are a *just* system of punishment or the mad world of being treated like sick or healthy animals, we do in fact have a right to a system of punishment of this kind. But this hardly shows that we have a right *simpliciter* to punishment as we do, say, to be free. Indeed, it does not even show a right to a just system of punishment, for surely we can, without too much difficulty, imagine situations in which the alternatives to punishment are not this mad world but a world in which we are still treated as persons and there is, for example, not the pain and suffering attendant upon punishment. One such world is one in which there are rules but responses to their violation is not the deprivation of some good but forgiveness. Still another type of world would be one in which violation of the rules were responded to by merely comparing the conduct of the person to something commonly regarded as low or filthy, and thus, producing by this mode of moral criticism, feelings of shame rather than feelings of guilt.

I am prepared to allow that these objections have a point. While granting force to the above objections I want to offer a few additional comments with respect to each of them. First, any existent legal system permits the punishment of individuals under circumstances where the conditions I have set forth for a just system have not been satisfied. A glaring example of this would be criminal strict liability which is to be found in our own legal system. Nevertheless, I think it would be difficult to present any

system we should regard as a system of punishment that
would not still have a great advantage over our imagined
therapy system. The system of punishment we imagine may
more and more approximate a system of sheer terror in which
human beings are treated as animals to be intimidated and
prodded. To the degree that the system is of this character it is, in my judgment, not simply an unjust system but
one that diverges from what we normally understand by a
system of punishment. At least some deference to the
choice of individuals is built into the idea of punishment.
So there would be some truth in saying we have a right to
any system of punishment if the only alternative to it was
therapy.

Second, people may imagine systems in which there are
rules and in which the response to their violation is not
punishment but pardoning, the legal analogue of forgiveness.
Surely this is a system to which we would claim a right as
against one in which we are made to suffer for violating
the rules. There are several comments that need to be made
about this. It may be, of course, that a high incidence of
pardoning would increase the incidence of rule violations.
Further, the difficulty with suggesting pardoning as a general response is that pardoning presupposes the very responses that it is suggested it supplant. A system of deprivations, or a practice of deprivations on the happening of
certain actions, underlies the practice of pardoning and
forgiving, for it is only where we possess the idea of a
wrong to be made up or of a debt owed to others, ideas we
acquire within a world in which there have been deprivations for wrong acts, that we have the idea of pardoning
for the wrong or forgiving the debt.

Finally, if we look at the responses I suggested would
give rise to feelings of shame, we may rightly be troubled
with the appropriateness of this response in any community
in which each person assumes burdens so that each may derive benefits. In such situations might it not be that
individuals have a right to a system of punishment so that
each person could be assured that inequities in the distribution of benefits and burdens are unlikely to occur and if
they do, procedures exist for correcting them? Further, it
may well be that, everything considered, we should prefer
the pain and suffering of a system of punishment to a world
in which we only experience shame on the doing of wrong
acts, for with guilt there are relatively simple ways of
ridding outselves of the feeling we have, that is, gaining
forgiveness or taking the punishment, but with shame we
have to bear it until we no longer are the person who has
behaved in the shameful way. Thus, I suggest that we have,

wherever there is a distribution of benefits and burdens of
the kind I have described, a right to a system of punishment.

I want also to make clear in concluding this section
that I have argued, though very indirectly, not just for a
right to a system of punishment, but for a right to be punished once there is in existence such a system. Thus, a
man has the right to be punished rather than treated if he
is guilty of some offense. And, indeed, one can imagine a
case in which, even in the face of an offer of a pardon, a
man claims and ought to have acknowledged his right to be
punished.

2. The primary reason for preferring the system of
punishment as against the system of therapy might have been
expressed in terms of the one system treating one as a person and the other not. In invoking the right to be punished, one justifies one's claim by reference to a more
fundamental right. I want now to turn attention to this
fundamental right and attempt to shed light—it will have
to be little, for the topic is immense—on what is meant by
'treating an individual as a person.'

When we talk of not treating a human being as a person
or 'showing no respect for one as a person' what we imply
by our words is a contrast between the manner in which one
acceptably responds to human beings and the manner in which
one acceptably responds to animals and inanimate objects.
When we treat a human being merely as an animal or some inanimate object our responses to the human being are determined, not by his choices, but ours in disregard of or with
indifference to his. And when we 'look upon' a person as
less than a person or not a person, we consider the person
as incapable of a rational choice. In cases of not treating a human being as a person we interfere with a person in
such a way that what is done, even if the person is involved in the doing, is done not by the person but by the
user of the person. In extreme cases there may even be an
elision of a causal chain so that we might say that X
killed Z even though Y's hand was the hand that held the
weapon, for Y's hand may have been entirely in X's control.
The one agent is in some way treating the other as a mere
link in a causal chain. There is, of course, a wide range
of cases in which a person is used to accomplish the aim of
another and in which the person used is less than fully
free. A person may be grabbed against his will and used as
a shield. A person may be drugged or hypnotized and then
employed for certain ends. A person may be deceived into
doing other than he intends doing. A person may be ordered
to do something and threatened with harm if he does not and

coerced into doing what he does not want to. There is
still another range of cases in which individuals are not
used, but in which decisions by others are made that affect
them in circumstances where they have the capacity for
choice and where they are not being treated as persons.

But it is particularly important to look at coercion,
for I have claimed that a just system of punishment treats
human beings as persons; and it is not immediately apparent
how ordering someone to do something and threatening harm
differs essentially from having rules supported by threats
of harm in case of noncompliance.

There are affinities between coercion and other cases
of not treating someone as a person, for it is not the coerced person's choices but the coercer's that are responsible for what is done. But unlike other indisputable cases
of not treating one as a person, for example using someone
as a shield, there is some choice involved in coercion.
And if this is so, why does the coercer stand in any different relation to the coerced person than the criminal law
stands to individuals in society?

Suppose the person who is threatened disregards the
order and gets the threatened harm. Now suppose he is told,
"Well, you did after all bring it upon yourself." There is
clearly something strange in this. It is the person doing
the threatening and not the person threatened who is responsible. But our reaction to punishment, at least in a
system that resembles the one I have described, is precisely that the person violating the rules brought it upon himself. What lies behind these different reactions?

There exist situations in the law, of course, which
resemble coercion situations. There are occasions when in
the law a person might justifiably say "I am not being
treated as a person but being used" and where he might
properly react to the punishment as something "he was hardly responsible for." But it is possible to have a system
in which it would be misleading to say, over a wide range
of cases of punishment for noncompliance, that we are using
persons. The clearest case in which it would be inappropriate to so regard punishment would be one in which there
were explicit agreement in advance that punishment should
follow on the voluntary doing of certain acts. Even if one
does not have such conditions satisfied, and obviously such
explicit agreements are not characteristic, one can see
significant differences between our system of just punishment and a coercion situation.

First, unlike the case with one person coercing another 'to do his will,' the rules in our system apply to all,
with the benefits and burdens equally distributed. About

such a system it cannot be said that some are being subordinated to others or are being used by others or gotten to do things by others. To the extent that the rules are thought to be to the advantage of only some or to the extent there is a maldistribution of benefits and burdens, the difference between coercion and law disappears.

Second, it might be argued that at least any person inclined to act in a manner violative of the rules stands to all others as the person coerced stands to his coercer, and that he, at least, is a person disadvantaged as others are not. It is important here, I think, that he is part of a system in which it is commonly agreed that forbearance from the acts proscribed by the rules provides advantages for all. This system is the accepted setting; it is the norm. Thus, in any coercive situation, it is the coercer who deviates from the norm, with the responsibility of the person he is attempting to coerce defeated. In a just punishment situation, it is the person deviating from the norm, indeed he might be a coercer, who is responsible, for it is the norm to restrain oneself from acts of that kind. A voluntary agent diverging in his conduct from what is expected or what the norm is, on general causal principles, is regarded as the cause of what results from his conduct.

There is, then, some plausibility in the claim that, in a system of punishment of the kind I have sketched, a person chooses the punishment that is meted out to him. If, then, we can say in such a system that the rules provide none with advantages that others do not have, and further, that what happens to a person is conditioned by that person's choice and not that of others, then we can say that it is a system responding to one as a person.

We treat a human being as a person provided: first, we permit the person to make the choices that will determine what happens to him, and second, our responses to the person are responses respecting the person's choices. When we respond to a person's illness by treating the illness it is neither a case of treating or not treating the individual as a person. When we give a person a gift we are neither treating or not treating him as a person, unless, of course, he does not wish it, chooses not to have it, but we compel him to accept it.

3. This right to be treated as a person is a fundamental human right belonging to all human beings by virtue of their being human. It is also a natural, inalienable, and absolute right. I want now to defend these claims so reminiscent of an era of philosophical thinking about rights that many consider to have been seriously confused.

If the right is one that we possess by virtue of being human beings, we are immediately confronted with an apparent dilemma. If, to treat another as a person requires that we provide him with reasons for acting and avoid force or deception, how can we justify the force and deception we exercise with respect to children and the mentally ill? If they, too, have a right to be treated as persons are we not constantly infringing their rights? One way out of this is simply to restrict the right to those who satisfy the conditions of being a person. Infants and the insane, it might be argued, do not meet these conditions, and they would not then have the right. Another approach would be to describe the right they possess as a prima facie right to be treated as a person. This right might then be outweighed by other considerations. This approach generally seems to me, as I shall later argue, inadequate.

I prefer this tack. Children possess the right to be treated as persons but they possess this right as an individual might be said in the law of property to possess a future interest. There are advantages in talking of individuals as having a right though complete enjoyment of it is postponed. Brought to our attention, if we ascribe to them the right, is the legitimacy of their complaint if they are not provided with opportunities and conditions assuring their full enjoyment of the right when they acquire the characteristics of persons. More than this, all persons are charged with the sensitive task of not denying them the right to be a person and to be treated as a person by failing to provide the conditions for their becoming individuals who are able freely and in an informed way to choose and who are prepared themselves to assume responsibility for their choices. There is an obligation imposed upon us all, unlike that we have with respect to animals, to respond to children in such a way as to maximize the chances of their becoming persons. This may well impose upon us the obligation to treat them as persons from a very early age, that is, to respect their choices and to place upon them the responsibility for the choices to be made. There is no need to say that there is a close connection between how we respond to them and what they become. It also imposes upon us all the duty to display constantly the qualities of a person, for what they become they will largely become because of what they learn from us is acceptable behavior.

In claiming that the right is a right that human beings have by virtue of being human, there are several other features of the right that should be noted, perhaps better

conveyed by labelling them 'natural.' First, it is a right
we have apart from any voluntary agreement into which we
have entered. Second, it is not a right that derives from
some defined position or status. Third, it is equally apparent that one has the right regardless of the society or
community of which one is a member. Finally, it is a right
linked to certain features of a class of beings. Were we
fundamentally different than we now are, we would not have
it. But it is more than that, for the right is linked to a
feature of human beings which, were that feature absent—
the capacity to reason and to choose on the basis of reasons—, profound conceptual changes would be involved in
the thought about human beings. It is a right, then, connected with a feature of men that sets men apart from other
natural phenomena.

The right to be treated as a person is inalienable.
To say of a right that it is inalienable draws attention
not to limitations placed on what others may do with respect to the possessor of the right but rather to limitations placed on the dispositive capacities of the possessor
of the right. Something is to be gained in keeping the issues of alienability and absoluteness separate.

There are a variety of locutions qualifying what pos-
sessors of rights may and may not do. For example, on this
issue of alienability, it would be worthwhile to look at,
among other things, what is involved in abandoning, abdi-
cating, conveying, giving up, granting, relinquishing, surrendering, transferring, and waiving one's rights. And
with respect to each of these concepts we should also have
to be sensitive to the variety of uses of the term 'rights.'
What it is, for example, to waive a Hohfeldian 'right' in
his strict sense will differ from what it is to waive a
right in his 'privilege' sense.

Let us look at only two concepts very briefly, those
of transferring and waiving rights. The clearest case of
transferring rights is that of transferring rights with respect to specific objects. I own a watch and owning it I
have a complicated relationship, captured in this area
rather well I think by Hohfeld's four basic legal relationships, to all persons in the world with respect to the
watch. We crudely capture these complex relationships by
talking of my 'property rights' in or with respect to the
watch. If I sell the watch, thus exercising a capacity
provided by the rules of property, I have transferred
rights in or with respect to the watch to someone else, the
buyer, and the buyer now stands, as I formerly did, to all
persons in the world in a series of complex relationships
with respect to the watch.

While still the owner, I may have given to another permission to use it for several days. Had there not been the permission and had the person taken the watch, we should have spoken of interfering with or violating or, possibly, infringing my property rights. Or, to take a situation in which transferring rights is inappropriate, I may say to another "go ahead and slap me—you have my permission." In these types of situations philosophers and others have spoken of 'surrendering' rights or, alternatively and, I believe, less strangely, of 'waiving one's rights.' And recently, of course, the whole topic of 'waiving one's right to remain silent' in the context of police interrogation of suspects has been a subject of extensive litigation and discussion.

I confess to feeling that matters are not entirely perspicuous with respect to what is involved in 'waiving' or 'surrendering' rights. In conveying to another permission to take a watch or slap one, one makes legally permissible what otherwise would not have been. But in saying those words that constitute permission to take one's watch one is, of course, exercising precisely one of those capacities that leads us to say he has, while others have not, property rights with respect to the watch. Has one then waived his right in Hohfeld's strict sense in which the correlative is a duty to forbear on the part of others?

We may wish to distinguish here waiving the right to have others forbear to which there is a corresponding duty on their part to forbear, from placing oneself in a position where one has no legitimate right to complain. If I say the magic words "take the watch for a couple of days" or "go ahead and slap me," have I waived my right not to have my property taken or a right not to be struck or have I, rather, in saying what I have, simply stepped into a relation in which the rights no longer apply with respect to a specified other person? These observations find support in the following considerations. The right is that which gives rise, when infringed, to a legitimate claim against another person. What this suggests is that the right is that sphere interference with which entitles us to complain or gives us a right to complain. From this it seems to follow that a right to bodily security should be more precisely described as 'a right that others not interfere without permission.' And there is the corresponding duty not to interfere unless provided permission. Thus when we talk of waiving our rights or 'giving up our rights' in such cases we are not waiving or giving up our right to property nor our right to bodily security, for we still, of course, possess the right not to have our watch taken without permission. We have rather placed ourselves in a position where we do not possess the capacity, sometimes called a right, to complain if the person takes the watch or slaps us.

There is another type of situation in which we may speak of waiving our rights. If someone without permission slaps me, there is an infringement of my right to bodily security. If I now acquiesce or go further and say "forget it" or "you are forgiven," we might say that I had waived my right to complain. But here, too, I feel uncomfortable about what is involved. For I do have the right to complain (a right without a corresponding duty) in the event I am slapped and I have that right whether I wish it or not. If I say to another after the slap, "you are forgiven" what I do is not waive the right to complain but rather make illegitimate my subsequent exercise of that right.

Now, if we turn to the right to be treated as a person, the claim that I made was that it was inalienable, and what I meant to convey by that word of respectable age is that (a) it is a right that cannot be transferred to another in the way one's right with respect to objects can be transferred and (b) that it cannot be waived in the ways in which people talk of waiving rights to property or waiving, within certain limitations, one's right to bodily security. While the rules of the law of property are such that persons may, satisfying certain procedures, transfer rights, the right to be treated as a person logically cannot be transferred any more than one person can transfer to another his right to life or privacy. What, indeed, would it be like for another to have our right to be treated as a person? We can understand transferring a right with respect to certain objects. The new owner stands where the old owner stood. But with a right to be treated as a person what could this mean? My having the right meant that my choices were respected. Now if I transfer it to another this will mean that he will possess the right that my choices be respected? This is nonsense. It is only each person himself that can have his choices respected. It is no more possible to transfer this right than it is to transfer one's right to life.

Nor can the right be waived. It cannot be waived because any agreement to being treated as an animal or an instrument does not provide others with the moral permission to so treat us. One can volunteer to be a shield, but then it is one's choice on a particular occasion to be a shield. If without our permission, without our choosing it, someone used us as a shield, we may, I should suppose, forgive the person for treating us as an object. But we do not thereby waive our right to be treated as a person, for that is a right that has been infringed and what we have at most done is put ourselves in a position where it is inappropriate any longer to exercise the right to complain.

This is the sort of right, then, such that the moral rules defining relationships among persons preclude anyone from morally giving others legitimate permissions or rights with respect to one by doing or saying certain things. One stands, then, with respect to one's person as the nonowner of goods stands to those goods. The nonowner cannot, given the rule-defined relationships, convey to others rights and privileges that only the owner possesses. Just as there are agreements nonenforceable because void is contrary to public policy, so there are permissions our moral outlook regards as without moral force. With respect to being treated as a person, one is 'disabled' from modifying relations of others to one.

The right is absolute. This claim is bound to raise eyebrows. I have an innocuous point in mind in making this claim.

In discussing alienability we focused on incapacities with respect to disposing of rights. Here what I want to bring out is a sense in which a right exists despite considerations for refusing to accord the person his rights. As with the topic of alienability there are a host of concepts that deserve a close look in this area. Among them are according, acknowledging, annulling, asserting, claiming, denying, destroying, exercising, infringing, insisting upon, interfering with, possessing, recognizing, and violating.

The claim that rights are absolute has been construed to mean that 'assertions of rights cannot, for any reason under any circumstances, be denied.' When there are considerations which warrant refusing to accord persons their rights, there are two prevalent views as to how this should be described: there is, first, the view that the person does not have the right, and second, the view that he has rights but of a prima facie kind and that these have been outweighed or overcome by the other considerations. "We can conceive times when such rights must give way, and, therefore, they are only prima facie and not absolute rights." (Brandt)

Perhaps there are cases in which a person claims a right to do a certain thing, say with his property, and argues that his property rights are absolute, meaning by this he has a right to do whatever he wishes with his property. Here, no doubt, it has to be explained to the person that the right he claims he has, he does not in fact possess. In such a case the person does not have and never did have,

given a certain description of the right, a right that was
prima facie or otherwise, to do what he claimed he had the
right to do. If the assertion that a right is absolute implies that we have a right to do whatever we wish to do, it
is an absurd claim and as such should not really ever have
been attributed to political theorists arguing for absolute
rights. But, of course, the claim that we have a prima
facie right to do whatever we wish to do is equally absurd.
The right is not prima facie either, for who would claim,
thinking of the right to be free, that one has a prima
facie right to kill others, if one wishes, unless there are
moral considerations weighing against it?

There are, however, other situations in which it is
accepted by all that a person possesses rights of a certain
kind, and the difficulty we face is that of according the
person the right he is claiming when this will promote more
evil than good. The just act is to give the man his due
and giving a man what it is his right to have is giving him
his due. But it is a mistake to suppose that justice is
the only dimension of morality. It may be justifiable not
to accord to a man his rights. But it is no less a wrong
to him, no less an infringement. It is seriously misleading to turn all justifiable infringements into noninfringe-
ments by saying that the right is only prima facie, as if
we have, in concluding that we should not accord a man his
rights, made out a case that he had none. To use the language of 'prima facie rights' misleads, for it suggests
that a presumption of the existence of a right has been
overcome in these cases where all that can be said is that
the presumption in favor of according a man his rights has
been overcome. If we begin to think the right itself is
prima facie, we shall, in cases in which we are justified
in not according it, fail sufficiently to bring out that we
have interfered where justice says we should not. Our moral framework is unnecessarily and undesirably impoverished
by the theory that there are such rights.

When I claim, then, that the right to be treated as a
person is absolute what I claim is that given that one is a
person, one always has the right so to be treated, and that
while there may possibly be occasions morally requiring not
according a person this right, this fact makes it no less
true that the right exists and would be infringed if the
person were not accorded it.

4. Having said something about the nature of this fundamental right I want now, in conclusion, to suggest that
the denial of this right entails the denial of all moral
rights and duties. This requires bringing out what is surely intuitively clear—that any framework of rights and duties

presupposes individuals that have the capacity to choose on the basis of reasons presented to them, and that what makes legitimate actions within such a system are the free choices of individuals. There is, in other words, a distribution of benefits and burdens in accord with a respect for the freedom of choice and freedom of action of all. I think that the best way to make this point may be to sketch some of the features of a world in which rights and duties are possessed.

First, rights exist only when there is some conception of some things valued and others not. Secondly, and implied in the first point, is the fact that there are dispositions to defend the valued commodities. Third, the valued commodities may be interfered with by others in this world. A group of animals might be said to satisfy these first three conditions. Fourth, rights exist when there are recognized rules establishing the legitimacy of some acts and ruling out others. Mistakes in the claim of rights are possible. Rights imply the concepts of interference and infringement, concepts the elucidation of which requires the concept of a rule applying to the conduct of persons. Fifth, to possess a right is to possess something that constitutes a legitimate restraint on the freedom of action of others. It is clear, for example, that if individuals were incapable of controlling their actions we would have no notion of a legitimate claim that they do so. If, for example, we were all disposed to object or disposed to complain, as the elephant seal is disposed to object when his territory is invaded, then the objection would operate in a causal way, or approximating a causal way, in getting the behavior of noninterference. In a system of rights, on the other hand, there is a point to appealing to the rules in legitimating one's complaint. Implied, then, in any conception of rights is the existence of individuals capable of choosing and capable of choosing on the basis of considerations with respect to rules. The distribution of freedom throughout such a system is determined by the free choice of individuals. Thus any denial of the right to be treated as a person would be a denial undercutting the whole system, for the system rests on the assumption that spheres of legitimate and illegitimate conduct are to be delimited with regard to the choices made by persons.

This conclusion stimulates one final reflection on the therapy world we imagined.

The denial of this fundamental right will also carry with it, ironically, the denial of the right to treatment to those who are ill. In the world as we now understand it, there are those who do wrong and who have a right to be

responded to as persons who have done wrong. And there are
those who have not done wrong but who are suffering from
illnesses that in a variety of ways interfere with their
capacity to live their lives as complete persons. These
persons who are ill have a claim upon our compassion. But
more than this they have, as animals do not, a right to be
treated as persons. When an individual is ill he is entitled to that assistance which will make it possible for
him to resume his functioning as a person. If it is an injustice to punish an innocent person, it is no less an injustice, and a far more significant one in our day, to fail
to promote as best we can through adequate facilities and
medical care the treatment of those who are ill. Those human beings who fill our mental institutions are entitled to
more than they do in fact receive; they should be viewed as
possessing the right to be treated as a person so that our
responses to them may increase the likelihood that they
will enjoy fully the right to be so treated. Like the
child the mentally ill person has a future interest we cannot rightly deny him. Society is today sensitive to the
infringement of justice in punishing the innocent; elaborate rules exist to avoid this evil. Society should be no
less sensitive to the injustice of failing to bring back to
the community of persons those whom it is possible to bring
back.

PUNISHMENT AND UTILITY

Jeremy Bentham

OF THE PRINCIPLE OF UTILITY

I.   Nature has placed mankind under the governance of
two sovereign masters, *pain* and *pleasure*. It is for them

From Chapters I, III, VII, XIII, and XIV of *An Introduction
to the Principles of Morals and Legislation* (1823 edition).
Some footnotes have been omitted.

alone to point out what we ought to do, as well as to determine what we shall do. On the one hand the standard of
right and wrong, on the other the chain of causes and effects, are fastened to their throne. They govern us in all
we do, in all we say, in all we think: every effort we can
make to throw off our subjection, will serve but to demonstrate and confirm it. In words a man may pretend to ab-
jure their empire: but in reality he will remain subject to
it all the while. The *principle of utility*[1] recognises
this subjection, and assumes it for the foundation of that
system, the object of which is to rear the fabric of felicity by the hands of reason and law. Systems which attempt
to question it, deal in sounds instead of sense, in caprice
instead of reason, in darkness instead of light.

But enough of metaphor and declamation: it is not by
such means that moral science is to be improved.

II. The principle of utility is the foundation of the
present work: it will be proper therefore at the outset to
give an explicit and determinate account of what is meant
by it. By the principle of utility is meant that principle
which approves or disapproves of every action whatsoever,
according to the tendency which it appears to have to

---

[1]Note by the Author, July 1822.
To this denomination has of late been added, or substituted, the *greatest happiness* or *greatest felicity* principle: this for shortness, instead of saying at length *that
principle* which states the greatest happiness of all those
whose interest is in question, as being the right and proper, and only right and proper and universally desirable,
end of human action: of human action in every situation,
and in particular in that of a functionary or set of func-
tionaries exercising the powers of Government. The word
utility does not so clearly point to the ideas of *pleasure*
and *pain* as the words *happiness* and *felicity* do: nor does
it lead us to the consideration of the *number*, of the interests affected; to the *number*, as being the circumstance,
which contributes, in the largest proportion, to the forma-
tion of the standard here in question; the *standard of
right and wrong*, by which alone the propriety of human conduct, in every situation, can with propriety be tried.
This want of a sufficiently manifest connexion between the
ideas of *happiness* and *pleasure* on the one hand, and the
idea of *utility* on the other, I have every now and then
found operating, and with but too much efficiency, as a
bar to the acceptance, that might otherwise have been given,
to this principle.

augment or diminish the happiness of the party whose interest is in question: or, what is the same thing in other words, to promote or to oppose that happiness. I say of every action whatsoever; and therefore not only of every action of a private individual, but of every measure of government.

III. By utility is meant that property in any object, whereby it tends to produce benefit, advantage, pleasure, good, or happiness, (all this in the present case comes to the same thing) or (what comes again to the same thing) to prevent the happening of mischief, pain, evil, or unhappiness to the party whose interest is considered: if that party be the community in general, then the happiness of the community: if a particular individual, then the happiness of that individual.

IV. The interest of the community is one of the most general expressions that can occur in the phraseology of morals: no wonder that the meaning of it is often lost. When it has a meaning, it is this. The community is a fictitious *body*, composed of the individual persons who are considered as constituting as it were its *members*. The interest of the community then is, what?—the sum of the interests of the several members who compose it.

V. It is in vain to talk of the interest of the community, without understanding what is the interest of the individual. A thing is said to promote the interest, or to be *for* the interest, of an individual, when it tends to add to the sum total of his pleasures: or, what comes to the same thing, to diminish the sum total of his pains.

VI. An action then may be said to be conformable to the principle of utility, or, for shortness sake, to utility, (meaning with respect to the community at large) when the tendency it has to augment the happiness of the community is greater than any it has to diminish it.

VII. A measure of government (which is but a particular kind of action, performed by a particular person or persons) may be said to be conformable to or dictated by the principle of utility, when in like manner the tendency which it has to augment the happiness of the community is greater than any which it has to diminish it.

VIII. When an action, or in particular a measure of government, is supposed by a man to be conformable to the principle of utility, it may be convenient, for the purposes of discourse, to imagine a kind of law or dictate, called a law or dictate of utility: and to speak of the action in question, as being conformable to such a law or dictate. . . .

OF THE FOUR SANCTIONS OR SOURCES OF PAIN AND PLEASURE

I.   It has been shown that the happiness of the individuals, of whom a community is composed, that is their
pleasures and their security, is the end and the sole end
which the legislator ought to have in view: the sole standard, in conformity to which each individual ought, as far
as depends upon the legislator, to be *made* to fashion his
behaviour. But whether it be this or any thing else that
is to be *done*, there is nothing by which a man can ultimately be *made* to do it, but either pain or pleasure.
Having taken a general view of these two grand objects
(*viz*. pleasure, and what comes to the same thing, immunity
from pain) in the character of *final* causes; it will be
necessary to take a view of pleasure and pain itself, in
the character of *efficient* causes or means.

II.   There are four distinguishable sources from which
pleasure and pain are in use to flow: considered separately,
they may be termed the *physical*, the *political*, the *moral*,
and the *religious*: and inasmuch as the pleasures and pains
belonging to each of them are capable of giving a binding
force to any law or rule of conduct, they may all of them
be termed *sanctions*. . . .

IV.   If at the hands of a *particular* person or set of
persons in the community, who under names correspondent to
that of *judge*, are chosen for the particular purpose of
dispensing it, according to the will of the sovereign or
supreme ruling power in the state, it may be said to issue
from the *political sanction*. . . .

OF HUMAN ACTIONS IN GENERAL

I.   The business of government is to promote the happiness of the society, by punishing and rewarding. That
part of its business which consists in punishing, is more
particularly the subject of penal law. In proportion as an
act tends to disturb that happiness, in proportion as the
tendency of it is pernicious, will be the demand it creates
for punishment. What happiness consists of we have already seen: enjoyment of pleasures, security from pains.

II.   The general tendency of an act is more or less
pernicious, according to the sum total of its consequences:
that is, according to the difference between the sum of
such as are good, and the sum of such as are evil.

III.   It is to be observed, that here, as well as
henceforward, wherever consequences are spoken of, such

only are meant as are *material*. Of the consequences of any
act, the multitude and variety must needs be infinite: but
such of them only as are material are worth regarding. Now
among the consequences of an act, be they what they may,
such only, by one who views them in the capacity of a legislator, can be said to be material, as either consist of
pain or pleasure, or have an influence in the production of
pain or pleasure. . . .

CASES UNMEET FOR PUNISHMENT

1. *General View of Cases Unmeet for Punishment*

I. The general object which all laws have, or ought
to have, in common, is to augment the total happiness of
the community; and therefore, in the first place, to exclude, as far as may be, every thing that tends to subtract
from that happiness: in other words, to exclude mischief.
II. But all punishment is mischief: all punishment in
itself is evil. Upon the principle of utility, if it ought
at all to be admitted, it ought only to be admitted in as
far as it promises to exclude some greater evil.[2]

[2]What follows, relative to the subject of punishment, ought
regularly to be preceded by a distinct chapter on the ends
of punishment. But having little to say on that particular
branch of the subject, which has not been said before, it
seemed better, in a work, which will at any rate be but too
voluminous, to omit this title, reserving it for another,
hereafter to be published intituled *The Theory of Punishment*. To the same work I must refer the analysis of the
several possible modes of punishment, a particular and minute examination of the nature of each, and of its advantages and disadvantages, and various other disquisitions,
which did not seem absolutely necessary to be inserted here.
A very few words, however, concerning the *ends* of punishment, can scarcely be dispensed with.
The immediate principal end of punishment is to control action. This action is either that of the offender,
or of others: that of the offender it controls by its influence, either on his will, in which case it is said to
operate in the way of *reformation*; or on his physical power,
in which case it is said to operate by *disablement*: that of
others it can influence no otherwise than by its influence
over their wills; in which case it is said to operate in

III. It is plain, therefore, that in the following cases punishment ought not to be inflicted.

1. Where it is *groundless*: where there is no mischief for it to prevent; the act not being mischievous upon the whole.

2. Where it must be *inefficacious*: where it cannot act so as to prevent the mischief.

3. Where it is *unprofitable*, or too *expensive*: where the mischief it would produce would be greater than what it prevented.

4. Where it is *needless*: where the mischief may be prevented, or cease of itself, without it: that is, at a cheaper rate.

2. *Cases in Which Punishment Is Groundless*

These are,

IV. 1. Where there has never been any mischief: where no mischief has been produced to any body by the act in question. Of this number are those in which the act was such as might, on some occasions, be mischievous or disagreeable, but the person whose interest it concerns gave his *consent* to the performance of it. This consent, provided it be free, and fairly obtained, is the best proof

---

[2](cont.) the way of *example*. A kind of collateral end, which it has a natural tendency to answer, is that of affording a pleasure or satisfaction to the party injured, where there is one, and, in general, to parties whose ill-will, whether on a self-regarding account, or on the account of sympathy or antipathy, has been excited by the offence. This purpose, as far as it can be answered *gratis*, is a beneficial one. But no punishment ought to be allotted merely to this purpose, because (setting aside its effects in the way of control) no such pleasure is ever produced by punishment as can be equivalent to the pain. The punishment, however, which is allotted to the other purpose, ought, as far as it can be done without expense, to be accommodated to this. Satisfaction thus administered to a party injured, in the shape of a dissocial pleasure, may be styled a vindictive satisfaction or compensation: as a compensation, administered in the shape of a self-regarding profit, or stock of pleasure, may be styled a lucrative one. See B. I. tit. vi. [Compensation]. Example is the most important end of all, in proportion as the *number* of the persons under temptation to offend is to *one*.

that can be produced, that, to the person who gives it, no mischief, at least no immediate mischief upon the whole, is done. For no man can be so good a judge as the man himself, what it is gives him pleasure or displeasure.

V. 2. Where the mischief was *outweighed*: although a mischief was produced by that act, yet the same act was necessary to the production of a benefit which was of greater value than the mischief. This may be the case with any thing that is done in the way of precaution against instant calamity, as also with any thing that is done in the exercise of the several sorts of powers necessary to be established in every community, to wit, domestic, judicial, military, and supreme.

VI. 3. Where there is a certainty of an adequate compensation: and that in all cases where the offence can be committed. This supposes two things: 1. That the offence is such as admits of an adequate compensation: 2. That such a compensation is sure to be forthcoming. Of these suppositions, the latter will be found to be a merely ideal one: a supposition that cannot, in the universality here given to it, be verified by fact. It cannot, therefore, in practice, be numbered amongst the grounds of absolute impunity. It may, however, be admitted as a ground for an abatement of that punishment, which other considerations, standing by themselves, would seem to dictate.

3. *Cases in Which Punishment Must Be Inefficacious*

These are,

VII. 1. Where the penal provision is *not established* until after the act is done. Such are the cases, 1. Of an *ex-post-facto* law; where the legislator himself appoints not a punishment till after the act is done. 2. Of a sentence beyond the law; where the judge, of his own authority, appoints a punishment which the legislator had not appointed.

VIII. 2. Where the penal provision, though established, is *not conveyed* to the notice of the person on whom it seems intended that it should operate. Such is the case where the law has omitted to employ any of the expedients which are necessary, to make sure that every person whatsoever, who is within the reach of the law, be apprized of all the cases whatsoever, in which (being in the station of life he is in) he can be subjected to the penalties of the law.

IX. 3. Where the penal provision, though it were conveyed to a man's notice, *could produce no effect* on him,

with respect to the preventing him from engaging in any act
of the *sort* in question. Such is the case, 1. In extreme
infancy; where a man has not yet attained that state or disposition of mind in which the prospect of evils so distant
as those which are held forth by the law, has the effect of
influencing his conduct. 2. In *insanity*; where the person,
if he has attained to that disposition, has since been deprived of it through the influence of some permanent though
unseen cause. 3. In *intoxication*; where he has been deprived of it by the transient influence of a visible cause:
such as the use of wine, or opium, or other drugs, that act
in this manner on the nervous system: which condition is
indeed neither more nor less than a temporary insanity produced by an assignable cause.[3]

X. 4. Where the appeal provision (although, being conveyed to the party's notice, it might very well prevent his
engaging in acts of the sort in question, provided he knew
that it related to those acts) could not have this effect,
with regard to the *individual* act he is about to engage in:
to wit, because he knows not that it is of the number of
those to which the penal provision relates. This may happen, 1. In the case of *unintentionality*; where he intends
not to engage, and thereby knows not that he is about to engage, in the *act* in which eventually he is about to engage.

---

[3]Notwithstanding what is here said, the cases of infancy
and intoxication (as we shall see hereafter) cannot be
looked upon in practice as affording sufficient grounds for
absolute impunity. But this exception in point of practice
is no objection to the propriety of the rule in point of
theory. The ground of the exception is neither more nor
less than the difficulty there is of ascertaining the matter of fact: viz. whether at the requisite point of time
the party was actually in the state in question; that is,
whether a given case comes really under the rule. Suppose
the matter of fact capable of being perfectly ascertained,
without danger or mistake, the impropriety of punishment
would be as indubitable in these cases as in any other.

The reason that is commonly assigned for the establishing an exemption from punishment in favour of infants, insane persons, and persons under intoxication, is either
false in fact, or confusedly expressed. The phrase is,
that the will of these persons concurs not with the act;
that they have no vicious will; or, that they have not the
free use of their will. But suppose all this to be true?
What is it to the purpose? Nothing: except in as far as it
implies the reason given in the text.

2. In the case of *unconsciousness*; where, although he may know that he is about to engage in the *act* itself, yet, from not knowing all the material *circumstances* attending it, he knows not of the *tendency* it has to produce that mischief, in contemplation of which it has been made penal in most instances.   3. In the case of *missupposal*; where, although he may know of the tendency the act has to produce that degree of mischief, he supposes it, though mistakenly, to be attended with some circumstance, or set of circumstances, which, if it had been attended with, it would either not have been productive of that mischief, or have been productive of such a greater degree of good, as has determined the legislator in such a case not to make it penal.

XI. 5.   Where, though the penal clause might exercise a full and prevailing influence, were it to act alone, yet by the *predominant* influence of some opposite cause upon the will, it must necessarily be ineffectual; because the evil which he sets himself about to undergo, in the case of his *not* engaging in the act, is so great, that the evil denounced by the penal clause, in case of his engaging in it, cannot appear greater.   This may happen, 1. In the case of *physical danger*; where the evil is such as appears likely to be brought about by the unassisted powers of *nature*. 2. In the case of a *threatened mischief*; where it is such as appears likely to be brought about through the intentional and conscious agency of *man*. [4]

XII. 6.   Where (though the penal clause may exert a full and prevailing influence over the *will* of the party) yet his *physical faculties* (owing to the predominant influence of some physical cause) are not in a condition to follow the determination of the will: insomuch that the act is absolutely *involuntary*.   Such is the case of physical

---

[4]The influences of the *moral* and *religious* sanctions, or, in other words, of the motives of *love of reputation* and *religion*, are other causes, the force of which may, upon particular occasions, come to be greater than that of any punishment which the legislator is *able*, or at least which he will *think proper*, to apply.   These, therefore, it will be proper for him to have his eye upon.   But the force of these influences is variable and different in different times and places: the force of the foregoing influences is constant and the same, at all times and every where.   These, therefore, it can never be proper to look upon as safe grounds for establishing absolute impunity: owing (as in the above-mentioned cases of infancy and intoxication) to the impracticability of ascertaining the matter of fact.

compulsion or *restraint*, by whatever means brought about; where the man's hand, for instance, is pushed against some object which his will disposes him *not* to touch; or tied down from touching some object which his will disposes him to touch.

4. *Cases Where Punishment Is Unprofitable*

These are,

XIII. 1. Where, on the one hand, the nature of the offence, on the other hand, that of the punishment, are, *in the ordinary state of things*, such, that when compared together, the evil of the latter will turn out to be greater than that of the former.

XIV. Now the evil of the punishment divides itself into four branches, by which so many different sets of persons are affected. 1. The evil of *coercion* or *restraint*: or the pain which it gives a man not to be able to do the act, whatever it be, which by the apprehension of the punishment he is deterred from doing. This is felt by those by whom the law is *observed*. 2. The evil of *apprehension*: or the pain which a man, who has exposed himself to punishment, feels at the thoughts of undergoing it. This is felt by those by whom the law has been *broken*, and who feel themselves in *danger* of its being executed upon them. 3. The evil of *sufferance*: or the pain which a man feels, in virtue of the punishment itself, from the time when he begins to undergo it. This is felt by those by whom the law is broken, and upon whom it comes actually to be executed. 4. The pain of sympathy, and the other *derivative* evils resulting to the persons who are in *connection* with the several classes of original sufferers just mentioned. Now of these four lots of evil, the first will be greater or less, according to the nature of the act from which the party is restrained: the second and third according to the nature of the punishment which stands annexed to that offence.

XV. On the other hand, as to the evil of the offence, this will also, of course, be greater or less, according to the nature of each offence. The proportion between the one evil and the other will therefore be different in the case of each particular offence. The cases, therefore, where punishment is unprofitable on this ground, can by no other means be discovered, than by an examination of each particular offence; which is what will be the business of the body of the work.

XVI. 2. Where, although in the *ordinary state* of things, the evil resulting from the punishment is not

greater than the benefit which is likely to result from the
force with which it operates, during the same space of time,
towards the excluding the evil of the offences, yet it may
have been rendered so by the influence of some *occasional
circumstances*.   In the number of these circumstances may be,
1. The multitude of delinquents at a particular juncture;
being such as would increase, beyond the ordinary measure,
the *quantum* of the second and third lots, and thereby also
of a part of the fourth lot, in the evil of the punishment.
2. The extraordinary value of the services of some one de-
linquent; in the case where the effect of the punishment
would be to deprive the community of the benefit of those
services. 3. The displeasure of the *people*; that is, of an
indefinite number of the members of the *same* community, in
cases where (owing to the influence of some occasional incident) they happen to conceive, that the offence or the
offender ought not to be punished at all, or at least ought
not to be punished in the way in question.   4. The displeasure of *foreign powers*; that is, of the governing body,
or a considerable number of the members of some *foreign*
community or communities, with which the community in question is connected.

5. *Cases Where Punishment Is Needless*

These are,
XVII. 1.   Where the purpose of putting an end to the
practice may be attained as effectually at a cheaper rate:
by instruction, for instance, as well as by terror: by in-
forming the understanding; as well as by exercising an immediate influence on the will.   This seems to be the case
with respect to all those offences which consist in the
disseminating pernicious principles in matters of *duty*; of
whatever kind the duty be; whether political, or moral, or
religious.   And this, whether such principles be dissemi-
nated *under*, or even *without*, a sincere persuasion of their
being beneficial.   I say, even *without*: for though in such
a case it is not instruction that can prevent the writer
from endeavouring to inculcate his principles, yet it may
the readers from adopting them: without which, his endeavouring to inculcate them will do no harm.   In such a case,
the sovereign will commonly have little need to take an active part: if it be the interest of *one* individual to inculcate principles that are pernicious, it will as surely be
the interest of *other* individuals to expose them.   But if
the sovereign must needs take a part in the controversy,
the pen is the proper weapon to combat error with, not the
sword.

OF THE PROPORTION BETWEEN PUNISHMENTS AND OFFENCES

I. We have seen that the general object of all laws is to prevent mischief; that is to say, when it is worth while; but that, where there are no other means of doing this than punishment, there are four cases in which it is *not* worth while.

II. When it *is* worth while, there are four subordinate designs or objects, which, in the course of his endeavours to compass, as far as may be, that one general object, a legislator, whose views are governed by the principle of utility, comes naturally to propose to himself.

III. 1. His first, most extensive, and most eligible object, is to prevent, in as far as it is possible, and worth while, all sorts of offences whatsoever:[5] in other words, so to manage, that no offence whatsoever may be committed.

IV. 2. But if a man must needs commit an offence of some kind or other, the next object is to induce him to commit an offence *less* mischievous, *rather* than one *more* mischievous: in other words, to choose always the *least* mischievous, of two offences that will either of them suit his purpose.

V. 3. When a man has resolved upon a particular offence, the next object is to dispose him to do *no more* mischief than is *necessary* to his purpose: in other words, to do as little mischief as is consistent with the benefit he has in view.

VI. 4. The last object is, whatever the mischief be, which it is proposed to prevent, to prevent it at as *cheap* a rate as possible.

VII. Subservient to these four objects, or purposes, must be the rules or canons by which the proportion of punishments to offences is to be governed.

VIII. Rule I. 1. The first object, it has been seen, is to prevent, in as far as it is worth while, all sorts of offences; therefore,

The value of the punishment must not be less in any case than what is sufficient to outweigh that of the profit[6] *of the offence.*

---

[5]By *offences* I mean, at present, acts which appear to him to have a tendency to produce mischief.

[6]By the profit of an offence, is to be understood, not merely the pecuniary profit, but the pleasure or advantage, of whatever kind it be, which a man reaps, or expects to reap, from the gratification of the desire which prompted him to

If it be, the offence (unless some other considerations, independent of the punishment, should intervene and operate efficaciously in the character of tutelary motives) will be sure to be committed notwithstanding: the whole lot of punishment will be thrown away: it will be altogether *inefficacious*.

IX. The above rule has been often objected to, on account of its seeming harshness: but this can only have happened for want of its being properly understood. The strength of the temptation, *cæteris paribus*, is as the profit of the offence: the quantum of the punishment must rise with the profit of the offence: *cæteris paribus*, it must therefore rise with the strength of the temptation. This there is no disputing. True it is, that the stronger the temptation, the less conclusive is the indication which the act of delinquency affords of the depravity of the offender's disposition. So far then as the absence of any aggravation, arising from extraordinary depravity of disposition, may operate, or at the utmost, so far as the presence of a ground of extenuation, resulting from the innocence or beneficence of the offender's disposition, can operate, the strength of the temptation may operate in abatement of the demand for punishment. But it can never operate so far as to indicate the propriety of making the punishment ineffectual, which it is sure to be when brought below the level of the apparent profit of the offence.

The partial benevolence which should prevail for the reduction of it below this level, would counteract as well those purposes which such a motive would actually have in

---

[6](cont.) engage in the offence. It is the profit (that is, the expectation of the profit) of the offence that constitutes the *impelling* motive, or, where there are several, the sum of the impelling motives, by which a man is prompted to engage in the offence. It is the punishment, that is, the expectation of the punishment, that constitutes the *restraining* motive, which, either by itself, or in conjunction with others, is to act upon him in a *contrary* direction, so as to induce him to abstain from engaging in the offence. Accidental circumstances apart, the strength of the temptation is as the force of the seducing, that is, of the impelling motive or motives. To say then, as authors of great merit and great name have said, that the punishment ought not to increase with the strength of the temptation, is as much as to say in mechanics, that the moving force or *momentum* of the *power* need not increase in proportion to the momentum of the *burthen*.

view, as those more extensive purposes which benevolence
ought to have in view: it would be cruelty not only to the
public, but to the very persons in whose behalf it pleads:
in its effects, I mean, however opposite in its intention.
Cruelty to the public, that is cruelty to the innocent, by
suffering them, for want of an adequate protection, to lie
exposed to the mischief of the offence: cruelty even to the
offender himself, by punishing him to no purpose, and without the chance of compassing that beneficial end, by which
alone the introduction of the evil of punishment is to be
justified.

 X. Rule 2. But whether a given offence shall be prevented in a given degree by a given quantity of punishment,
is never any thing better than a chance; for the purchasing
of which, whatever punishment is employed, is so much ex-
pended in advance. However, for the sake of giving it the
better chance of outweighing the profit of the offence,

*The greater the mischief of the offence, the greater
is the expense, which it may be worth while to be at, in
the way of punishment.*

 XI. Rule 3. The next object is, to induce a man to
choose always the least mischievous of two offences; therefore

*Where two offences come in competition, the punishment
for the greater offence must be sufficient to induce a man
to prefer the less.*

 XII. Rule 4. When a man has resolved upon a particular offence, the next object is, to induce him to do no
more mischief than what is necessary for his purpose: therefore

*The punishment should be adjusted in such manner to
each particular offence, that for every part of the mischief there may be a motive to restrain the offender from
giving birth to it.*

 XIII. Rule 5. The last object is, whatever mischief
is guarded against, to guard against it at as cheap a rate
as possible: therefore

*The punishment ought in no case to be more than what
is necessary to bring it into conformity with the rules
here given.*

 XIV. Rule 6. It is further to be observed, that owing to the different manners and degrees in which persons
under different circumstances are affected by the same exciting cause, a punishment which is the same in name will
not always either really produce, or even so much as appear
to others to produce, in two different persons the same degree of pain: therefore

*That the quantity actually inflicted on each individu-
al offender may correspond to the quantity intended for*

similar offenders in general, the several circumstances influencing sensibility ought always to be taken into account.

XV. Of the above rules of proportion, the four first, we may perceive, serve to mark out the limits on the side of diminution; the limits *below* which a punishment ought not to be *diminished*: the fifth, the limits on the side of increase; the limits *above* which it ought not to be *increased*. The five first are calculated to serve as guides to the legislator: the sixth is calculated, in some measure, indeed, for the same purpose; but principally for guiding the judge in his endeavours to conform, on both sides, to the intentions of the legislator.

XVI. Let us look back a little. The first rule, in order to render it more conveniently applicable to practice, may need perhaps to be a little more particularly unfolded. It is to be observed, then, that for the sake of accuracy, it was necessary, instead of the word *quantity* to make use of the less perspicuous term *value*. For the word *quantity* will not properly include the circumstances either of certainty or proximity: circumstances which, in estimating the value of a lot of pain or pleasure, must always be taken into the account. Now, on the one hand, a lot of punishment is a lot of pain; on the other hand, the profit of an offence is a lot of pleasure, or what is equivalent to it. But the profit of the offence *is* commonly more *certain* than the punishment, or, what comes to the same thing, *appears* so at least to the offender. It is at any rate commonly more *immediate*. It follows, therefore, that, in order to maintain its superiority over the profit of the offence, the punishment must have its value made up in some other way, in proportion to that whereby it falls short in the two points of *certainty* and *proximity*. Now there is no other way in which it can receive any addition to its *value*, but by receiving an addition in point of *magnitude*. Wherever then the value of the punishment falls short, either in point of *certainty*, or of *proximity*, of that of the profit of the offence, it must receive a proportionable addition in point of *magnitude*.[7]

XVII. Yet farther. To make sure of giving the value of the punishment the superiority over that of the offence, it may be necessary, in some cases, to take into

---

[7]It is for this reason, for example, that simple compensation is never looked upon as sufficient punishment for theft or robbery.

the account the profit not only of the *individual* offence
to which the punishment is to be annexed, but also of such
other offences of the *same sort* as the offender is likely
to have already committed without detection. This random
mode of calculation, severe as it is, it will be impossible
to avoid having recourse to, in certain cases: in such, to
wit, in which the profit is pecuniary, the chance of detection very small, and the obnoxious act of such a nature as
indicates a habit: for example, in the case of frauds
against the coin. If it be *not* recurred to, the practice
of committing the offence will be sure to be, upon the balance of the account, a gainful practice. That being the
case, the legislator will be absolutely sure of *not* being
able to suppress it, and the whole punishment that is be-
stowed upon it will be thrown away. In a word (to keep to
the same expressions we set out with) that whole quantity
of punishment will be *inefficacious*.

XVIII.   Rule 7.   These things being considered, the
three following rules may be laid down by way of supplement
and explanation to Rule 1.

*To enable the value of the punishment to outweigh
that of the profit of the offence, it must be increased,
in point of magnitude, in proportion as it falls short
in point of certainty.*

XIX.   Rule 8.   *Punishment must be further increased
in point of magnitude, in proportion as it falls short in
point of proximity.*

XX.   Rule 9.   *Where the act is conclusively indicative
of a habit, such an increase must be given to the punishment as may enable it to outweigh the profit not only of
the individual offence, but of such other like offences as
are likely to have been committed with impunity by the same
offender.*

XXI.   There may be a few other circumstances or considerations which may influence, in some small degree, the demand for punishment: but as the propriety of these is either not so demonstrable, or not so constant, or the application of them not so determinate, as that of the foregoing,
it may be doubted whether they be worth putting on a level
with the others.

XXII.   Rule 10.   *When a punishment, which in point of
quality is particularly well calculated to answer its intention, cannot exist in less than a certain quantity, it may
sometimes be of use, for the sake of employing it, to
stretch a little beyond that quantity which, on other accounts, would be strictly necessary.*

XXIII.   Rule 11.   *In particular, this may sometimes be
the case, where the punishment proposed is of such a nature*

*as to be particularly well calculated to answer the purpose
of a moral lesson.*[8]

XXIV. Rule 12. The tendency of the above considerations is to dictate an augmentation in the punishment: the
following rule operates in the way of diminution. There
are certain cases (it has been seen) in which, by the influence of accidental circumstances, punishment may be rendered unprofitable in the whole: in the same cases it may
chance to be rendered unprofitable as to a part only. Accordingly,

*In adjusting the quantum of punishment, the circum-
stances, by which all punishment may be rendered unprofitable, ought to be attended to.*

XXV. Rule 13. It is to be observed, that the more
various and minute any set of provisions are, the greater
the chance is that any given article in them will not be
borne in mind: without which, no benefit can ensue from it.
Distinctions, which are more complex than what the conceptions of those whose conduct it is designed to influence
can take in, will even be worse than useless. The whole
system will present a confused appearance: and thus the effect, not only of the proportions established by the articles in question, but of whatever is connected with them,
will be destroyed. To draw a precise line of direction in
such case seems impossible. However, by way of memento, it
may be of some use to subjoin the following rule.

*Among provisions designed to perfect the proportion
between punishments and offences, if any occur, which, by
their own particular good effects, would not make up for
the harm they would do by adding to the intricacy of the
Code, they should be omitted.*

XXVI. It may be remembered, that the political sanction, being that to which the sort of punishment belongs,
which in this chapter is all along in view, is but one of
four sanctions, which may all of them contribute their
share towards producing the same effects. It may be expected, therefore, that in adjusting the quantity of political punishment, allowance should be made for the assistance it may meet with from those other controlling powers.

---

[8]A punishment may be said to be calculated to answer the
purpose of a moral lesson, when, by reason of the ignominy
it stamps upon the offence, it is calculated to inspire the
public with sentiments of aversion towards those pernicious
habits and dispositions with which the offence appears to
be connected; and thereby to inculcate the opposite beneficial habits and dispositions.

True it is, that from each of these several sources a very
powerful assistance may sometimes be derived. But the case
is, that (setting aside the moral sanction, in the case
where the force of it is expressly adopted into and modified by the political) the force of those other powers is
never determinate enough to be depended upon. It can never
be reduced, like political punishment, into exact lots, nor
meted out in number, quantity, and value. The legislator
is therefore obliged to provide the full complement of punishment, as if he were sure of not receiving any assistance
whatever from any of those quarters. If he does, so much
the better: but lest he should not, it is necessary he
should, at all events, make that provision which depends
upon himself.

XXVII. It may be of use, in this place, to recapitulate the several circumstances, which, in establishing the
proportion betwixt punishments and offences, are to be attended to. These seem to be as follows:

I. *On the part of the offence:*
   1. The profit of the offence;
   2. The mischief of the offence;
   3. The profit and mischief of other great-
      er or lesser offences, of different
      sorts, which the offender may have to
      choose out of;
   4. The profit and mischief of other of-
      fences, of the same sort, which the
      same offender may probably have been
      guilty of already.

II. *On the part of the punishment:*
   5. The magnitude of the punishment: com-
      posed of its intensity and duration;
   6. The deficiency of the punishment in point
      of certainty;
   7. The deficiency of the punishment in point
      of proximity;
   8. The quality of the punishment;
   9. The accidental advantage in point of
      quality of a punishment, not strictly
      needed in point of quantity;
   10. The use of a punishment of a particular
       quality, in the character of a moral
       lesson.

III. *On the part of the offender:*
   11. The responsibility of the class of per-
       sons in a way to offend;
   12. The sensibility of each particular
       offender;

        13. The particular merits or useful quali-
           ties of any particular offender, in case
           of a punishment which might deprive the
           community of the benefit of them;
        14. The multitude of offenders on any partic-
           ular occasion.
  IV. *On the part of the public*, at any particular
      conjuncture:
        15. The inclinations of the people, for or
           against any quantity or mode of punish-
           ment;
        16. The inclinations of foreign powers.
   V. *On the part of the law*: that is, of the pub-
      lic for a continuance:
        17. The necessity of making small sacrifices,
           in point of proportionality, for the sake
           of simplicity.

   XXVIII.   There are some, perhaps, who, at first sight, may look upon the nicety employed in the adjustment of such rules, as so much labour lost: for gross ignorance, they will say, never troubles itself about laws, and passion does not calculate. But the evil of ignorance admits of cure: and as to the proposition that passion does not calculate, this, like most of these very general and oracular propositions, is not true. When matters of such importance as pain and pleasure are at stake, and these in the highest degree (the only matters, in short, that can be of importance) who is there that does not calculate? Men calculate, some with less exactness, indeed, some with more: but all men calculate. I would not say, that even a madman does not calculate.[9] Passion calculates, more or less, in every man: in different men, according to the warmth or coolness of their dispositions: according to the firmness or irritability of their minds: according to the nature of the motives by which they are acted upon. Happily, of all passions, that is the most given to calculation, from the excesses of which, by reason of its strength, constancy, and universality, society has most to apprehend: I mean that which corresponds to the motive of pecuniary interest: so that these niceties, if such they are to be called, have the best chance of being efficacious, where efficacy is of the most importance.

---

[9]There are few madmen but what are observed to be afraid of the strait waistcoat.

PUNISHMENT AS A PRACTICE

John Rawls

The subject of punishment, in the sense of attaching legal penalties to the violation of legal rules, has always been a troubling moral question. The trouble about it has not been that people disagree as to whether or not punishment is justifiable. Most people have held that, freed from certain abuses, it is an acceptable institution. Only a few have rejected punishment entirely, which is rather surprising when one considers all that can be said against it. The difficulty is with the justification of punishment: various arguments for it have been given by moral philosophers, but so far none of them has won any sort of general acceptance; no justification is without those who detest it. I hope to show that the use of the aforementioned distinction[1] enables one to state the utilitarian view in a way which allows for the sound points of its critics.

For our purposes we may say that there are two justifications of punishment. What we may call the retributive view is that punishment is justified on the grounds that wrongdoing merits punishment. It is morally fitting that a

---

Excerpted from John Rawls, "Two Concepts of Rules," *The Philosophical Review* 64 (1955), pp. 3-32. Reprinted with permission of *The Philosophical Review* and the author. The footnotes have been renumbered and some have been omitted. John Rawls is a Professor of Philosophy at Harvard University and is the author of *A Theory of Justice*, Harvard, 1971.

[1] [Rawls begins his paper by claiming that he wants to show "the importance of the distinction between justifying a practice and justifying a particular action falling under it. . . . The word 'practice' is used throughout as a sort of technical term meaning any form of activity specified by a system of rules which defines offices, roles, moves, penalties, defenses, and so on, and which gives the activity its structure. As examples one may think of games and rituals, trials and parliaments." The importance of the distinction, Rawls argues, lies in "the way it strengthens the utilitarian view regardless of whether or not that view is completely defensible." Ed.]

person who does wrong should suffer in proportion to his wrongdoing. That a criminal should be punished follows from his guilt, and the severity of the appropriate punishment depends on the depravity of his act. The state of affairs where a wrongdoer suffers punishment is morally better than the state of affairs where he does not; and it is better irrespective of any of the consequences of punishing him.

What we may call the utilitarian holds that on the principle that bygones are bygones and that only future consequences are material to present decisions, punishment is justifiable only by reference to the probable consequences of maintaining it as one of the devices of the social order. Wrongs committed in the past are, as such, not relevant considerations for deciding what to do. If punishment can be shown to promote effectively the interest of society it is justifiable, otherwise it is not.

I have stated these two competing views very roughly to make one feel the conflict between them: one feels the force of *both* arguments and one wonders how they can be reconciled. From my introductory remarks it is obvious that the resolution which I am going to propose is that in this case one must distinguish between justifying a practice as a system of rules to be applied and enforced, and justifying a particular action which falls under these rules; utilitarian arguments are appropriate with regard to questions about practices, while retributive arguments fit the application of particular rules to particular cases.

We might try to get clear about this distinction by imagining how a father might answer the question of his son. Suppose the son asks, "Why was J put in jail yesterday?" The father answers, "Because he robbed the bank at B. He was duly tried and found guilty. That's why he was put in jail yesterday." But suppose the son had asked a different question, namely, "Why do people put other people in jail?" Then the father might answer, "To protect good people from bad people" or "To stop people from doing things that would make it uneasy for all of us; for otherwise we wouldn't be able to go to bed at night and sleep in peace." There are two very different questions here. One question emphasizes the proper name: it asks why J was punished rather than someone else, or it asks what he was punished for. The other question asks why we have the institution of punishment: why do people punish one another rather than, say, always forgiving one another?

Thus the father says in effect that a particular man is punished, rather than some other man, because he is guilty, and he is guilty because he broke the law (past tense). In his case the law looks back, the judge looks back, the jury looks back, and a penalty is visited upon him for something he did. That a man is to be punished, and what his punishment is to be, is settled by its being shown that he broke the law and that the law assigns that penalty for the violation of it.

On the other hand we have the institution of punishment itself, and recommend and accept various changes in it, because it is thought by the (ideal) legislator and by those to whom the law applies that, as a part of a system of law impartially applied from case to case arising under it, it will have the consequence, in the long run, of furthering the interests of society.

One can say, then, that the judge and the legislator stand in different positions and look in different directions: one to the past, the other to the future. The justification of what the judge does, *qua* judge, sounds like the retributive view; the justification of what the (ideal) legislator does, *qua* legislator, sounds like the utilitarian view. Thus both views have a point (this is as it should be since intelligent and sensitive persons have been on both sides of the argument); and one's initial confusion disappears once one sees that these views apply to persons holding different offices with different duties, and situated differently with respect to the system of rules that make up the criminal law.

One might say, however, that the utilitarian view is more fundamental since it applies to a more fundamental office, for the judge carries out the legislator's will so far as he can determine it. Once the legislator decides to have laws and to assign penalties for their violation (as things are there must be both the law and the penalty) an institution is set up which involves a retributive conception of particular cases. It is part of the concept of the criminal law as a system of rules that the application and enforcement of these rules in particular cases should be justifiable by arguments of a retributive character. The decision whether or not to use law rather than some other mechanism of social control, and the decision as to what laws to have and what penalties to assign, may be settled by utilitarian arguments; but if one decides to have laws then one has decided on something whose working in particular cases is retributive in form.

The answer, then, to the confusion engendered by the two views of punishment is quite simple: one distinguishes two offices, that of the judge and that of the legislator, and one distinguishes their different stations with respect to the system of rules which make up the law; and then one notes that the different sorts of considerations which would usually be offered as reasons for what is done under the cover of these offices can be paired off with the competing justifications of punishment. One reconciles the two views by the time-honored device of making them apply to different situations.

But can it really be this simple? Well, this answer allows for the apparent intent of each side. Does a person who advocates the retributive view necessarily advocate, as an *institution*, legal machinery whose essential purpose is to set up and preserve a correspondence between moral turpitude and suffering? Surely not. What retributionists have rightly insisted upon is that no man can be punished unless he is guilty, that is, unless he has broken the law. Their fundamental criticism of the utilitarian account is that, as they interpret it, it sanctions an innocent person's being punished (if one may call it that) for the benefit of society.

On the other hand, utilitarians agree that punishment is to be inflicted only for the violation of law. They regard this much as understood from the concept of punishment itself. The point of the utilitarian account concerns the institution as a system of rules: utilitarianism seeks to limit its use by declaring it justifiable only if it can be shown to foster effectively the good of society. Historically it is a protest against the indiscriminate and ineffective use of the criminal law. It seeks to dissuade us from assigning to penal institutions the improper, if not sacrilegious, task of matching suffering with moral turpitude. Like others, utilitarians want penal institutions designed so that, as far as humanly possible, only those who break the law run afoul of it. They hold that no official should have discretionary power to inflict penalties whenever he thinks it for the benefit of society; for on utilitarian grounds an institution granting such power could not be justified.

The suggested way of reconciling the retributive and the utilitarian justifications of punishment seems to account for what both sides have wanted to say. There are, however, two further questions which arise, and I shall devote the remainder of this section to them.

First, will not a difference of opinion as to the proper criterion of just law make the proposed reconciliation unacceptable to retributionists? Will they not question whether, if the utilitarian principle is used as the criterion, it follows that those who have broken the law are guilty in a way which satisfies their demand that those punished deserve to be punished? To answer this difficulty, suppose that the rules of the criminal law are justified on

utilitarian grounds (it is only for laws that meet his criterion that the utilitarian can be held responsible). Then
it follows that the actions which the criminal law specifies as offenses are such that, if they were tolerated,
terror and alarm would spread in society. Consequently,
retributionists can only deny that those who are punished
deserve to be punished if they deny that such actions are
wrong. This they will not want to do.

The second question is whether utilitarianism doesn't
justify too much. One pictures it as an engine of justification which, if consistently adopted, could be used to
justify cruel and arbitrary institutions. Retributionists
may be supposed to concede that utilitarians *intend* to reform the law and to make it more humane; that utilitarians
do not *wish* to justify any such thing as punishment of the
innocent; and that utilitarians may appeal to the fact that
punishment presupposes guilt in the sense that by punishment one understands an institution attaching penalties to
the infraction of legal rules, and therefore that it is
logically absurd to suppose that utilitarians in justifying
punishment might also have justified punishment (if we may
call it that) of the innocent. The real question, however,
is whether the utilitarian, in justifying punishment,
hasn't used arguments which commit him to accepting the infliction of suffering on innocent persons if it is for the
good of society (whether or not one calls this punishment).
More generally, isn't the utilitarian committed in principle to accepting many practices which he, as a morally sensitive person, wouldn't want to accept? Retributionists
are inclined to hold that there is no way to stop the utilitarian principle from justifying too much except by adding
to it a principle which distributes certain rights to individuals. Then the amended criterion is not the greatest
benefit of society *simpliciter*, but the greatest benefit of
society subject to the constraint that no one's rights may
be violated. Now while I think that the classical utilitarians proposed a criterion of this more complicated sort,
I do not want to argue that point here.[2] What I want to
show is that there is *another* way of preventing the utilitarian principle from justifying too much, or at least of
making it much less likely to do so: namely, by stating
utilitarianism in a way which accounts for the distinction
between the justification of an institution and the justification of a particular action falling under it.

---

[2]By the classical utilitarians I understand Hobbes, Hume,
Bentham, J. S. Mill, and Sidgwick.

I begin by defining the institution of punishment as follows: a person is said to suffer punishment whenever he is legally deprived of some of the normal rights of a citizen on the ground that he has violated a rule of law, the violation having been established by trial according to the due process of law, provided that the deprivation is carried out by the recognized legal authorities of the state, that the rule of law clearly specifies both the offense and the attached penalty, that the courts construe statutes strictly, and that the statute was on the books prior to the time of the offense. This definition specifies what I shall understand by punishment. The question is whether utilitarian arguments may be found to justify institutions widely different from this and such as one would find cruel and arbitrary.

This question is best answered, I think, by taking up a particular accusation. Consider the following from Carritt:

> . . . the utilitarian must hold that we are justified in inflicting pain always and only to prevent worse pain or bring about greater happiness. This, then, is all we need to consider in so-called punishment, which must be purely preventive. But if some kind of very cruel crime becomes common, and none of the criminals can be caught, it might be highly expedient, as an example, to hang an innocent man, if a charge against him could be so framed that he were universally thought guilty; indeed this would only fail to be an ideal instance of utilitarian 'punishment' because the victim himself would not have been so likely as a real felon to commit such a crime in the future; in all other respects it would be perfectly deterrent and therefore felicific.[3]

Carritt is trying to show that there are occasions when a utilitarian argument would justify taking an action which would be generally condemned; and thus that utilitarianism justifies too much. But the failure of Carritt's argument lies in the fact that he makes no distinction between the justification of the general system of rules which constitutes penal institutions and the justification of particular applications of these rules to particular cases by the

---

[3]*Ethical and Political Thinking* (Oxford, 1947), p. 65.

various officials whose job it is to administer them. This
becomes perfectly clear when one asks who the "we" are of
whom Carritt speaks. Who is this who has a sort of absolute authority on particular occasions to decide that an
innocent man shall be "punished" if everyone can be convinced that he is guilty? Is this person the legislator,
or the judge, or the body of private citizens, or what? It
is utterly crucial to know who is to decide such matters,
and by what authority, for all of this must be written into
the rules of the institution. Until one knows these things
one doesn't know what the institution is whose justification is being challenged; and as the utilitarian principle
applies to the institution one doesn't know whether it is
justifiable on utilitarian grounds or not.

Once this is understood it is clear what the counter-
move to Carritt's argument is. One must describe more
carefully what the *institution* is which his example suggests, and then ask oneself whether or not it is likely
that having this institution would be for the benefit of
society in the long run. One must not content oneself with
the vague thought that, when it's a question of *this* case,
it would be a good thing if *somebody* did something even if
an innocent person were to suffer.

Try to imagine, then, an institution (which we may
call "telishment") which is such that the officials set up
by it have authority to arrange a trial for the condemnation of an innocent man whenever they are of the opinion
that doing so would be in the best interests of society.
The discretion of officials is limited, however, by the
rule that they may not condemn an innocent man to undergo
such an ordeal unless there is, at the time, a wave of offenses similar to that with which they charge him and telish him for. We may imagine that the officials having the
discretionary authority are the judges of the higher courts
in consultation with the chief of police, the minister of
justice, and a committee of the legislature.

Once one realizes that one is involved in setting up
an *institution*, one sees that the hazards are very great.
For example, what check is there on the officials? How is
one to tell whether or not their actions are authorized?
How is one to limit the risks involved in allowing such sys-
tematic deception? How is one to avoid giving anything
short of complete discretion to the authorities to telish
anyone they like? In addition to these considerations, it
is obvious that people will come to have a very different
attitude towards their penal system when telishment is ad-
joined to it. They will be uncertain as to whether a convicted man has been punished or telished. They will wonder

whether or not they should feel sorry for him. They will
wonder whether the same fate won't at any time fall on them.
If one pictures how such an institution would actually work,
and the enormous risks involved in it, it seems clear that
it would serve no useful purpose. A utilitarian justification for this institution is most unlikely.

It happens in general that as one drops off the defining features of punishment one ends up with an institution
whose utilitarian justification is highly doubtful. One
reason for this is that punishment works like a kind of
price system: by altering the prices one has to pay for the
performance of actions it supplies a motive for avoiding
some actions and doing others. The defining features are
essential if punishment is to work in this way; so that an
institution which lacks these features, e.g., an institution
which is set up to "punish" the innocent, is likely to have
about as much point as a price system (if one may call it
that) where the prices of things change at random from day
to day and one learns the price of something after one has
agreed to buy it.[4]

If one is careful to apply the utilitarian principle
to the institution which is to authorize particular actions,

-----

[4]The analogy with the price system suggests an answer to
the question of how utilitarian considerations insure that
punishment is proportional to the offense. It is interesting to note that Sir David Ross, after making the distinction between justifying a penal law and justifying a particular application of it, and after stating that utilitarian
considerations have a large place in determining the former,
still holds back from accepting the utilitarian justification of punishment on the grounds that justice requires
that punishment be proportional to the offense, and that
utilitarianism is unable to account for this. Cf. *The
Right and the Good*, pp. 61-62. I do not claim that utilitarianism can account for this requirement as Sir David
might wish, but it happens, nevertheless, that if utilitarian considerations are followed penalties will be proportional to offenses in this sense: the order of offenses according to seriousness can be paired off with the order of
penalties according to severity. Also the absolute level
of penalties will be as low as possible. This follows from
the assumption that people are rational (i.e., that they
are able to take into account the "prices" the state puts
on actions), the utilitarian rule that a penal system
should provide a motive for preferring the less serious offense, and the principle that punishment as such is an evil.
All this was carefully worked out by Bentham in *The Principles of Morals and Legislation*, chs. xiii-xv.

then there is *less* danger of its justifying too much. Carritt's example gains plausibility by its indefiniteness and
by its concentration on the particular case. His argument
will only hold if it can be shown that there are utilitarian arguments which justify an institution whose publicly
ascertainable offices and powers are such as to permit officials to exercise that kind of discretion in particular
cases. But the requirement of having to build the arbitrary features of the particular decision into the institutional practice makes the justification much less likely to
go through. . . .

CAPITAL PUNISHMENT

Karl Marx

                    London, Friday, January 28, 1853
The Times of January 25 contains the following observations under the head of "Amateur Hanging":

> It has often been remarked that in this coun-
> try a public execution is generally followed close-
> ly by instances of death by hanging, either suici-
> dal or accidental, in consequence of the powerful
> effect which the execution of a noted criminal pro-
> duces upon a morbid and unmatured mind.

Of the several cases which are alleged by *The Times* in
illustration of this remark, one is that of a lunatic at
Sheffield, who, after talking with other lunatics respecting the execution of Barbour, put an end to his existence
by hanging himself. Another case is that of a boy of fourteen years, who also hanged himself.

This brief essay appeared in the New York *Daily Tribune* on
February 18, 1853. In spite of its title, it contains re-
flections on punishment in general and is not limited solely to capital punishment. There is no sustained philosophical examination of punishment in the writings of Marx, but
a brief discussion may be found in *The Holy Family* (with
Engels, 1845), Chapter 8, Section 3.

The doctrine to which the enumeration of these facts was intended to give its support is one which no reasonable man would be likely to guess, it being no less than a direct apotheosis of the hangman, while capital punishment is extolled as the *ultima ratio* of society.   This is done in a leading article of the "leading journal."

The Morning Advertiser, in some very bitter but just strictures on the hanging predilections and bloody logic of *The Times*, has the following interesting data on forty-three days of the year 1849:

Executions of		*Murders and Suicides*	
Millan	March 20	Hannah Saddles	March 22
Petley	March 20	M. G. Newton	March 22
		J. G. Gleeson—4 Murders at Liverpool	March 27
Smith	March 27	Murder and Suicide at Leicester	April 2
Howe	March 31	Poisoning at Bath	April 7
		W. Bailey	April 8
		J. Ward murders his mother	April 13
Landish	April 9	Yardley	April 14
Sarah Thomas	May 9	Doxy, parricide	April 14
		J. Bailey kills his two children and himself	April 17
J. Griffiths	April 18	Chas. Overton	April 18
J. Rush	April 21	Daniel Holmston	May 2

This table, as *The Times* concedes, shows not only suicides, but also murders of the most atrocious kind, following closely upon the execution of criminals.   It is astonishing that the article in question does not produce even a single argument or pretext for indulging in the savage theory therein propounded; and it would be very difficult, if not altogether impossible, to establish any principle upon which the justice of expediency of capital punishment could be founded in a society glorying in its civilization.   Punishment in general has been defended as a means either of ameliorating or of intimidating.   Now what right have you to punish me for the amelioration or intimidation of others? And besides there is history—there is such a thing as statistics—which prove with the most complete evidence that since Cain the world has been neither intimidated nor ameliorated by punishment. Quite the contrary. From the point of view of abstract right, there is only one theory of punishment which recognizes human dignity in the abstract, and that is the theory of Kant, especially in the more rigid formula given to it by Hegel. Hegel says:

> Punishment is the *right* of the criminal. It is an act of his own will. The violation of right has been proclaimed by the criminal as his own right. His crime is the negation of right. Punishment is the negation of this negation, and consequently an affirmation of right, solicited and forced upon the criminal by himself.

There is no doubt something specious in this formula, inasmuch as Hegel, instead of looking upon the criminal as the mere object, the slave of justice, elevates him to the position of a free and self-determined being. Looking, however, more closely into the matter, we discover that German idealism here, as in most other instances, has but given a transcendental sanction to the rules of existing society. Is it not a delusion to substitute for the individual with his real motives, with multifarious social circumstances pressing upon him, the abstraction of "free will"—one among the many qualities of man for man himself? This theory, considering punishment as the result of the criminal's own will, is only a metaphysical expression for the old *jus talionis*; eye against eye, tooth against tooth, blood against blood. Plainly speaking, and dispensing with all paraphrases, punishment is nothing but a means of society to defend itself against the infraction of its vital conditions, whatever may be their character. Now what a state of society is that which knows of no better instrument for its own defense than the hangman, and which proclaims, through the "leading journal of the world," its own brutality as eternal law?

Mr. A. Quételet, in his excellent and learned work, *L'Homme et ses Facultés*, says:

> There is a *budget* which we pay with frightful regularity—it is that of prisons, dungeons, and scaffolds. . . . We might even predict how many individuals will stain their hands with the blood of their fellow men, how many will be forgers, how many will deal in poison, pretty nearly the same way as we may foretell the annual births and deaths.

And Mr. Quételet, in a calculation of the probabilities of crime published in 1829, actually predicted with astonishing certainty not only the amount but all the different kinds of crimes committed in France in 1830. That it is not so much the particular political institutions of a country as the fundamental conditions of modern *bourgeois* society in general which produce an average amount of crime in a given national fraction of society may be seen from the following table, communicated by Quételet, for the years 1822-24. We find in a number of one hundred condemned criminals in America and France:

Age	Philadelphia	France
Under twenty-one years	19	19
Twenty-one to thirty	44	35
Thirty to forty	23	23
Above forty	14	23
Total	100	100

Now, if crimes observed on a great scale thus show, in their amount and their classification, the regularity of physical phenomena—if, as Mr. Quételet remarks: "It would be difficult to decide in respect to which of the two [the physical world and the social system] the acting causes produce their effect with the utmost regularity"—is there not a necessity for deeply reflecting upon an alteration of the system that breeds these crimes, instead of glorifying the hangman who executes a lot of criminals to make room only for the supply of new ones?

TWO MODELS OF THE CRIMINAL PROCESS

Herbert L. Packer

INTRODUCTION

People who commit crimes appear to share the prevalent
impression that punishment is an unpleasantness that is
best avoided. They ordinarily take care to avoid being
caught. If arrested, they ordinarily deny their guilt and
otherwise try not to cooperate with the police. If brought
to trial, they do whatever their resources permit to resist
being convicted. And even after they have been convicted
and sent to prison, their efforts to secure their freedom
do not cease. It is a struggle from start to finish. This
struggle is often referred to as the criminal process, a
compendious term that stands for all the complexes of activity that operate to bring the substantive law of crime to
bear (or to keep it from coming to bear) on persons who are
suspected of having committed crimes. It can be described,
but only partially and inadequately, by referring to the
rules of law that govern the apprehension, screening, and
trial of persons suspected of crime. It consists at least
as importantly of patterns of official activity that correspond only in the roughest kind of way to the prescriptions
of procedural rules. As a result of recent emphasis on empirical research into the administration of criminal justice, we are just beginning to be aware how very rough the
correspondence is.

At the same time, and perhaps in part as a result of
this new accretion of knowledge, some of our lawmaking institutions—particularly the Supreme Court of the United
States—have begun to add measurably to the prescriptions
of law that are meant to govern the operation of the

From Herbert L. Packer, *The Limits of the Criminal Sanction*
(Stanford, Calif.: Stanford University Press, 1968),
pp. 149-173. (Footnotes have been renumbered and some have
been omitted.) © 1968 by Herbert L. Packer. Reprinted
with permission of the publisher. The late Herbert L.
Packer was a Professor of Law at Stanford University.

criminal process. This accretion has become, in the last
few years, exponential in extent and velocity. We are
faced with an interesting paradox: the more we learn about
the Is of the criminal process, the more we are instructed
about its Ought and the greater the gulf between Is and
Ought appears to become. We learn that very few people get
adequate legal representation in the criminal process; we
are simultaneously told that the Constitution requires people to be afforded adequate legal representation in the
criminal process. We learn that coercion is often used to
extract confessions from suspected criminals; we are then
told that convictions based on coerced confessions may not
be permitted to stand. We discover that the police often
use methods in gathering evidence that violate the norms
of privacy protected by the Fourth Amendment; we are told
that evidence obtained in this way must be excluded from
the criminal trial. But these prescriptions about how the
process ought to operate do not automatically become part
of the patterns of official behavior in the criminal process. Is and Ought share an increasingly uneasy coexistence.
Doubts are stirred about the kind of criminal process we
want to have.

The kind of criminal process we have is an important
determinant of the kind of behavior content that the criminal law ought rationally to comprise. Logically, the substantive question may appear to be prior: decide what kinds
of conduct one wants to reach through the criminal process,
and then decide what kind of process is best calculated to
deal with those kinds of conduct. It has not worked that
way. On the whole, the process has been at least as much a
given as the content of the criminal law. But it is far
from being a given in any rigid sense.

The shape of the criminal process affects the substance of the criminal law in two general ways. First, one
would want to know, before adding a new category of behavior to the list of crimes and therefore placing an additional burden on the process, whether it is easy or hard to
employ the criminal process. The more expeditious the
process, the greater the number of people with whom it can
deal and, therefore, the greater the variety of antisocial
conduct that can be confided in whole or in part to the
criminal law for inhibition. On the other hand, the harder
the process is to use, the smaller the number of people who
can be handled by it at any given level of resources for
staffing and operating it. The harder it is to put a suspected criminal in jail, the fewer the number of cases that
can be handled in a year by a given number of policemen,
prosecutors, defense lawyers, judges and jurymen, probation

officers, etc., etc. A second and subtler relationship exists between the characteristic functioning of the process
and the kinds of conduct with which it can efficiently deal.
Perhaps the clearest example, but by no means the only one,
is in the area of what have been referred to as victimless
crimes, i.e., offenses that do not result in anyone's feeling that he has been injured so as to impel him to bring
the offense to the attention of the authorities. The offense of fornication is an example. In a jurisdiction
where it is illegal for two persons not married to each
other to have sexual intercourse, there is a substantial
enforcement problem (or would be, if the law were taken seriously) because people who voluntarily have sexual intercourse with each other often do not feel that they have
been victimized and therefore often do not complain to the
police. Consensual transactions in gambling and narcotics
present the same problem, somewhat exacerbated by the fact
that we take these forms of conduct rather more seriously
than fornication. To the difficulties of apprehending a
criminal when it is known that he has committed a crime are
added the difficulties of knowing that a crime has been committed. In this sense, the victimless crime always presents a greater problem to the criminal process than does
the crime with an ascertainable victim. But this problem
may be minimized if the criminal process has at its dispos-
al measures designed to increase the probability that the
commission of such offenses will become known. If suspects
may be entrapped into committing offenses, if the police
may arrest and search a suspect without evidence that he
has committed an offense, if wiretaps and other forms of
electronic surveillance are permitted, it becomes easier to
detect the commission of offenses of this sort. But if
these measures are prohibited and if the prohibitions are
observed in practice, it becomes more difficult, and eventually there may come a point at which the capacity of the
criminal process to deal with victimless offenses becomes
so attenuated that a failure of enforcement occurs.

Thus, a pragmatic approach to the central question of
what the criminal law is good for would require both a general assessment of whether the criminal process is a high-
speed or a low-speed instrument of social control, and a
series of specific assessments of its fitness for handling
particular kinds of antisocial behavior. Such assessments
are necessary if we are to have a basis for elaborating the
criteria that ought to affect legislative invocation of the
criminal sanction. How can we provide ourselves with an
understanding of the criminal process that pays due regard
to its static and dynamic elements? There are, to be sure,

aspects of the criminal process that vary only inconsequentially from place to place and from time to time. But its dynamism is clear—clearer today, perhaps, than ever before. We need to have an idea of the potentialities for change in the system and the probable direction that change is taking and may be expected to take in the future. We need to detach ourselves from the welter of more or less connected details that describe the myriad ways in which the criminal process does operate or may be likely to operate in mid-twentieth-century America, so that we can begin to see how the system as a whole might be able to deal with the variety of missions we confide to it.

One way to do this kind of job is to abstract from reality, to build a model. In a sense, a model is just what an examination of the constitutional and statutory provisions that govern the operation of the criminal process would produce. This in effect is the way analysis of the legal system has traditionally proceeded. It has considerable utility as an index of current value choices; but it produces a model that will not tell us very much about some important problems that the system encounters and that will only fortuitously tell us anything useful about how the system actually operates. On the other hand, the kind of model that might emerge from an attempt to cut loose from the law on the books and to describe, as accurately as possible, what actually goes on in the real-life world of the criminal process would so subordinate the inquiry to the tyranny of the actual that the existence of competing value choices would be obscured. The kind of criminal process we have depends importantly on certain value choices that are reflected, explicitly or implicitly, in its habitual functioning. The kind of model we need is one that permits us to recognize explicitly the value choices that underlie the details of the criminal process. In a word, what we need is a *normative* model or models. It will take more than one model, but it will not take more than two.

Two models of the criminal process will let us perceive the normative antinomy at the heart of the criminal law. These models are not labeled Is and Ought, nor are they to be taken in that sense. Rather, they represent an attempt to abstract two separate value systems that compete for priority in the operation of the criminal process. Neither is presented as either corresponding to reality or representing the ideal to the exclusion of the other. The two models merely afford a convenient way to talk about the operation of a process whose day-to-day functioning involves a constant series of minute adjustments between the competing demands of two value systems and whose normative future likewise involves a series of resolutions of the tensions between competing claims.

I call these two models the Due Process Model and the Crime Control Model. In the rest of this chapter I shall sketch their animating presuppositions, and in succeeding chapters I shall show how the two models apply to a selection of representative problems that arise at successive stages of the criminal process. As we examine the way the models operate in each successive stage, we will raise two further inquiries: first, where on a spectrum between the extremes represented by the two models do our present practices seem approximately to fall; second, what appears to be the direction and thrust of current and foreseeable trends along each such spectrum?

There is a risk in an enterprise of this sort that is latent in any attempt to polarize. It is, simply, that values are too various to be pinned down to yes-or-no answers. The models are distortions of reality. And, since they are normative in character, there is a danger of seeing one or the other as Good or Bad. The reader will have his preferences, as I do, but we should not be so rigid as to demand consistently polarized answers to the range of questions posed in the criminal process. The weighty questions of public policy that inhere in any attempt to discern where on the spectrum of normative choice the "right" answer lies are beyond the scope of the present inquiry. The attempt here is primarily to clarify the terms of discussion by isolating the assumptions that underlie competing policy claims and examining the conclusions that those claims, if fully accepted, would lead to.

VALUES UNDERLYING THE MODELS

Each of the two models we are about to examine is an attempt to give operational content to a complex of values underlying the criminal law. As I have suggested earlier, it is possible to identify two competing systems of values, the tension between which accounts for the intense activity now observable in the development of the criminal process. The actors in this development—lawmakers, judges, police, prosecutors, defense lawyers—do not often pause to articulate the values that underlie the positions that they take on any given issue. Indeed, it would be a gross oversimplification to ascribe a coherent and consistent set of values to any of these actors. Each of the two competing schemes of values we will be developing in this section contains components that are demonstrably present some of the time in some of the actors' preferences regarding the criminal process. No one person has ever identified himself as holding all of the values that underlie these two models. The models are polarities, and so are the schemes of value that underlie them. A person who subscribed to all of the values underlying one model to the exclusion of all of the values underlying the other would be rightly viewed as a fanatic. The values are presented here as an aid to analysis, not as a program for action.

Some Common Ground

However, the polarity of the two models is not absolute. Although it would be possible to construct models that exist in an institutional vacuum, it would not serve our purposes to do so. We are postulating, not a criminal process that operates in any kind of society at all, but rather one that operates within the framework of contemporary American society. This leaves plenty of room for polarization, but it does require the observance of some limits. A model of the criminal process that left out of account relatively stable and enduring features of the American legal system would not have much relevance to our central inquiry. For convenience, these elements of stability and continuity can be roughly equated with minimal agreed limits expressed in the Constitution of the United States and, more importantly, with unarticulated assumptions that can be perceived to underlie those limits. Of course, it is true that the Constitution is constantly appealed to by proponents and opponents of many measures that affect the criminal process. And only the naive would deny that there are few conclusive positions that can be reached by appeal to the Constitution. Yet there are assumptions about the criminal process that are widely shared and that may be viewed as common ground for the operation of any model of the criminal process. Our first task is to clarify these assumptions.

First, there is the assumption, implicit in the ex post facto clause of the Constitution, that the function of defining conduct that may be treated as criminal is separate from and prior to the process of identifying and dealing with persons as criminals. How wide or narrow the definition of criminal conduct must be is an important question of policy that yields highly variable results depending on the values held by those making the relevant decisions. But that there must be a means of definition that is in some sense separate from and prior to the operation

of the process is clear. If this were not so, our efforts
to deal with the phenomenon of organized crime would appear
ludicrous indeed (which is not to say that we have by any
means exhausted the possibilities for dealing with that
problem within the limits of this basic assumption).

A related assumption that limits the area of controversy is that the criminal process ordinarily ought to be
invoked by those charged with the responsibility for doing
so when it appears that a crime has been committed and that
there is a reasonable prospect of apprehending and convicting its perpetrator. Although police and prosecutors are
allowed broad discretion for deciding not to invoke the
criminal process, it is commonly agreed that these officials have no general dispensing power. If the legislature
has decided that certain conduct is to be treated as criminal, the decision-makers at every level of the criminal
process are expected to accept that basic decision as a
premise for action. The controversial nature of the occasional case in which the relevant decision-makers appear
not to have played their appointed role only serves to highlight the strength with which the premise holds. This assumption may be viewed as the other side of the ex post
facto coin. Just as conduct that is not proscribed as criminal may not be dealt with in the criminal process, so conduct that has been denominated as criminal must be treated
as such by the participants in the criminal process acting
within their respective competences.

Next, there is the assumption that there are limits to
the powers of government to investigate and apprehend persons suspected of committing crimes. I do not refer to the
controversy (settled recently, at least in broad outline)
as to whether the Fourth Amendment's prohibition against unreasonable searches and seizures applies to the states with
the same force with which it applies to the federal government.[1] Rather, I am talking about the general assumption
that a degree of scrutiny and control must be exercised
with respect to the activities of law enforcement officers,
that the security and privacy of the individual may not be
invaded at will. It is possible to imagine a society in
which even lip service is not paid to this assumption.
Nazi Germany approached but never quite reached this position. But no one in our society would maintain that any
individual may be taken into custody at any time and held
without any limitation of time during the process of

---

[1]Mapp v. Ohio, 367 U.S. 643 (1961); Kerr v. California, 374
U.S. 23 (1963).

investigating his possible commission of crimes, or would
argue that there should be no form of redress for violation
of at least some standards for official investigative conduct. Although this assumption may not appear to have much
in the way of positive content, its absence would render
moot some of our most hotly controverted problems. If
there were not general agreement that there must be some
limits on police power to detain and investigate, the highly controversial provisions of the Uniform Arrest Act, permitting the police to detain a person for questioning for a
short period even though they do not have grounds for making an arrest, would be a magnanimous concession by the all-
powerful state rather than, as it is now perceived, a substantial expansion of police power.

Finally, there is a complex of assumptions embraced by
terms such as "the adversary system," "procedural due process," "notice and an opportunity to be heard," and "day in
court." Common to them all is the notion that the alleged
criminal is not merely an object to be acted upon but an
independent entity in the process who may, if he so desires, force the operators of the process to demonstrate to
an independent authority (judge and jury) that he is guilty
of the charges against him. It is a minimal assumption.
It speaks in terms of "may" rather than "must." It permits
but does not require the accused, acting by himself or
through his own agent, to play an active role in the process. By virtue of that fact the process becomes or has the
capacity to become a contest between, if not equals, at
least independent actors. As we shall see, much of the
space between the two models is occupied by stronger or
weaker notions of how this contest is to be arranged, in
what cases it is to be played, and by what rules. The
Crime Control Model tends to de-emphasize this adversary
aspect of the process; the Due Process Model tends to make
it central. The common ground, and it is important, is the
agreement that the process has, for everyone subjected to
it, at least the potentiality of becoming to some extent an
adversary struggle.

So much for common ground. There is a good deal of it,
even in the narrowest view. Its existence should not be
overlooked, because it is, by definition, what permits partial resolutions of the tension between the two models to
take place. The rhetoric of the criminal process consists
largely of claims that disputed territory is "really" common ground: that, for example, the premise of an adversary
system "necessarily" embraces the appointment of counsel
for everyone accused of crime, or conversely, that the obligation to pursue persons suspected of committing crimes

"necessarily" embraces interrogation of suspects without
the intervention of counsel. We may smile indulgently at
such claims; they are rhetoric, and no more. But the form
in which they are made suggests an important truth: that
there *is* a common ground of value assumption about the criminal process that makes continued discourse about its problems possible.

Crime Control Values

The value system that underlies the Crime Control
Model is based on the proposition that the repression of
criminal conduct is by far the most important function to
be performed by the criminal process. The failure of law
enforcement to bring criminal conduct under tight control
is viewed as leading to the breakdown of public order and
thence to the disappearance of an important condition of
human freedom. If the laws go unenforced—which is to say,
if it is perceived that there is a high percentage of failure to apprehend and convict in the criminal process—a
general disregard for legal controls tends to develop. The
law-abiding citizen then becomes the victim of all sorts of
unjustifiable invasions of his interests. His security of
person and property is sharply diminished, and, therefore,
so is his liberty to function as a member of society. The
claim ultimately is that the criminal process is a positive
guarantor of social freedom. In order to achieve this high
purpose, the Crime Control Model requires that primary attention be paid to the efficiency with which the criminal
process operates to screen suspects, determine guilt, and
secure appropriate dispositions of persons convicted of
crime.

Efficiency of operation is not, of course, a criterion
that can be applied in a vacuum. By "efficiency" we mean
the system's capacity to apprehend, try, convict, and dispose of a high proportion of criminal offenders whose offenses become known. In a society in which only the
grossest forms of antisocial behavior were made criminal
and in which the crime rate was exceedingly low, the criminal process might require the devotion of many more man-
hours of police, prosecutorial, and judicial time per case
than ours does, and still operate with tolerable efficiency.
A society that was prepared to increase even further the
resources devoted to the suppression of crime might cope
with a rising crime rate without sacrifice of efficiency
while continuing to maintain an elaborate and time-
consuming set of criminal processes. However, neither of

these possible characteristics corresponds with social reality in this country. We use the criminal sanction to cover an increasingly wide spectrum of behavior thought to be antisocial, and the amount of crime is very high indeed, although both level and trend are hard to assess.[2] At the same time, although precise measures are not available, it does not appear that we are disposed in the public sector of the economy to increase very drastically the quantity, much less the quality, of the resources devoted to the suppression of criminal activity through the operation of the criminal process. These factors have an important bearing on the criteria of efficiency, and therefore on the nature of the Crime Control Model.

The model, in order to operate successfully, must produce a high rate of apprehension and conviction, and must do so in a context where the magnitudes being dealt with are very large and the resources for dealing with them are very limited. There must then be a premium on speed and finality. Speed, in turn, depends on informality and on uniformity; finality depends on minimizing the occasions for challenge. The process must not be cluttered up with ceremonious rituals that do not advance the progress of a case. Facts can be established more quickly through interrogation in a police station than through the formal process of examination and cross-examination in a court. It follows that extrajudicial processes should be preferred to judicial processes, informal operations to formal ones. But informality is not enough; there must also be uniformity. Routine, stereotyped procedures are essential if large numbers are being handled. The model that will operate successfully on these presuppositions must be an administrative, almost a managerial, model. The image that comes to mind is an assembly-line conveyor belt down which moves an endless stream of cases, never stopping, carrying the cases to workers who stand at fixed stations and who perform on each case as it comes by the same small but essential operation that brings it one step closer to being a finished product, or, to exchange the metaphor for the reality, a closed file. The criminal process, in this model, is seen as a screening process in which each successive stage—pre-arrest investigation, arrest, post-arrest investigation, preparation for trial, trial or entry of plea, conviction, disposition—involves a series of

---

[2] See President's Commission on Law Enforcement and Administration of Justice, *The Challenge of Crime in a Free Society* (Washington, D.C., 1967), chap. 2.

routinized operations whose success is gauged primarily by their tendency to pass the case along to a successful conclusion.

What is a successful conclusion? One that throws off at an early stage those cases in which it appears unlikely that the person apprehended is an offender and then secures, as expeditiously as possible, the conviction of the rest, with a minimum of occasions for challenge, let alone post-audit. By the application of administrative expertness, primarily that of the police and prosecutors, an early determination of probable innocence or guilt emerges. Those who are probably innocent are screened out. Those who are probably guilty are passed quickly through the remaining stages of the process. The key to the operation of the model regarding those who are not screened out is what I shall call a presumption of guilt. The concept requires some explanation, since it may appear startling to assert that what appears to be the precise converse of our generally accepted ideology of a presumption of innocence can be an essential element of a model that does correspond in some respects to the actual operation of the criminal process.

The presumption of guilt is what makes it possible for the system to deal efficiently with large numbers, as the Crime Control Model demands. The supposition is that the screening processes operated by police and prosecutors are reliable indicators of probable guilt. Once a man has been arrested and investigated without being found to be probably innocent, or, to put it differently, once a determination has been made that there is enough evidence of guilt to permit holding him for further action, then all subsequent activity directed toward him is based on the view that he is probably guilty. The precise point at which this occurs will vary from case to case; in many cases it will occur as soon as the suspect is arrested, or even before, if the evidence of probable guilt that has come to the attention of the authorities is sufficiently strong. But in any case the presumption of guilt will begin to operate well before the "suspect" becomes a "defendant."

The presumption of guilt is not, of course, a thing. Nor is it even a rule of law in the usual sense. It simply is the consequence of a complex of attitudes, a mood. If there is confidence in the reliability of informal administrative fact-finding activities that take place in the early stages of the criminal process, the remaining stages of the process can be relatively perfunctory without any loss in operating efficiency. The presumption of guilt, as it operates in the Crime Control Model, is the operational expression of that confidence.

It would be a mistake to think of the presumption of guilt as the opposite of the presumption of innocence that we are so used to thinking of as the polestar of the criminal process and that, as we shall see, occupies an important position in the Due Process Model. The presumption of innocence is not its opposite; it is irrelevant to the presumption of guilt; the two concepts are different rather than opposite ideas. The difference can perhaps be epitomized by an example. A murderer, for reasons best known to himself, chooses to shoot his victim in plain view of a large number of people. When the police arrive, he hands them his gun and says, "I did it and I'm glad." His account of what happened is corroborated by several eyewitnesses. He is placed under arrest and led off to jail. Under these circumstances, which may seem extreme but which in fact characterize with rough accuracy the evidentiary situation in a large proportion of criminal cases, it would be plainly absurd to maintain that more probably than not the suspect did not commit the killing. But that is not what the presumption of innocence means. It means that until there has been an adjudication of guilt by an authority legally competent to make such an adjudication, the suspect is to be treated, for reasons that have nothing whatever to do with the probable outcome of the case, as if his guilt is an open question.

The presumption of innocence is a direction to officials about how they are to proceed, not a prediction of outcome. The presumption of guilt, however, is purely and simply a prediction of outcome. The presumption of innocence is, then, a direction to the authorities to ignore the presumption of guilt in their treatment of the suspect. It tells them, in effect, to close their eyes to what will frequently seem to be factual probabilities. The reasons why it tells them this are among the animating presuppositions of the Due Process Model, and we will come to them shortly. It is enough to note at this point that the presumption of guilt is descriptive and factual; the presumption of innocence is normative and legal. The pure Crime Control Model has no truck with the presumption of innocence, although its real-life emanations are, as we shall see, brought into uneasy compromise with the dictates of this dominant ideological position. In the presumption of guilt this model finds a factual predicate for the position that the dominant goal of repressing crime can be achieved through highly summary processes without any great loss of efficiency (as previously defined), because of the probability that, in the run of cases, the preliminary screening processes operated by the police and the prosecuting officials contain adequate guarantees of reliable fact-finding. Indeed, the model takes an even stronger position. It is that subsequent processes, particularly those of a formal adjudicatory nature, are unlikely to produce as reliable fact-finding as the expert administrative process that precedes them is capable of. The criminal process thus must put special weight on the quality of administrative fact-finding. It becomes important, then, to place as few restrictions as possible on the character of the administrative fact-finding processes and to limit restrictions to such as enhance reliability, excluding those designed for other purposes. As we shall see, this view of restrictions on administrative fact-finding is a consistent theme in the development of the Crime Control Model.

In this model, as I have suggested, the center of gravity for the process lies in the early, administrative fact-finding stages. The complementary proposition is that the subsequent stages are relatively unimportant and should be truncated as much as possible. This, too, produces tensions with presently dominant ideology. The pure Crime Control Model has very little use for many conspicuous features of the adjudicative process, and in real life works out a number of ingenious compromises with them. Even in the pure model, however, there have to be devices for dealing with the suspect after the preliminary screening process has resulted in a determination of probable guilt. The focal device, as we shall see, is the plea of guilty; through its use, adjudicative fact-finding is reduced to a minimum. It might be said of the Crime Control Model that, when reduced to its barest essentials and operating at its most successful pitch, it offers two possibilities: an administrative fact-finding process leading (1) to exoneration of the suspect or (2) to the entry of a plea of guilty.

Due Process Values

If the Crime Control Model resembles an assembly line, the Due Process Model looks very much like an obstacle course. Each of its successive stages is designed to present formidable impediments to carrying the accused any further along in the process. Its ideology is not the converse of that underlying the Crime Control Model. It does not rest on the idea that it is not socially desirable to repress crime, although critics of its application have been known to claim so. Its ideology is composed of a complex of ideas, some of them based on judgments about the efficacy of crime control devices, others having to do with

quite different considerations. The ideology of due process is far more deeply impressed on the formal structure of
the law than is the ideology of crime control; yet an accurate tracing of the strands that make it up is strangely
difficult. What follows is only an attempt at an approxi-
mation.

The Due Process Model encounters its rival on the
Crime Control Model's own ground in respect to the reliability of fact-finding processes. The Crime Control Model,
as we have suggested, places heavy reliance on the ability
of investigative and prosecutorial officers, acting in an
informal setting in which their distinctive skills are
given full sway, to elicit and reconstruct a tolerably accurate account of what actually took place in an alleged
criminal event. The Due Process Model rejects this premise
and substitutes for it a view of informal, nonadjudicative
fact-finding that stresses the possibility of error. People are notoriously poor observers of disturbing events—
the more emotion-arousing the context, the greater the possibility that recollection will be incorrect; confessions
and admissions by persons in police custody may be induced
by physical or psychological coercion so that the police
end up hearing what the suspect thinks they want to hear
rather than the truth; witnesses may be animated by a bias
or interest that no one would trouble to discover except
one specially charged with protecting the interests of the
accused (as the police are not). Considerations of this
kind all lead to a rejection of informal fact-finding processes as definitive of factual guilt and to an insistence
on formal, adjudicative, adversary fact-finding processes
in which the factual case against the accused is publicly
heard by an impartial tribunal and is evaluated only after
the accused has had a full opportunity to discredit the
case against him. Even then, the distrust of fact-finding
processes that animates the Due Process Model is not dis-
sipated. The possibilities of human error being what they
are, further scrutiny is necessary, or at least must be
available, in case facts have been overlooked or suppressed
in the heat of battle. How far this subsequent scrutiny
must be available is a hotly controverted issue today. In
the pure Due Process Model the answer would be: at least as
long as there is an allegation of factual error that has
not received an adjudicative hearing in a fact-finding context. The demand for finality is thus very low in the Due
Process Model.

This strand of due process ideology is not enough to
sustain the model. If all that were at issue between the
two models was a series of questions about the reliability

of fact-finding processes, we would have but one model of
the criminal process, the nature of whose constituent elements would pose questions of fact not of value. Even if
the discussion is confined, for the moment, to the question
of reliability, it is apparent that more is at stake than
simply an evaluation of what kinds of fact-finding processes, alone or in combination, are likely to produce the
most nearly reliable results. The stumbling block is this:
how much reliability is compatible with efficiency? Granted that informal fact-finding will make some mistakes that
can be remedied if backed up by adjudicative fact-finding,
the desirability of providing this backup is not affirmed
or negated by factual demonstrations or predictions that
the increase in reliability will be x per cent or x plus n
per cent. It still remains to ask how much weight is to be
given to the competing demands of reliability (a high degree of probability in each case that factual guilt has
been accurately determined) and efficiency (expeditious
handling of the large numbers of cases that the process in-
gests). The Crime Control Model is more optimistic about
the improbability of error in a significant number of cases;
but it is also, though only in part therefore, more toler-
ant about the amount of error that it will put up with.
The Due Process Model insists on the prevention and elimination of mistakes to the extent possible; the Crime Control Model accepts the probability of mistakes up to the
level at which they interfere with the goal of repressing
crime, either because too many guilty people are escaping
or, more subtly, because general awareness of the unreliability of the process leads to a decrease in the deterrent
efficacy of the criminal law. In this view, reliability
and efficiency are not polar opposites but rather complementary characteristics. The system is reliable *because*
efficient; reliability becomes a matter of independent concern only when it becomes so attenuated as to impair efficiency. All of this the Due Process Model rejects. If
efficiency demands shortcuts around reliability, then absolute efficiency must be rejected. The aim of the process
is at least as much to protect the factually innocent as it
is to convict the factually guilty. It is a little like
quality control in industrial technology: tolerable deviation from standard varies with the importance of conformity
to standard in the destined uses of the product. The Due
Process Model resembles a factory that has to devote a substantial part of its input to quality control. This necessarily cuts down on quantitative output.

     All of this is only the beginning of the ideological
difference between the two models. The Due Process Model

could disclaim any attempt to provide enhanced reliability
for the fact-finding process and still produce a set of institutions and processes that would differ sharply from
those demanded by the Crime Control Model. Indeed, it may
not be too great an oversimplification to assert that in
point of historical development the doctrinal pressures
emanating from the demands of the Due Process Model have
tended to evolve from an original matrix of concern for the
maximization of reliability into values quite different and
more far-reaching. These values can be expressed in, although not adequately described by, the concept of the pri-
macy of the individual and the complementary concept of
limitation on official power.

The combination of stigma and loss of liberty that is
embodied in the end result of the criminal process is
viewed as being the heaviest deprivation that government
can inflict on the individual. Furthermore, the processes
that culminate in these highly afflictive sanctions are
seen as in themselves coercive, restricting, and demeaning.
Power is always subject to abuse—sometimes subtle, other
times, as in the criminal process, open and ugly. Precisely because of its potency in subjecting the individual to
the coercive power of the state, the criminal process must,
in this model, be subjected to controls that prevent it
from operating with maximal efficiency. According to this
ideology, maximal efficiency means maximal tyranny. And,
although no one would assert that minimal efficiency means
minimal tyranny, the proponents of the Due Process Model
would accept with considerable equanimity a substantial
diminution in the efficiency with which the criminal process operates in the interest of preventing official oppres-
sion of the individual.

The most modest-seeming but potentially far-reaching
mechanism by which the Due Process Model implements these
antiauthoritarian values is the doctrine of legal guilt.
According to this doctrine, a person is not to be held
guilty of crime merely on a showing that in all probability,
based upon reliable evidence, he did factually what he is
said to have done. Instead, he is to be held guilty if and
only if these factual determinations are made in procedural-
ly regular fashion and by authorities acting within competences duly allocated to them. Furthermore, he is not to
be held guilty, even though the factual determination is or
might be adverse to him, if various rules designed to protect him and to safeguard the integrity of the process are
not given effect: the tribunal that convicts him must have
the power to deal with his kind of case ("jurisdiction")
and must be geographically appropriate ("venue"); too long

a time must not have elapsed since the offense was committed ("statute of limitations"); he must not have been previously convicted or acquitted of the same or a substantially similar offense ("double jeopardy"); he must not fall within a category of persons, such as children or the insane, who are legally immune to conviction ("criminal responsibility"); and so on. None of these requirements has anything to do with the factual question of whether the person did or did not engage in the conduct that is charged as the offense against him; yet favorable answers to any of them will mean that he is legally innocent. Wherever the competence to make adequate factual determinations lies, it is apparent that only a tribunal that is aware of these guilt-defeating doctrines and is willing to apply them can be viewed as competent to make determinations of legal guilt. The police and the prosecutors are ruled out by lack of competence, in the first instance, and by lack of assurance of willingness, in the second. Only an impartial tribunal can be trusted to make determinations of legal as opposed to factual guilt.

In this concept of legal guilt lies the explanation for the apparently quixotic presumption of innocence of which we spoke earlier. A man who, after police investigation, is charged with having committed a crime can hardly be said to be presumptively innocent, if what we mean is factual innocence. But if what we mean is that it has yet to be determined if any of the myriad legal doctrines that serve in one way or another the end of limiting official power through the observance of certain substantive and procedural regularities may be appropriately invoked to exculpate the accused man, it is apparent that as a matter of prediction it cannot be said with confidence that more probably than not he will be found guilty.

Beyond the question of predictability this model posits a functional reason for observing the presumption of innocence: by forcing the state to prove its case against the accused in an adjudicative context, the presumption of innocence serves to force into play all the qualifying and disabling doctrines that limit the use of the criminal sanction against the individual, thereby enhancing his opportunity to secure a favorable outcome. In this sense, the presumption of innocence may be seen to operate as a kind of self-fulfilling prophecy. By opening up a procedural situation that permits the successful assertion of defenses having nothing to do with factual guilt, it vindicates the proposition that the factually guilty may nonetheless be legally innocent and should therefore be given a chance to qualify for that kind of treatment.

The possibility of legal innocence is expanded enormously when the criminal process is viewed as the appropriate forum for correcting its own abuses. This notion may well account for a greater amount of the distance between the two models than any other. In theory the Crime Control Model can tolerate rules that forbid illegal arrests, unreasonable searches, coercive interrogations, and the like. What it cannot tolerate is the vindication of those rules in the criminal process itself through the exclusion of evidence illegally obtained or through the reversal of convictions in cases where the criminal process has breached the rules laid down for its observance. And the Due Process Model, although it may in the first instance be addressed to the maintenance of reliable fact-finding techniques, comes eventually to incorporate prophylactic and deterrent rules that result in the release of the factually guilty even in cases in which blotting out the illegality would still leave an adjudicative fact-finder convinced of the accused person's guilt. Only by penalizing errant police and prosecutors within the criminal process itself can adequate pressure be maintained, so the argument runs, to induce conformity with the Due Process Model.

Another strand in the complex of attitudes underlying the Due Process Model is the idea—itself a shorthand statement for a complex of attitudes—of equality. This notion has only recently emerged as an explicit basis for pressing the demands of the Due Process Model, but it appears to represent, at least in its potential, a most powerful norm for influencing official conduct. Stated most starkly, the ideal of equality holds that "there can be no equal justice where the kind of trial a man gets depends on the amount of money he has."[3] The factual predicate underlying this assertion is that there are gross inequalities in the financial means of criminal defendants as a class, that in an adversary system of criminal justice an effective defense is largely a function of the resources that can be mustered on behalf of the accused, and that the very large proportion of criminal defendants who are, operationally speaking, "indigent" will thus be denied an effective defense. This factual premise has been strongly reinforced by recent studies that in turn have been both a cause and an effect of an increasing emphasis upon norms for the criminal process based on the premise.

The norms derived from the premise do not take the form of an insistence upon governmental responsibility to

---

[3]Griffin v. Illinois, 351 U.S. 12, 19 (1956).

provide literally equal opportunities for all criminal defendants to challenge the process. Rather, they take as
their point of departure the notion that the criminal process, initiated as it is by government and containing as it
does the likelihood of severe deprivations at the hands of
government, imposes some kind of public obligation to ensure that financial inability does not destroy the capacity
of an accused to assert what may be meritorious challenges
to the processes being invoked against him. At its most
gross, the norm of equality would act to prevent situations
in which financial inability forms an absolute barrier to
the assertion of a right that is in theory generally available, as where there is a right to appeal that is, however,
effectively conditional upon the filing of a trial transcript obtained at the defendant's expense. Beyond this, it
may provide the basis for a claim whenever the system theo-
retically makes some kind of challenge available to an accused who has the means to press it. If, for example, a
defendant who is adequately represented has the opportunity
to prevent the case against him from coming to the trial
stage by forcing the state to its proof in a preliminary
hearing, the norm of equality may be invoked to assert that
the same kind of opportunity must be available to others as
well. In a sense the system as it functions for the small
minority whose resources permit them to exploit all its de-
fensive possibilities provides a benchmark by which its
functioning in all other cases is to be tested: not, perhaps, to guarantee literal identity but rather to provide a
measure of whether the process as a whole is recognizably
of the same general order. The demands made by a norm of
this kind are likely by their very nature to be quite sweeping. Although the norm's imperatives may be initially limited to determining whether in a particular case the accused was injured or prejudiced by his relative inability
to make an appropriate challenge, the norm of equality very
quickly moves to another level on which the demand is that
the process in general be adapted to minimize discrimina-
tions rather than that a mere series of post hoc determinations of discrimination be made or makeable.

It should be observed that the impact of the equality
norm will vary greatly depending upon the point in time at
which it is introduced into a model of the criminal process.
If one were starting from scratch to decide how the process
ought to work, the norm of equality would have nothing very
important to say on such questions as, for example, whether
an accused should have the effective assistance of counsel
in deciding whether to enter a plea of guilty. One could
decide, on quite independent considerations, that it is or

is not a good thing to afford that facility to the general-
ity of persons accused of crime. But the impact of the
equality norm becomes far greater when it is brought to
bear on a process whose contours have already been shaped.
If our model of the criminal process affords defendants who
are in a financial position to do so the right to consult a
lawyer before entering a plea, then the equality norm ex-
erts powerful pressure to provide such an opportunity to
all defendants and to regard the failure to do so as a mal-
functioning of the process of whose consequences the accused is entitled to be relieved. In a sense, this has
been the role of the equality norm in affecting the real-
world criminal process. It has made its appearance on the
scene comparatively late, and has therefore encountered a
system in which the relative financial inability of most
persons accused of crime results in treatment very different from that accorded the small minority of the financial-
ly capable. For this reason, its impact has already been
substantial and may be expected to be even more so in the
future.

There is a final strand of thought in the Due Process
Model that is often ignored but that needs to be candidly
faced if thought on the subject is not to be obscured.
This is a mood of skepticism about the morality and utility of the criminal sanction, taken either as a whole or in
some of its applications. The subject is a large and complicated one, comprehending as it does much of the intellectual history of our times. It is properly the subject of
another essay altogether. To put the matter briefly, one
cannot improve upon the statement by Professor Paul Bator:

> In summary we are told that the criminal law's
> notion of just condemnation and punishment is a
> cruel hypocrisy visited by a smug society on the
> psychologically and economically crippled; that
> its premise of a morally autonomous will with at
> least some measure of choice whether to comply
> with the values expressed in a penal code is un-
> scientific and outmoded; that its reliance on
> punishment as an educational and deterrent agent
> is misplaced, particularly in the case of the
> very members of society most likely to engage
> in criminal conduct; and that its failure to pro-
> vide for individualized and humane rehabilitation
> of offenders is inhuman and wasteful.[4]

[4]*Finality in Criminal Law and Federal Habeas Corpus for
State Prisoners,* 76 Harv. L. Rev. 441, 442 (1963).

This skepticism, which may be fairly said to be widespread among the most influential and articulate contemporary leaders of informed opinion, leads to an attitude toward the processes of the criminal law that, to quote Mr. Bator again, engenders "a peculiar receptivity toward claims of injustice which arise within the traditional structure of the system itself; fundamental disagreement and unease about the very bases of the criminal law has, inevitably, created acute pressure at least to expand and liberalize those of its processes and doctrines which serve to make more tentative its judgments or limit its power." In short, doubts about the ends for which power is being exercised create pressure to limit the discretion with which that power is exercised.

The point need not be pressed to the extreme of doubts about or rejection of the premises upon which the criminal sanction in general rests. Unease may be stirred simply by reflection on the variety of uses to which the criminal sanction is put and by a judgment that an increasingly large proportion of those uses may represent an unwise invocation of so extreme a sanction. It would be an interesting irony if doubts about the propriety of certain uses of the criminal sanction prove to contribute to a restrictive trend in the criminal process that in the end requires a choice among uses and finally an abandonment of some of the very uses that stirred the original doubts, but for a reason quite unrelated to those doubts.

There are two kinds of problems that need to be dealt with in any model of the criminal process. One is what the rules shall be. The other is how the rules shall be implemented. The second is at least as important as the first. As we shall see time and again in our detailed development of the models, the distinctive difference between the two models is not only in the rules of conduct that they lay down but also in the sanctions that are to be invoked when a claim is presented that the rules have been breached and, no less importantly, in the timing that is permitted or required for the invocation of those sanctions.

As I have already suggested, the Due Process Model locates at least some of the sanctions for breach of the operative rules in the criminal process itself. The relation between these two aspects of the process—the rules and the sanctions for their breach—is a purely formal one unless there is some mechanism for bringing them into play with each other. The hinge between them in the Due Process Model is the availability of legal counsel. This has a double aspect. Many of the rules that the model requires are couched in terms of the availability of counsel to do various things at various stages of the process—this is the conventionally recognized aspect; beyond it, there is a pervasive assumption that counsel is necessary in order to invoke sanctions for breach of any of the rules. The more freely available these sanctions are, the more important is the role of counsel in seeing to it that the sanctions are appropriately invoked. If the process is seen as a series of occasions for checking its own operation, the role of counsel is a much more nearly central one than is the case in a process that is seen as primarily concerned with expeditious determination of factual guilt. And if equality of operation is a governing norm, the availability of counsel to some is seen as requiring it for all. Of all the controverted aspects of the criminal process, the right to counsel, including the role of government in its provision, is the most dependent on what one's model of the process looks like, and the least susceptible of resolution unless one has confronted the antinomies of the two models.

I do not mean to suggest that questions about the right to counsel disappear if one adopts a model of the process that conforms more or less closely to the Crime Control Model, but only that such questions become absolutely central if one's model moves very far down the spectrum of possibilities toward the pure Due Process Model. The reason for this centrality is to be found in the assumption underlying both models that the process is an adversary one in which the initiative in invoking relevant rules rests primarily on the parties concerned, the state, and the accused. One could construct models that placed central responsibility on adjudicative agents such as committing magistrates and trial judges. And there are, as we shall see, marginal but nonetheless important adjustments in the role of the adjudicative agents that enter into the models with which we are concerned. For present purposes it is enough to say that these adjustments are marginal, that the animating presuppositions that underlie both models in the context of the American criminal system relegate the adjudicative agents to a relatively passive role, and therefore place central importance on the role of counsel.

One last introductory note before we proceed to a detailed examination of some aspects of the two models in operation. What assumptions do we make about the sources of authority to shape the real-world operations of the criminal process? Recognizing that our models are only models, what agencies of government have the power to pick and choose between their competing demands? Once again, the limiting features of the American context come into play. Ours is not a system of legislative supremacy. The distinc-

tively American institution of judicial review exercises a
limiting and ultimately a shaping influence on the criminal
process.   Because the Crime Control Model is basically an
affirmative model, emphasizing at every turn the existence
and exercise of official power, its validating authority is
ultimately legislative (although proximately administrative).   Because the Due Process Model is basically a negative model, asserting limits on the nature of official power and on the modes of its exercise, its validating authority is judicial and requires an appeal to supra-legislative
law, to the law of the Constitution.   To the extent that
tensions between the two models are resolved by deference
to the Due Process Model, the authoritative force at work
is the judicial power, working in the distinctively judicial mode of invoking the sanction of nullity.   That is at
once the strength and the weakness of the Due Process Model:
its strength because in our system the appeal to the Constitution provides the last and the overriding work; its weakness because saying no in specific cases is an exercise in
futility unless there is a general willingness on the part
of the officials who operate the process to apply negative
prescriptions across the board.   It is no accident that
statements reinforcing the Due Process Model come from the
courts, while at the same time facts denying it are established by the police and prosecutors.

CRIMINAL PSYCHODYNAMICS: A PLATFORM

Benjamin Karpman

Criminal psychodynamics has for its purpose the study of the genesis, development, and motivation of that aspect of human behavior that conflicts with accepted social norms and standards. The Archives of Criminal Psychodynamics will encourage research into the psychodynamics of existing knowledge on the subject, promotion of superior legal and humane understanding of the relations between the criminal and society, and the betterment of the condition of the criminal as an individual.

With this as a prior formulation, let us see where we stand today as compared with fifteen years ago, when I prepared a platform for the *Journal of Criminal Psychopathology*, edited by the late Dr. V. C. Branham.

I. PSYCHODYNAMICS AND CRIMINAL MOTIVATIONS

No marked improvement can be reported in the contributions to criminal psychopathology made by criminology, academic psychology, physical anthropology, and law, which emphasize mass aspects of the situation, generally failing to appreciate the significance of the individual.

In conventional psychiatry, an advance has been made through the increased number of converts to psychodynamics. But many psychiatrists still operate at the descriptive level, seeing behavior as consisting of deliberately chosen, conscious acts and seemingly unable to grasp the meaning of unconscious motivations.

Reprinted with permission from the *Journal of Criminal Law, Criminology and Police Science* 47 (1956), pp. 8-17. Copyright © 1956 by Northwestern University School of Law. This article is a condensation of a much longer article which originally appeared in the *Archives of Criminal Psychodynamics* (1955). The author is a psychotherapist on the staff of St. Elizabeth's Hospital, Washington, D.C.

II. RELATION TO GENERAL PSYCHODYNAMICS

Criminal psychodynamics is a direct descendent of general psychodynamics and subscribes to the same tenets. A close relationship between crime and insanity has long been evident. The insane contribute a much larger proportion of crime than an equal number of the general population; and a proportionately far greater number of criminals than members of the population as a whole develop insanity. It remained for the psychoanalytic school of psychiatry to seek a clearer understanding of the meaning of this relationship.

It was discovered that neuroses are expressive of conflicts between instinctive drives and opposing pressures of society; that the neurotic was a cryptic criminal, whose neurosis was a method of protecting himself from committing a crime; and that the unconscious mental life of neurotics was thoroughly tinged with criminality. Now and then these defenses would prove inadequate, the instinct would get the upper hand for a moment, and the neurotic turn antisocial. From such considerations the justification for regarding criminality as a form of neurosis was derived. Thousands of such persons now fill our penal institutions, although they need treatment for their psychic illness, not punishment.

Basically, criminality is but a symptom of insanity, using the term in its widest generic sense to express unacceptable social behavior based on unconscious motivation flowing from a disturbed instinctive and emotional life, whether this appears in frank psychoses, or in less obvious form in neuroses and unrecognized psychoses. This conclusion is having revolutionary effects. If criminals are products of early environmental influences in the same sense that psychotics and neurotics are, then it should be possible to reach them psychotherapeutically. Only a bare beginning has been made in this respect, but the results are most encouraging, for criminals have been cured through psychotherapy, often when other means have completely failed.

III.   MENTAL DEFICIENCIES AND CRIME

Despite commonly held beliefs to the contrary, it is not at all certain that mental defectives commit crimes more often than do other groups in proportion to their numbers. They commit as wide a variety of crimes and for the same basic reasons as people of better intelligence. A foundation for neurosis often is present in mental

defectives because their disadvantage in relation to their
environment results in emotional conflicts.

IV. THE CONTRIBUTION OF PSYCHOSES TO CRIMINALITY

A. *The Paranoiac*. Kraepelin's definition, which I
accept, limits true paranoia to intellectual disturbances,
with delusions of persecution well systematized and logically presented. In its criminal forms it is extremely
dangerous; for example, most regicides are paranoiacs. The
problem is insufficiently discussed or understood among psychiatrists, partly because it is relatively rare and many
paranoiacs escape commitment and partly because definitions
of paranoia differ, some including less well systematized
or hallucinating patients.

B. *The Schizophrenias*. The average psychiatrist appears to associate criminality among paranoiacs or paranoid
praecoxes solely with murder or assault with intent to kill.
Yet they may be guilty of any type of offense. Catatonics
often commit murders of even greater brutality than paranoid praecoxes. Many hebephrenics and simple praecoxes are
inclined to various types of crimes, but we know practically nothing about how the criminal praecox differs from the
non-criminal praecox. The delusions of psychotics often
show strong potential criminality which is not otherwise
expressed, the patient having escaped into his psychosis.

C. *The Manic-Depressive Psychoses*. A wide range of
criminal offenses is found in manic-depressive psychoses,
though sexual offenses as such seem to be lacking or not
conspicuous. Minor social difficulties are often part of
the on-coming manic attack, while such serious crimes as
murder may be committed in the hypomanic or manic stage.

D. *Epilepsy and Alcoholism*. We often associate brutal crimes with epilepsy, alcoholism, and alcoholic psychoses, but these are only the most conspicuous cases. Because epilepsy is not fully recognized as a mental disease,
many epileptics are imprisoned for offenses caused by their
disease. Alcohol may create inhibitions or reduce them.
The unconscious tendency toward a criminal act often leads
to alcoholic indulgence, rather than the reverse.

E. *Organic Brain Disease.* The contribution of these diseases to criminality has been little investigated psychodynamically. Typically, the criminal acts of paretics are minor, but there are persons with no antisocial history prior to the disease who embark on a consistent criminal career when paresis destroys the frontal lobes which are the seat of inhibitions and the sense of guilt. Any type of crime may be committed in arteriosclerotic psychoses, while paedophilia or other sexual offenses are most typical in senile dementia. Sexual offenses and predatory crimes are not uncommon in encephalitic lethargica. These crimes may be forerunners of latent encephalitis. Many undetected sufferers from organic brain diseases are serving prison sentences when they should be hospitalized.

V. CRIMINALITY WITHIN THE FRAMEWORK OF NEUROSES

A. *Neuroses vs. Psychopathic Personality.* On the assumption that neurotics "by definition" do not commit crimes, the hospital diagnosis of a psychoneurotic who commits a crime is likely to be psychopathic personality. Yet many neurotics do commit crimes when the safeguards provided by their neuroses prove insufficient. In the majority of so-called psychopathic personalities I have analyzed, their antisocial behavior was traceable to psychogenetic situations, and they were cured when the emotional difficulties were analytically resolved. Only the few remaining were true psychopaths. Obsessive and compulsive neuroses, with their overwhelming sense of guilt, furnish the smallest contribution to crime.

B. *The Sexual Offenses.* It is the writer's opinion that neurotic criminals far outnumber psychotic criminals, as neuroses in general outnumber psychoses. A larger concept of neurosis is needed, however, to include the vast number of reactions which are not as grossly hysterical as paralysis and convulsions and do not display the "major symptoms of hysteria," but do exhibit the basic core of neurosis: emotional lability and immaturity, dependence, and so forth. Second, we must include the large group of reactions which superficially seem psychopathic—the secondary psychopathic reactions.

The paraphilias (perversions), to which the greatest number of sexual offenses belong, must also be included, for they have all the earmarks of neuroses and are amenable to psychotherapy. Unlike the psychopath, the paraphiliac invariably carries a greater or lesser burden of guilt.

VI. PSYCHOPATHY AND CRIMINALITY

Some progress has been made in the past fifteen years in the clinical delineation of psychopathy. I personally view psychopathy as a specific mental disease, even more distinct from neuroses than neuroses are from psychoses. At the present the term is a sort of wastebasket, used with a number of meanings and often denoting any mental abnormality otherwise not specifically limited. It is also often used over-specifically to mean "antisocial."

One may submit here that any behavior, criminal or entirely harmless socially, that flows out of (unconscious) psychogenic difficulties belongs to neuroses or psychoses, not to psychopathies. In a recent study, I made an exhaustive examination of 24 hospital admissions, mostly from penal institutions, in which the diagnosis included "psychopathic personality," with or without psychosis. In only four cases was the description justified. In each of the other cases we were unquestionably dealing with either a neurosis or a psychosis, the label "psychopathic personality" supported only by the fact that there was a criminal record.

VII. PSYCHODYNAMICS OF SPECIFIC CRIME ACTIVITIES

A. *Overt Crime and Vicarious Intent*. Conventionally, the law groups crimes according to their object, as crimes against property, morals, persons, or the state. Such grouping does not consider motivation, and the surface action of a crime may give little clue to the dynamics behind it. For example, a man who enters a house and steals a woman's clothing, with the aid of which he will masturbate, is charged with housebreaking and larceny, where at root this is a sexual offense.

B. *Is the Criminal a Responsible Agent?* All offenses against society are commonly regarded as willfully planned, for personal gain or from sheer viciousness. The individual is considered a free and responsible agent. Psychodynamics submits that in the main criminal acts result from emotional states which find an outlet in aggressive acts which are symbols of unconscious motivations, often having the same psychic significance as neurotic symptoms.

C. *Crimes against Property.* This widely varying group of crimes furnishes the largest class of "habitual" criminality. It includes arson and murder where the motive appears to be predatory. We have made much progress in the recognition that offenses by kleptomaniacs and pyromaniacs are symptoms of mental disease and to be treated as such. But under intensive study of causation, the fine line between neurotic kleptomania and pyromania and common thieving and arson begins to vanish. In studying a larger number of habitual, hard-boiled "jailbirds," excepting a few true psychopaths, the author found their criminal activity to be expressive of unconscious emotional problems. Naturally, there are certain differences which leave one neurotic without antisocial involvements while another is driven to socially unacceptable actions. Situations in early life are highly significant. Not only the broken home, but the oppressive, joyless home, or the home where there is constant conflict often contributes to a criminal situation with a definitely neurotic background, through an intense though usually unconscious urge toward compensation.

D. *Crimes against Morals.* Despite the lack of superficial resemblance between crimes against property and sexual offenses, common features begin to emerge as one searches for underlying mechanisms. Many of these offenses, such as fetishism and exhibitionism, present little actual threat to society, while others such as rape, sadism, and paedophilia are extremely serious. Sexual offenses also must not be taken at face value but understood as symbols of other sexual situations or crimes for which they represent a symptomatic compromise. Punishment has no effect in preventing repetitions of sexual offenses after release from prison, since it leaves the emotional factors untouched.

E. *Crimes against Persons: Murder and Related Phenomena.* Murder, whether the so-called murder from passion or murder for profit, must be viewed as a highly complicated form of behavior, a result of deeply rooted difficulties rather than immediate circumstances. Murders are often committed by the frankly insane, the most frequent example being the paranoid individual who kills an innocent person he regards as his persecutor. Such murders are actually symbolic, however, the paranoiac trying to kill his own homosexual component. Pathological jealousy, usually related to feelings of (sexual) inferiority, and incest wishes are other motives which may lie beneath the surface in murder. In any case, a severe conflict between instinctive forces and conscience is present. To commit murder, whatever the superficial or underlying incentives toward it, one of the strongest of all cultural repressions must be overcome. Suicide is sometimes chosen as a means of avoiding murder.

Most murders are committed in an acute emotional state that knows only the irresistible need to discharge itself, despite the claim that all mercenary murders and most passion murders are committed with deliberation and that the individual is responsible for his deed, which he could have controlled if he wanted to. Though the individual may seemingly be able to distinguish right and wrong, his choice is actually determined by emotional motivations outside conscious control by intelligence. Even in cases of mercenary murder, this is a deeper motivation which is emotional. Where mental illness is not immediately apparent, careful analytic exploration is necessary before the question of deliberateness and hence responsibility can be fairly settled.

Psychodynamics, unlike the law, is concerned with underlying rather than superficial and conscious motivations for murder. In "passion" murders, it is the deeper motives behind such obvious motives as jealousy and revenge that give insight into the act. Sometimes, particularly in psychosis, no motive is apparent, and if the patient is inaccessible to analysis, even the psychiatrist can only speculate on the process involved. It must be remembered that many individuals face situations which are externally provocative of the desire to kill; yet few will actually kill. A knowledge of superficial motivations cannot explain this.

Among predatory murderers there is the psychopathic group, already mentioned, with a minimum of emotional content. A larger group fails to reveal an overt emotional background, but one may be found on careful analysis. In another type, one finds inner deep-seated emotional motives of which the murder is only a superficial or even accidental expression.

F. *Child and Juvenile Delinquency.* No detailed consideration of the important problem of childhood and adolescent delinquency will be undertaken here. However, it may be mentioned that tendencies toward antisocial behavior may be observed even in very young children, and few of us escape some minor defiances of authority. But these trends toward expression of hostility are normally balanced by the great deal of affection given to most children. The recent increase in juvenile delinquency is probably due to the deterioration of the home situation attendant upon the war and its aftermath, and the insecurity which currently pervades our lives.

VIII. ADVANCES IN TYPOLOGY AND PSYCHODYNAMICS OF PSYCHOPATHY

The past fifteen years have seen a gradual narrowing of the concept of psychopathy toward a diagnostic entity, a disease *sui generis*, and a corresponding broadening of the concept of neurosis. In 1946 I outlined two basic subtypes of psychopathy: *aggressive-predatory* and *passive-parasitic*.

The life of an individual in the first subgroup is characterized by continuous aggression. He lives only for himself and for the moment, is unteachable and unmanageable, without conscience or sense of guilt. In contrast to neurotics, these people have a most shallow unconscious; complex emotional reactions are beyond them, although they may express intense but fleeting emotional reactions. In early life, either drastic rejection and privation or overprotection, with resulting infantilization may create the foundation for aggressive psychopathy.

Members of the second subgroup also extract what they want from the environment, but they are parasitic and "sponge" on other people without conscience, remorse, or appreciation of help received. They often appear as helpless individuals, arousing others' sympathy. Actually, there are many gradations between these two subgroups.

There are intermediate types between psychopathy and neurosis in which hysterical reactions may well intrude. If the original privations or rejections have been complete, clear-cut psychopathy will result; but in cases with modifying circumstances such as an individual other than the parent who takes an interest in the child, a modicum of normality may be provided.

A. *Spurious or Deceptive Types of Psychopathy*. There is another group of individuals whose criminal and psychopathic behavior in no way appears to differ from that of the aggressive psychopath. Careful analytic scrutiny, however, will disclose that behind the wall of aggression,

hostility, and unremitting criminal behavior is a full-
fledged neurosis. A major contributory cause is refused
love, generating hatred which is repressed and reappears
in later years as criminal behavior.

B. *Present Consensus of Genesis of Primary Psychopathy.* Findings favor the conception that primary psychopathy is likely to be environmentally conditioned. Current
opinion holds that its roots may be found in the first five
years of life, some narrowing it to the first year or two.
The condition appears when close adult-child relationships
are lacking at this critical age, most frequently in institutional children, those moved from one foster home to another, left with frequently-changed servants, or those
whose mothers exhibit such rapidly changing attitudes toward the children as to prevent establishment of reliable
object relations. Without early opportunity for identification, the ability to identify is lost, and the normal
personality cannot continue to develop. Anxiety and guilt,
which arise when object relations are threatened, are unknown to the psychopathic child, since he has established
no such relations.

IX. DIVERGENT TRENDS IN LAW AND PSYCHIATRY

A. *Meeting the Criticisms: Basic Misunderstandings.*
A professor of law has stated that lawyers are skeptical of
psychiatry, among other reasons, because of the unreliability of psychiatric diagnosis, the uncertainty of psychotherapy, the fantastic character of some psychiatric court testimony, and the widespread disagreements among medical
psychologists about fundamental problems of theory and practice, which raise doubts as to the scientific validity of
psychiatry. Only a full-fledged, obligatory course in psychiatry in law schools will give lawyers the understanding
necessary for a rapprochement between the two disciplines.
When there is serious disagreement as to diagnosis, it
usually occurs because the psychiatrists are given too little time to elicit and evaluate the necessary data concerning an individual. The problem would be largely solved if
persons charged with major crimes—or even lesser offenses—
could be sent to an institution for observation and diagnosis.
The results of psychotherapy are no more uncertain
than therapy in other branches of medicine. No other

branch has made such remarkable strides since World War I
as psychiatry, as evidenced by the enormously increased
number of psychiatric casualties returned to military duty.
     The only reason psychiatric testimony may appear "fan-
tastic" is that lawyers do not understand the steps by
which psychiatrists reach their conclusions, and the psychiatrist rarely has an opportunity to bring out all the material which supports his findings.
     Psychiatry is by no means the only scientific disci-
pline in which widespread disagreements occur. Why single
it out for criticism? The law is far less genuinely scientific, as evidenced by the great differences between laws
in different states and the wide variety of sentences meted
out by different judges for similar offenses.

     B. *Differences in Viewpoints on Specific Problems.*
Law assumes that punishment is the best deterrent of crime,
despite abundant evidence to the contrary, for the chronic
repeater is the rule in crime. The following considerations are offered with a view to clearing up existing mis-
conceptions regarding punishment as a treatment, and showing how many psychological factors conspire to nullify the
effects of the treatment offered by law and even to make
the situation worse.
     Law focuses upon the crime and its results—the deed,
not the doer—and punishment is differentiated on the basis
of results rather than intent. Since it is the results
which directly affect the life of the community, why is
this emphasis not justifiable? Because the deed, like a
symptom in disease, is only the surface expression of a
large number of internal and external factors, and no deed
can be understood apart from the psychology of the doer.
Society, which is concerned with the abolition of misdeeds,
will never accomplish its aim by dealing with deeds alone,
for one must reach the deed through the doer. A radical
change is needed, and meanwhile crime continues unabated.
     Causation, which refers chiefly to physical, economic,
and other external factors, is considered more important in
criminal law than is motivation, which refers to factors
springing from the inner life of the individual. Little
more is sought in a criminal trial than the most immediate
causation or motive. Yet this gives no clue as to why under apparently identical social conditions one person becomes a criminal while another remains a respected citizen.
Only knowledge of their inner lives could account for the
difference, elucidate the meaning of the crime for the criminal, and indicate how to deal with the situation. Often

in criminal behavior, as in normal personality development, single specific motivations cannot be found, but rather an accumulation of many minute influences which in totality produce the effects.

Motivations and setting have an important bearing in the consideration of right and wrong and the problem of responsibility. It is not sufficient to say that the defendant knows or does not know the difference between right and wrong, or that he is guilty, not guilty, responsible, partly responsible, or not responsible. One must know whether he can choose right from wrong emotionally as well as intellectually: why and to what extent he is guilty and responsible. Modern psychiatry challenges the conception that every individual, unless he is definitely insane or feebleminded, has a perfect knowledge of right and wrong and responsibility. Overwhelming clinical evidence proves that human behavior is basically emotionally conditioned and intellectual activities emotionally determined. Hence an individual may know right from wrong in a conventional sense but be wholly unable to choose it emotionally.

Viewing crime on the basis of personalities and deeper motivations involved, two clearly defined types seem to emerge: the psychopathic, committed on a purely mercenary, predatory basis; and the psychogenic, in which a superficially similar crime may be found to have definite psychological roots, often deeply tied to the individual's emotional life. This distinction may make little difference to the victim of a crime, but it is important in terms of disposition of the case with an aim to prevent recurrence. Society cannot afford to treat these two types of criminals alike. The psychogenic cases should be treated, for many can be and have been cured. Ways of dealing with the psychopathic criminal must be devised. In the long run, this is the only approach that can truly solve the problem of crime.

C. *Specific Influences in Prison Negating Treatment.* On commission of a crime, especially a first offense, there may be some degree of repentance for the deed, as well as fear of consequences. However, the prisoner reacts to the physical and psychic insults of being jailed, tried, and sentenced with hatred, neutralizing any sense of guilt or penitence which may have been present. On conviction, he experiences a mixed feeling of revolt, sense of injustice (no matter how just the sentence), and a sense of degradation and loss of social esteem.

The intended purposes of imprisonment are to punish, to correct through fear of repeated punishment, to provide opportunity for penitence, and to protect society by isolating the criminal. In point of fact, antipathic emotions —notably hate and a desire for revenge—are a greater product of imprisonment than is fear. These emotions leave little room for penitence. Society's protection is limited to the time an individual is imprisoned, and the results of imprisonment make recidivism upon release more likely, not less so.

Confinement has major effects on the criminal in the physical, social, psychic, and sexual realms. Food is generally inadequate, daily routines monotonous, tasks performed with little incentive, and genuinely constructive recreation minimal. Irresponsibility is likely to result, as everything is pre-arranged for the prisoner, who is not supposed to assert his individuality. By precluding normal sexual outlets, imprisonment forces a great majority of prisoners to lower forms of adaptation, which may or may not be continued upon release. The constant prison discipline taxes all human endurance. The prisoner is never allowed to forget that he is one who must be punished. The hate which is engendered is essentially a defense reaction, a protective mechanism to save the prisoner's body and soul from destruction. All these factors lead to a degradation of personality and tend to drive the individual into abnormal introversion, substituting phantasy for bitter reality; hence the ease and frequency with which prisoners develop "prison psychosis."

Upon discharge, the prisoner meets a hostile world, vocationally and socially. It is all too easy to seek escape into the criminal group where his record is an admission card instead of a barrier.

The strong antipathies thus built up against anything connected with authority make an adequate psychotherapeutic approach all but impossible. This situation can only be corrected if punitive-corrective measures are reduced to a minimum and social rehabilitation made practicable.

X.   THE TASKS AHEAD

The reader may have gained the impression that knowledge of psychodynamics of crime has made a substantial advance in recent years. A careful study of the literature will show large gaps in this branch of knowledge and biased presentations, due partly to lack of adequate material. All too often, sweeping conclusions have been drawn from insufficient premises.

Much work is still ahead of us. The contribution of mental defectives to crime needs further study. Our present knowledge of their emotional life is meager. We may find that rather than there being something specific about defective criminals, they exhibit the same type of psychodynamic mechanisms as their normal brothers. Definitive studies of the contributions to crime of each of the psychoses are lacking, and the large field of organic brain diseases and crime awaits intelligent handling. But the neuroses offer the richest harvest. This reviewer feels that this group of secondary psychopaths furnishes the largest proportion of criminals. Perhaps most important of all is the study of true, primary psychopaths, who furnish such a large bulk of the criminal population. Finally, we know virtually nothing of the psychodynamics behind organized crime as against individual crime.

Even more important than an understanding of criminality in terms of clinical categories is an insight into the underlying mechanisms, the deeper emotions involved in criminal behavior. Just a few examples of the multitude of questions to be elucidated are: What are the roles of anxiety and unconscious guilt in criminal behavior? How does criminality differ from the forms of non-criminal aggression? What is the difference between a non-criminal neurotic who phantasies criminal acts and the criminal who impulsively perpetrates them? Is criminality a neurosis *sui generis* or a syndrome, a symptom complex? and so on. Such questions require clarification by solid, verifiable facts.

The sex life of criminals is virtually a *terra incognita* to us. Although this area of an individual's life may have most important bearing in the dynamics underlying his activities, it is at present not even considered important from the legal standpoint.

As long as our understanding of criminal psychodynamics depends on individual workers alone, relatively little progress can be made. Organized efforts are needed. I would suggest that every state should have a Criminological Institute whose function it would be to study intensively the lives of criminals. In the long run it would fully pay for itself, in such ways as helping to correct the travesties on justice and common sense perpetrated by parole and probation boards. These boards should consist of psychiatrists, with staffs to take histories. The warden should also be a psychiatrist. Guards should be replaced by nurses, and special prisons stressing rehabilitation should be built for the more harmless type of prisoner. Indeed, we might profit more if the entire system were turned over

to psychiatrists. They certainly could not do worse and
conceivably might do better.

CODA

Criminal psychodynamics sees criminality as basically
a psychiatric, extra-legal problem. It does not see the
criminal eye to eye with the public and the law as a vicious individual for whom the only treatment is punishment.
And it differs from conventional psychiatry in refusing to
accept the legal standards of insanity in place of well
tested, genuine, scientific psychiatric formulations. It
views the problems of right and wrong, of guilt and responsibility, of irresistible impulse not as abstract concepts
or transient trends in human behavior but as being deeply
rooted in the basic biological, instinctual-emotional, and
cultural-ethical make-up of the man. It views criminality,
however incidental it may seem on the surface, as a basic
human expression having a long history and evolution and a
pathology all its own. It sees in criminality a disease
sui generis, a severe disease which, however, can be cured
or prevented when and if proper psychotherapeutic measures
are taken.

It views skeptically the outworn tenets of partial
guilt, partial responsibility, and partial or temporary insanity because these consider only the deed and not the
doer, the intent and not the motivation, external rather
than internal factors, superficial intellectual rather than
deep-seated emotional factors.

The Archives will stimulate the organization of all
the psychiatric resources available and encourage making a
frontal attack on established but badly outworn concepts
that do not take into consideration the advances of science,
while at the same time sending thousands of emotionally innocent men and women to execution or imprisonment. It is
our basic tenet that the criminal is a product of a vicious,
emotionally unhealthy environment in the creation of which
he had no hand and over which he had no control. In so far
as society has done nothing or not enough to alleviate the
developing anti-sociality of the child, it may truly be
said that it deserves the criminals it has and that the
criminal is society's greatest crime. The punitive methods
adopted by society in treating criminals are least calculated to produce the desired results. Reformatories in
point of fact do not reform; there is nothing in penitentiaries to stimulate one to penitence; everything in the
prison only tends to harden criminality into a fixed form
of behavior. Society has failed to redeem its pledge.

The *Archives of Criminal Psychodynamics* will fight
vigorously for the recognition of the criminal as a very
sick person. The criminal is more sinned against than sin-
ning, and his present treatment only aggravates the condition, leading to further criminal behavior and creation of
a vicious circle. It is therefore, in a sense, a clarion
call to arms to all psychiatrists interested in criminality
to bring forth material that will stimulate advancement in
the field.

THERAPY, NOT PUNISHMENT

Karl Menninger

Since ancient times criminal law and penology have
been based upon what is called in psychology the pain-
pleasure principle. There are many reasons for inflicting
pain—to urge an animal to greater efforts, to retaliate
for pain received, to frighten, or to indulge in idle
amusement. Human beings, like all animals, tend to move
away from pain and toward pleasure. Hence the way to control behavior is to reward what is "good" and punish what
is "bad." This formula pervades our programs of child-
rearing, education, and social control of behavior.

With this concept three out of four readers will no
doubt concur.

"Why, of course," they will say. "Only common sense.
Take me for example. I know the speed limit and the penalty. Usually I drive moderately because I don't want to get
a ticket. One afternoon I was in a hurry; I had an appointment, I didn't heed the signs. I did what I knew was
forbidden and I got caught and received the punishment I

This article originally appeared under the title "Verdict
Guilty, Now What?" in *Harper's Magazine*, August, 1959, pp.
60-64. It is reprinted here with the permission of the
author. Karl Menninger is a distinguished American psychiatrist and is the author of numerous books and articles,
including *The Crime of Punishment* (New York: The Viking
Press, 1968).

deserved. Fair enough. It taught me a lesson. Since then
I drive more slowly in that area. And surely people are
deterred from cheating on their income taxes, robbing banks,
and committing rape by the fear of punishment. Why, if we
didn't have these crime road blocks we'd have chaos!"

This sounds reasonable enough and describes what most
people think—*part of the time*. But upon reflection we all
know that punishments and the threat of punishments do *not*
deter *some* people from doing forbidden things. Some of
them take a chance on not being caught, and this chance is
a very good one, too, better than five to one for most
crimes. Not even the fear of possible death, self-
inflicted, deters some speedsters. Exceeding the speed
limit is not really regarded as criminal behavior by most
people, no matter how dangerous and self-destructive. It
is the kind of a "crime" which respectable members of society commit and condone. This is not the case with rape,
bank-robbing, check-forging, vandalism, and the multitude
of offenses for which the prison penalty system primarily
exists. And from these offenses the average citizen, including the reader, is deterred by quite different restraints. For most of us it is our conscience, our self-
respect, and our wish for the good opinion of our neighbors
which are the determining factors in controlling our impulses toward misbehavior.

Today it is no secret that our official, prison-threat
theory of crime control is an utter failure. Criminologists have known this for years. When pocket-picking was
punishable by hanging, in England, the crowds that gathered
about the gallows to enjoy the spectacle of an execution
were particularly likely to have their pockets picked by
skillful operators who, to say the least, were not deterred
by the exhibition of "justice." We have long known that
the perpetrators of most offenses are never detected; of
those detected, only a fraction are found guilty and still
fewer serve a "sentence." Furthermore, we are quite certain now that of those who do receive the official punishment of the law, many become firmly committed thereby to a
continuing life of crime and a continuing feud with law
enforcement officers. Finding themselves ostracized from
society and blacklisted by industry they stick with the
crowd they have been introduced to in jail and try to play
the game of life according to this set of rules. In this
way society skillfully converts individuals of borderline
self-control into loyal members of the underground fra-
ternity.

The science of human behavior has gone far beyond
the common sense rubrics which dictated the early legal

statutes. We know now that one cannot describe rape or
bank-robbing or income-tax fraud simply as pleasure. Nor,
on the other hand, can we describe imprisonment merely as
pain. Slapping the hand of a beloved child as he reaches
to do a forbidden act is utterly different from the insti-
tutionalized process of official punishment. The offenders
who are chucked into our county and state and federal prisons are not anyone's beloved children; they are usually un-
loved children, grown-up physically but still hungry for
human concern which they never got or never get in normal
ways. So they pursue it in abnormal ways—abnormal, that
is, from *our* standpoint.

WHY OUR CRIME THERAPY HAS FAILED

What might deter the reader from conduct which his
neighbors would not like does not necessarily deter the
grown-up child of vastly different background. The latter's experiences may have conditioned him to believe that
the chances of winning by undetected cheating are vastly
greater than the probabilities of fair treatment and opportunity. He knows about the official threats and the social
disapproval of such acts. He knows about the hazards and
the risks. But despite all this "knowledge," he becomes
involved in waves of discouragement or cupidity or excite-
ment or resentment leading to episodes of social offensive-
ness.

These episodes may prove vastly expensive both to him
and to society. But sometimes they will have an aura of
success. Our periodicals have only recently described the
wealth and prominence for a time of a man described as a
murderer. Konrad Lorenz, the great psychiatrist and animal
psychologist, has beautifully described in geese what he
calls a "triumph reaction." It is sticking out of the
chest and flapping of the wings after an encounter with a
challenge. All of us have seen this primitive biological
triumph reaction—in some roosters, for example, in some
businessmen and athletes and others—*and* in some criminals.

In general, though, the gains and goals of the social
offender are not those which most men seek. Most offenders
whom we belabor are not very wise, not very smart, not even
very "lucky." It is not the successful criminal upon whom
we inflict our antiquated penal system. It is the unsuc-
cessful criminal, the criminal who really doesn't know how
to commit crimes, and who gets caught. Indeed, until he is
caught and convicted a man is technically not even called a
criminal. The clumsy, the desperate, the obscure, the

friendless, the defective, the diseased—these men who commit crimes that do not come off—are bad actors, indeed. But they are not the professional criminals, many of whom occupy high places. In some instances the crime is the merest accident or incident or impulse, expressed under unbearable stress. More often the offender is a persistently perverse, lonely, and resentful individual who joins the only group to which he is eligible—the outcasts and the anti-social.

And what do we do with such offenders? After a solemn public ceremony we pronounce them enemies of the people, and consign them for arbitrary periods to institutional confinement on the basis of laws written many years ago. Here they languish until time has ground out so many weary months and years. Then with a planlessness and stupidity only surpassed by that of their original incarceration they are dumped back upon society, regardless of whether any change has taken place in them for the better and with every assurance that changes have taken place in them for the worse. Once more they enter the unequal tussle with society. Proscribed for employment by most concerns, they are expected to invent a new way to make a living and to survive without any further help from society.

Intelligent members of society are well aware that the present system is antiquated, expensive, and disappointing, and that we are wasting vast quantities of manpower through primitive methods of dealing with those who transgress the law. In 1917 the famous Wickersham report of the New York State Prison Survey Committee recommended the abolition of jails, the institution of diagnostic clearing houses or classification centers, the development of a diversified institutional system and treatment program, and the use of indeterminate sentences. *Forty-two years have passed.* How little progress we have made! In 1933 the American Psychiatric Association, the American Bar Association, and the American Medical Association officially and jointly recommended psychiatric service for every criminal and juvenile court to assist the court and prison and parole officers with all offenders.

That was twenty-six years ago! Have these recommendations been carried out anywhere in the United States? With few exceptions offenders continue to be dealt with according to old-time instructions, written by men now dead who knew nothing about the present offender, his past life, the misunderstandings accumulated by him, or the provocation given to him.

The sensible, scientific question is: What kind of treatment could be instituted that would deter him or be

most likely to deter him?   Some of these methods are well
known.   For some offenders who have the money or the skillful legal counsel or the good luck to face a wise judge go
a different route from the prescribed routine.   Instead of
jail and deterioration, they get the sort of re-education
and re-direction associated with psychiatric institutions
and the psychiatric profession.   Relatively few wealthy offenders get their "treatment" in jail.   This does not mean
that justice is to be bought, or bought off.   But it does
mean that some offenders have relatives and friends who
care and who try to find the best possible solution to the
problem of persistent misbehavior, which is NOT the good
old jail-and-penitentiary and make-'em-sorry treatment.
It is a reflection on the democratic ideals of our country that these better ways are so often—indeed, *usually*—
denied to the poor, the friendless, and the ignorant.

SCIENCE VERSUS TRADITION

If we were to follow scientific methods, the convicted
offender would be detained indefinitely pending a decision
as to whether and how and when to reintroduce him successfully into society.   All the skill and knowledge of modern
behavioral science would be used to examine his personality
assets, his liabilities and potentialities, the environment
from which he came, its effects upon him, and his effects
upon it.
Having arrived at some diagnostic grasp of the offender's personality, those in charge can decide whether there
is a chance that he can be redirected into a mutually satisfactory adaptation to the world.   If so, the most suitable techniques in education, industrial training, group
administration, and psychotherapy should be selectively applied.   All this may be best done extramurally or intramu-
rally.   It may require maximum "security" or only minimum
"security."   If, in due time, perceptible change occurs,
the process should be expedited by finding a suitable spot
in society and industry for him, and getting him out of
prison control and into civil status (with parole control)
as quickly as possible.
The desirability of moving patients out of institutional control swiftly is something which we psychiatrists
learned the hard way, and recently.   Ten years ago, in the
state hospital I know best, the average length of stay was
five years; today it is three months.   Ten years ago few
patients were discharged under two years; today 90 per cent
are discharged within the first year.   Ten years ago the

hospital was overcrowded; today it has eight times the turn-
over it used to have; there are empty beds and there is no
waiting list.

But some patients do not respond to our efforts, and
they have to remain in the hospital, or return to it promptly after a trial home visit. And if the *prisoner*, like
some of the psychiatric patients, cannot be changed by genuine efforts to rehabilitate him, we must look *our* failure
in the face, and provide for his indefinitely continued
confinement, regardless of the technical reasons for it.
This we owe society for its protection.

There will be some offenders about whom the most experienced are mistaken, both ways. And there will be some
concerning whom no one knows what is best. There are many
problems for research. But what I have outlined is, I believe, the program of modern penology, the program now being carried out in some degree in California and a few other states, and in some of the federal prisons.

This civilized program, which would save so much now
wasted money, so much unused manpower, and so much injustice and suffering, is slow to spread. It is held back by
many things—by the continued use of fixed sentences in
many places; by unenlightened community attitudes toward
the offender whom some want tortured; by the prevalent popular assumption that burying a frustrated individual in a
hole for a short time will change his warped mind, and that
when he is certainly worse, he should be released because
his "time" has been served; by the persistent failure of
the law to distinguish between crime as an accidental, incidental, explosive event, crime as a behavior pattern expressive of chronic unutterable rage and frustration, and
crime as a business or elected way of life. Progress is
further handicapped by the lack of interest in the subject
on the part of lawyers, most of whom are proud to say that
they are not concerned with criminal law. It is handicapped by the lack of interest on the part of members of my
own profession. It is handicapped by the mutual distrust
of lawyers and psychiatrists.

The infestation or devil-possession theory of mental
disease is an outmoded, pre-medieval concept. Although
largely abandoned by psychiatry, it steadfastly persists
in the minds of many laymen, including, unfortunately,
many laymen.

On the other hand, most lawyers have no really clear
idea of the way in which a psychiatrist functions or of the
basic concepts to which he adheres. They cannot understand,
for example, why there is no such thing (for psychiatrists)
as "insanity." Most lawyers have no conception of the

meaning or methods of psychiatric case study and diagnosis.
They seem to think that psychiatrists can take a quick look
at a suspect, listen to a few anecdotes about him, and
thereupon be able to say, definitely, that the awful "it"—
the dreadful miasma of madness, the loathsome affliction of
"insanity"—is present or absent. Because we all like to
please, some timid psychiatrists fall in with this fallacy
of the lawyers and go through these preposterous antics.

AS THE PSYCHIATRIST SEES IT

It is true that almost any offender—like anyone else
—when questioned for a short time, even by the most skillful psychiatrist, can make responses and display behavior
patterns which will indicate that he is enough like the
rest of us to be called "sane." But a barrage of questions is not a psychiatric examination. Modern scientific
personality study depends upon various specialists—physical, clinical, and sociological as well as psychological.
It takes into consideration not only static and presently
observable factors, but dynamic and historical factors,
and factors of environmental interaction and change. It
also looks into the future for correction, re-education,
and prevention.

Hence, the same individuals who appear so normal to
superficial observation are frequently discovered in the
course of prolonged, intensive scientific study to have
tendencies regarded as "deviant," "peculiar," "unhealthy,"
"sick," "crazy," "senseless," "irrational," "insane."

But now you may ask, "Is it not possible to find such
tendencies in any individual if one looks hard enough? And
if this is so, if we are all a little crazy or potentially
so, what is the essence of your psychiatric distinctions?
Who is it that you want excused?"

And here is the crux of it all. We psychiatrists
don't want *anyone* excused. In fact, psychiatrists are much
more concerned about the protection of the public than are
the lawyers. I repeat; psychiatrists don't want anyone excused, certainly not anyone who shows anti-social tendencies. We consider them all responsible, which lawyers do
not. And we want the prisoner to take on that responsibility, or else deliver it to someone who will be concerned
about the protection of society and about the prisoner, too.
We don't want anyone excused, but neither do we want anyone
stupidly disposed of, futilely detained, or prematurely released. We don't want them tortured, either sensationally
with hot irons or quietly by long-continued and forced

idleness. In the psychiatrist's mind nothing should be
done in the name of punishment, though he is well aware
that the offender may regard either the diagnostic procedure or the treatment or the detention incident to the
treatment as punitive. But this is in *his* mind, not in
the psychiatrist's mind. And in our opinion it should not
be in the public's mind, because it is an illusion.

It is true that we psychiatrists consider that all
people have potentialities for anti-social behavior. The
law assumes this, too. Most of the time most people control their criminal impulses. But for various reasons and
under all kinds of circumstances some individuals become
increasingly disorganized or demoralized, and then they
begin to be socially offensive. The man who does criminal
things is less convincingly disorganized than the patient
who "looks" sick, because the former more nearly resembles
the rest of us, and seems to be indulging in acts that we
have struggled with and controlled. So we get hot under
the collar about the one and we call him "criminal" whereas we pityingly forgive the other and call him "lunatic."
But a surgeon uses the same principles of surgery whether
he is dealing with a "clean" case, say some cosmetic surgery on a face, or a "dirty" case which is foul-smelling
and offensive. What we are after is results and the emotions of the operator must be under control. Words like
"criminal" and "insane" have no place in the scientific
vocabulary any more than pejorative adjectives like "vicious," "psychopathic," "bloodthirsty," etc. The need is
to find all the *descriptive* adjectives that apply to the
case, and this is a scientific job—not a popular exercise
in name-calling. Nobody's insides are very beautiful; and
in the cases that require social control there has been a
great wound and some of the insides are showing.

Intelligent judges all over the country are increasingly surrendering the onerous responsibility of deciding
in advance what a man's conduct will be in a prison and
how rapidly his wicked impulses will evaporate there. With
more use of the indeterminate sentence and the establishment of scientific diagnostic centers, we shall be in a
position to make progress in the science of *treating* antisocial trends. Furthermore, we shall get away from the
present legal smog that hangs over the prisons, which lets
us detain with heartbreaking futility some prisoners fully
rehabilitated while others, whom the prison officials know
full well to be dangerous and unemployable, must be released, *against our judgment*, because a judge far away (who
has by this time forgotten all about it) said that five
years was enough. In my frequent visits to prisons I am

always astonished at how rarely the judges who have prescribed the "treatment" come to see whether or not it is
effective. What if doctors who sent their seriously ill
patients to hospitals never called to see them!

THE END OF TABOO

As more states adopt diagnostic centers directed toward getting the prisoners *out* of jail and back to work,
under modern, well-structured parole systems, the taboo on
jail and prison, like that on state hospitals, will begin
to diminish. Once it was a lifelong disgrace to have been
in either. Lunatics, as they were cruelly called, were
feared and avoided. Today only the ignorant retain this
phobia. Cancer was then considered a *shameful* thing to
have, and victims of it were afraid to mention it, or have
it correctly treated, because they did not want to be dis-
graced. The time will come when offenders, much as we
disapprove of their offenses, will no longer be unemployable untouchables.

To a physician discussing the wiser treatment of our
fellow men it seems hardly necessary to add that under no
circumstances should we kill them. It was never considered
right for doctors to kill their patients, no matter how
hopeless their condition. True, some patients in state institutions have undoubtedly been executed without benefit
of sentence. They were a nuisance, expensive to keep and
dangerous to release. Various people took it upon themselves to put an end to the matter, and I have even heard
them boast of it. The Hitler regime had the same philosophy.

But in most civilized countries today we have a higher
opinion of the rights of the individual and of the limits
to the state's power. We know, too, that for the most part
the death penalty is inflicted upon obscure, impoverished,
defective, and friendless individuals. We know that it in-
timidates juries in their efforts to determine guilt without prejudice. We know that it is being eliminated in one
state after another, most recently Delaware. We know that
in practice it has almost disappeared—for over seven thousand capital crimes last year there were less than one hundred executions. But vast sums of money are still being
spent—let us say wasted—in legal contests to determine
whether or not an individual, even one known to have been
mentally ill, is now healthy enough for the state to hang
him. (I am informed that such a case has recently cost the
State of California $400,000!)

Most of all, we know that no state employees—except perhaps some that ought to be patients themselves—want a job on the killing squad, and few wardens can stomach this piece of medievalism in their own prisons. For example, two officials I know recently quarreled because each wished to have the hanging of a prisoner carried out on the other's premises.

Capital punishment is, in my opinion, morally wrong. It has a bad effect on everyone, especially those involved in it. It gives a false sense of security to the public. It is vastly expensive. Worst of all it beclouds the entire issue of motivation in crime, which is so importantly relevant to the question of what to do for and with the criminal that will be most constructive to society as a whole. Punishing—and even killing—criminals may yield a kind of grim gratification; let us all admit that there are times when we are so shocked at the depredations of an offender that we persuade ourselves that this is a man the Creator didn't intend to create, and that we had better help correct the mistake. But playing God in this way has no conceivable moral or scientific justification.

Let us return in conclusion to the initial question: "Verdict guilty—now what?" My answer is that now we, the designated representatives of the society which has failed to integrate this man, which has failed him in some way, hurt him and been hurt by him, should take over. It is *our* move. And our move must be a constructive one, an intelligent one, a purposeful one—not a primitive, retaliatory, offensive move. We, the agents of society, must move to end the game of tit-for-tat and blow-for-blow in which the offender has foolishly and futiley engaged himself and us. We are not driven, as he is, to wild and impulsive actions. With knowledge comes power, and with power there is no need for the frightened vengeance of the old penology. In its place should go a quiet, dignified, therapeutic program for the rehabilitation of the disorganized one, if possible, the protection of society during his treatment period, and his guided return to useful citizenship, as soon as this can be effected.

PUNISHMENT

B. F. Skinner

A QUESTIONABLE TECHNIQUE

The commonest technique of control in modern life is
punishment. The pattern is familiar: if a man does not
behave as you wish, knock him down; if a child misbehaves,
spank him; if the people of a country misbehave, bomb them.
Legal and police systems are based upon such punishments
as fines, flogging, incarceration, and hard labor. Religious control is exerted through penances, threats of ex-
communication, and consignment to hell-fire. Education has
not wholly abandoned the birch rod. In everyday personal
contact we control through censure, snubbing, disapproval,
or banishment. In short, the degree to which we use punishment as a technique of control seems to be limited only
by the degree to which we can gain the necessary power.
All of this is done with the intention of reducing tendencies to behave in certain ways. Reinforcement builds up
these tendencies; punishment is designed to tear them down.

The technique has often been analyzed, and many familiar questions continue to be asked. Must punishment be
closely contingent upon the behavior punished? Must the
individual know what he is being punished for? What forms
of punishment are most effective and under what circumstances? This concern may be due to the realization that
the technique has unfortunate by-products. In the long
run, punishment, unlike reinforcement, works to the disadvantage of both the punished organism and the punishing
agency. The aversive stimuli which are needed generate

From B. F. Skinner, *Science and Human Behavior* (New York:
The Macmillan Company, 1953), pp. 182-193 and 446-449.
Copyright © 1953 by The Macmillan Company. Reprinted with
permission of The Macmillan Company. B. F. Skinner is a
Professor of Psychology at Harvard University and is the
author of numerous influential books and articles. His
latest book is *Beyond Freedom and Dignity* (New York: Alfred
A. Knopf, 1971).

emotions, including predispositions to escape or retaliate, and disabling anxieties. For thousands of years men have asked whether the method could not be improved or whether some alternative practice would not be better.

DOES PUNISHMENT WORK?

More recently, the suspicion has also arisen that punishment does not in fact do what it is supposed to do. An immediate effect in reducing a tendency to behave is clear enough, but this may be misleading. The reduction in strength may not be permanent. An explicit revision in the theory of punishment may be dated by the changes in the theories of E. L. Thorndike. Thorndike's first formulation of the behavior of his cats in a puzzle box appealed to two processes: the stamping in of rewarded behavior, or operant conditioning, and a converse process of stamping out as the effect of punishment. Thorndike's later experiments with human subjects required a change in this formulation. The rewards and punishments he used were the relatively mild, verbal conditioned reinforcers of "right" and "wrong." Thorndike found that although "right" strengthened the behavior that preceded it, "wrong" did not weaken it. The relatively trivial nature of the punishment was probably an advantage, since the collateral effects of severe punishment could be avoided and the absence of a weakening effect could therefore be observed without interference from other processes.

The difference between immediate and long-term effects of punishment is clearly shown in animal experiments. In the process of extinction the organism emits a certain number of responses which can be reasonably well predicted. As we have seen, the rate is at first high and then falls off until no significant responding occurs. The cumulative extinction curve is one way of representing the net effect of reinforcement, an effect which we may describe as a predisposition to emit a certain number of responses without further reinforcement. If we now punish the first few responses emitted in extinction, the theory of punishment would lead us to expect that the rest of the extinction curve would contain fewer responses. If we could choose a punishment which subtracted the same number of responses as are added by a reinforcement, then fifty reinforced responses followed by twenty-five punished responses should leave an extinction curve characteristic of twenty-five reinforced responses. When a similar experiment was performed, however, it was found that although punishing

responses at the beginning of an extinction curve reduced
the momentary rate of responding, the rate rose again when
punishment was discontinued and that eventually all responses came out.   The effect of punishment was a temporary
suppression of the behavior, not a reduction in the total
number of responses.   Even under severe and prolonged punishment, the rate of responding will rise when punishment
has been discontinued, and although under these circumstances it is not easy to show that all the responses originally available will eventually appear, it has been found
that after a given time the rate of responding is no lower
than if no punishment had taken place.

The fact that punishment does not permanently reduce
a tendency to respond is in agreement with Freud's discovery of the surviving activity of what he called repressed
wishes.   As we shall see later, Freud's observations can be
brought into line with the present analysis.

THE EFFECTS OF PUNISHMENT

If punishment is not the opposite of reward, if it
does not work by subtracting responses where reinforcement
adds them, what does it do?   We can answer this question
with the help of our analysis of escape and of avoidance
and anxiety.   The answer supplies not only a clear-cut picture of the effect of punishment but an explanation of its
unfortunate by-products.   The analysis is somewhat detailed,
but it is essential to the proper use of the technique and
to the therapy required to correct some of its consequences.

We must first define punishment without presupposing
any effect.   This may appear to be difficult.   In defining
a reinforcing stimulus we could avoid specifying physical
characteristics by appealing to the effect upon the strength
of the behavior.   If a punishing consequence is also defined without reference to its physical characteristics and
if there is no comparable effect to use as a touchstone,
what course is open to us?   The answer is as follows.   We
first define a positive reinforcer as any stimulus the *pre-
sentation* of which strengthens the behavior upon which it
is made contingent.   We define a negative reinforcer (an
aversive stimulus) as any stimulus the *withdrawal* of which
strengthens behavior.   Both are reinforcers in the literal
sense of reinforcing or strengthening a response.   Insofar
as scientific definition corresponds to lay usage, they are
both "rewards."   In solving the problem of punishment we
simply ask: What is the effect of *withdrawing* a *positive*
reinforcer or *presenting* a *negative*?   An example of the

former would be taking candy from a baby; an example of the latter, spanking a baby. We have not used any new terms in posing these questions and hence need not define any. Yet insofar as we are able to give a scientific definition of a lay term, these two possibilities appear to constitute the field of punishment. We do not presuppose any effect; we simply raise a question to be answered by appropriate experiments. The physical specifications of both kinds of consequences are determined in the case in which behavior is strengthened. Conditioned reinforcers, including the generalized reinforcers, fit the same definition: we punish by *dis*approving, by taking money away, as in a legal fine, and so on.

Although punishment is a powerful technique of social control, it is not necessarily administered by another individual. The burned child has been punished for touching flame. Eating unsuitable food is punished by indigestion. It is not necessary that the contingency represent an established functional relation, such as that between flames and burns or certain foods and indigestion. When a salesman in a midwestern city once approached a house and rang the doorbell, the rear of the house exploded. There was only an accidental and very rare contingency: gas had escaped into the kitchen, and the explosion was set off by sparks from the electric doorbell. The effect upon the subsequent behavior of the salesman as he rang other doorbells nevertheless falls within the present field.

A FIRST EFFECT OF PUNISHMENT

The first effect of the aversive stimuli used in punishment is confined to the immediate situation. It need not be followed by any change in behavior upon later occasions. When we stop a child from giggling in church by pinching it severely, the pinch elicits responses which are incompatible with laughing and powerful enough to suppress it. Although our action may have other consequences, we can single out the competing effect of the responses elicited by the punishing stimulus. The same effect is obtained with a conditioned stimulus when we stop the child with a threatening gesture. This requires earlier conditioning, but the current effect is simply the elicitation of incompatible behavior—the responses appropriate, for example, to fear. The formula can be extended to include emotional predispositions. Thus we may stop a man from running away by making him angry. The aversive stimulus which makes him angry may be unconditioned (for example,

stamping on his toe) or conditioned (for example, calling
him a coward). We may stop someone from eating his dinner
by frightening him with a sudden deafening noise or a grue-
some story.

It is not essential to have effect that the aversive
stimulus be contingent upon behavior in the standard punishing sequence. When that sequence is observed, however,
the effect still occurs and must be considered as one of
the results of punishment. It resembles other effects of
punishment in bringing undesirable behavior to an end; but
since this is temporary, it is not likely to be accepted as
typical of control through punishment.

A SECOND EFFECT OF PUNISHMENT

Punishment is generally supposed to have some abiding
effect. It is hoped that some change in behavior will be
observed in the future, even though further punishment is
withheld. One enduring effect, also not often considered
as typical, resembles the effect just considered. When a
child who has been pinched for giggling starts to giggle
upon a later occasion, his own behavior may supply conditioned stimuli which, like the mother's threatening gesture,
evoke opposed emotional responses. We have seen an adult
parallel in the use of drugs which induce nausea or other
aversive conditions as consequences of drinking alcoholic
beverages. As a result later drinking generates conditioned aversive stimuli which evoke responses incompatible
with further drinking. As an effect of the severe punishment of sexual behavior, the early stages of such behavior
generate conditioned stimuli giving rise to emotional responses which interfere with the completion of the behavior.
One difficulty with the technique is that punishment for
sexual behavior may interfere with similar behavior under
socially acceptable circumstances—for example, in marriage.
In general, then, as a second effect of punishment, behavior which has consistently been punished becomes the source
of conditioned stimuli which evoke incompatible behavior.

Some of this behavior involves glands and smooth muscles. Let us say, for example, that a child is consistently punished for lying. The behavior is not easily specified, since a verbal response is not necessarily in itself
a lie but can be defined as such only by taking into account the circumstances under which it is emitted. These
circumstances come to play a conspicuous role, however, so
that the total situation stimulates the child in a characteristic fashion. For reasons which we shall examine in

Chapter XVII, an individual is in general able to tell when
he is lying. The stimuli to which he responds when he does
so are conditioned to elicit responses appropriate to punishment: his palms may sweat, his pulse may speed up, and
so on. When he later lies during a lie-detection test,
these conditioned responses are recorded.

Strong emotional *predispositions* are also rearoused by
the beginnings of severely punished behavior. These are
the main ingredient of what we speak of as guilt, shame, or
a sense of sin. Part of what we feel when we feel guilty
are conditioned responses of glands and smooth muscles of
the kind reported by the lie detector, but we may also recognize a displacement of the normal probabilities of our
behavior. This is often the most conspicuous feature of
the guilt of others. The furtive look, the skulking manner,
the guilty way of speaking are emotional effects of the conditioned stimuli aroused by punished behavior. Comparable
effects are observed in lower animals: the guilty behavior
of a dog which is behaving in a way which has previously
been punished is a familiar spectacle. A case may be easily set up in the laboratory. If a rat has been conditioned
to press a lever by being reinforced with food and is then
punished by being lightly shocked as it presses the lever,
its behavior in approaching and touching the lever will be
modified. The early stages in the sequence generate conditioned emotional stimuli which alter the behavior previously established. Since the punishment is not directly
administered by another organism, the pattern does not resemble the more familiar behavior of guilt in the pet dog.

A condition of guilt or shame is generated not only
by previously punished behavior but by any consistent external occasion for such behavior. The individual may feel
guilty in a situation in which he has been punished. We
gain control by introducing stimuli for just this effect.
For example, if we punish a child for any behavior executed
after we have said "No, no!" this verbal stimulus will
later evoke an emotional state appropriate to punishment.
When this policy has been followed consistently, the behavior of the child may be controlled simply by saying "No,
no!" since the stimulus arouses an emotional condition
which conflicts with the response to be controlled.

Although the rearousal of responses appropriate to
aversive stimuli is again not the main effect of punishment, it works in the same direction. In none of these
cases, however, have we supposed that the punished response
is permanently weakened. It is merely temporarily suppressed, more or less effectively, by an emotional reaction.

A THIRD EFFECT OF PUNISHMENT

We come now to a much more important effect. If a given response is followed by an aversive stimulus, any stimulation which accompanies the response, whether it arises from the behavior itself or from concurrent circumstances, will be conditioned. We have just appealed to this formula in accounting for conditioned emotional reflexes and predispositions, but the same process also leads to the conditioning of aversive stimuli which serve as negative reinforcers. *Any behavior which reduces this conditioned aversive stimulation will be reinforced.* In the example just considered, as the rat approaches the lever to which its recent responses have been punished, powerful conditioned aversive stimuli are generated by the increasing proximity of the lever and by the rat's own behavior of approach. Any behavior which reduces these stimuli—turning or running away, for example—is reinforced. Technically we may say that further punishment is avoided.

The most important effect of punishment, then, is to establish aversive conditions which are avoided by any behavior of "doing something else." It is important—for both practical and theoretical reasons—to specify this behavior. It is not enough to say that what is strengthened is simply the opposite. Sometimes it is merely "doing nothing" in the form of actively holding still. Sometimes it is behavior appropriate to other current variables which are not, however, sufficient to explain the level of probability of the behavior without supposing that the individual is also acting "for the sake of keeping out of trouble."

The effect of punishment in setting up behavior which competes with, and may displace, the punished response is most commonly described by saying that the individual *represses* the behavior, but we need not appeal to any activity which does not have the dimensions of behavior. If there is any repressing force or agent, it is simply the incompatible response. The individual contributes to the process by executing this response. (In Chapter XVIII we shall find that another sort of repression involves the individual's knowledge of the repressed act.) No change in the strength of the punished response is implied.

If punishment is repeatedly avoided, the conditioned negative reinforcer undergoes extinction. Incompatible behavior is then less and less strongly reinforced, and the punished behavior eventually emerges. When punishment again occurs, the aversive stimuli are reconditioned, and the behavior of doing something else is then reinforced. If punishment is discontinued, the behavior may emerge in full strength.

When an individual is punished for not responding in a given way, conditioned aversive stimulation is generated when he is doing anything else. Only by behaving in a given way may he become free of "guilt." Thus one may avoid the aversive stimulation generated by "not doing one's duty" by simply doing one's duty. No moral or ethical problem is necessarily involved: a draft horse is kept moving according to the same formula. When the horse slows down, the slower pace (or the crack of a whip) supplies a conditioned aversive stimulus from which the horse escapes by increasing its speed. The aversive effect must be reinstated from time to time by actual contact with the whip.

Since punishment depends in large part upon the behavior of other people, it is likely to be intermittent. The action which is always punished is rare. All the schedules of reinforcement described in Chapter VI are presumably available.

SOME UNFORTUNATE BY-PRODUCTS OF PUNISHMENT

Severe punishment unquestionably has an immediate effect in reducing a tendency to act in a given way. This result is no doubt responsible for its widespread use. We "instinctively" attack anyone whose behavior displeases us —perhaps not in physical assault, but with criticism, disapproval, blame, or ridicule. Whether or not there is an inherited tendency to do this, the immediate effect of the practice is reinforcing enough to explain its currency. In the long run, however, punishment does not actually eliminate behavior from a repertoire, and its temporary achievement is obtained at tremendous cost in reducing the overall efficiency and happiness of the group.

One by-product is a sort of conflict between the response which leads to punishment and the response which avoids it. These responses are incompatible and they are both likely to be strong at the same time. The repressing behavior generated by even severe and sustained punishment often has very little advantage over the behavior it represses. The result of such a conflict is discussed in Chapter XIV. When punishment is only intermittently administered, the conflict is especially troublesome, as we see in the case of the child who "does not know when he will be punished and when he will get away with it." Responses which avoid punishment may alternate with punished responses in rapid oscillation or both may blend into an uncoordinated form. In the awkward, timorous, or "inhibited" person, standard behavior is interrupted by distracting responses, such as turning, stopping, and doing something else. The stutterer or stammerer shows a similar effect on a finer scale.

Another by-product of the use of punishment is even more unfortunate. Punished behavior is often strong, and certain incipient stages are therefore frequently reached. Even though the stimulation thus generated is successful in preventing a full-scale occurrence, it also evokes reflexes characteristic of fear, anxiety, and other emotions. Moreover, the incompatible behavior which blocks the punished response may resemble external physical restraint in generating rage or frustration. Since the variables responsible for these emotional patterns are generated by the organism itself, no appropriate escape behavior is available. The condition may be chronic and may result in "psychosomatic" illness or otherwise interfere with the effective behavior of the individual in his daily life (Chapter XXIV).

Perhaps the most troublesome result is obtained when the behavior punished is reflex—for example weeping. Here it is usually not possible to execute "just the opposite," since such behavior is not conditioned according to the operant formula. The repressing behavior must therefore work through a second stage, as in the operant control of "involuntary behavior" discussed in Chapter VI. Some examples will be considered in Chapter XXIV where the techniques of psychotherapy will be shown to be mainly concerned with the unfortunate by-products of punishment.

ALTERNATIVES TO PUNISHMENT

We may avoid the use of punishment by weakening an operant in other ways. Behavior which is conspicuously due to *emotional* circumstances, for example, is often likely to be punished, but it may often be more effectively controlled by modifying the circumstances. Changes brought about by *satiation*, too, often have the effect which is contemplated in the use of punishment. Behavior may often be eliminated from a repertoire, especially in young children, simply by allowing time to pass in accordance with a *developmental schedule*. If the behavior is largely a function of age, the child will, as we say, outgrow it. It is not always easy to put up with the behavior until this happens, especially under the conditions of the average household, but there is some consolation if we know that by carrying the child through a socially unacceptable stage we spare him the later complications arising from punishment.

Another way of weakening a conditioned response is simply to let time pass. This process of *forgetting* is not to be confused with extinction. Unfortunately it is generally slow and also requires that occasions for the behavior be avoided.

The most effective alternative process is probably *extinction*. This takes time but is much more rapid than allowing the response to be forgotten. The technique seems to be relatively free of objectionable by-products. We recommend it, for example, when we suggest that a parent "pay no attention" to objectionable behavior on the part of his child. If the child's behavior is strong only because it has been reinforced by "getting a rise out of" the parent, it will disappear when this consequence is no longer forthcoming.

Another technique is to *condition incompatible behavior*, not by withdrawing censure or guilt, but through positive reinforcement. We use this method when we control a tendency toward emotional display by reinforcing stoical behavior. This is very different from punishing emotional behavior, even though the latter also provides for the indirect reinforcement of stoical behavior through a reduction in aversive stimuli. Direct positive reinforcement is to be preferred because it appears to have fewer objectionable by-products.

Civilized man has made some progress in turning from punishment to alternative forms of control. Avenging gods and hell-fire have given way to an emphasis upon heaven and the positive consequences of the good life. In agriculture and industry, fair wages are recognized as an improvement over slavery. The birch rod has made way for the reinforcements naturally accorded the educated man. Even in politics and government the power to punish has been supplemented by a more positive support of the behavior which conforms to the interests of the governing agency. But we are still a long way from exploiting the alternatives, and we are not likely to make any real advance so long as our information about punishment and the alternatives to punishment remains at the level of casual observation. As a consistent picture of the extremely complex consequences of punishment emerges from analytical research, we may gain the confidence and skill needed to design alternative procedures in the clinic, in education, in industry, in politics, and in other practical fields. . . .

THE FATE OF THE INDIVIDUAL

Western thought has emphasized the importance and dignity of the individual. Democratic philosophies of

government, based upon the "rights of man," have asserted
that all individuals are equal under the law, and that the
welfare of the individual is the goal of government. In
similar philosophies of religion, piety and salvation have
been left to the individual himself rather than to a religious agency. Democratic literature and art have emphasized the individual rather than the type, and have often
been concerned with increasing man's knowledge and understanding of himself. Many schools of psychotherapy have
accepted the philosophy that man is the master of his own
fate. In education, social planning, and many other fields,
the welfare and dignity of the individual have received
first consideration.

The effectiveness of this point of view can scarcely
be denied. The practices associated with it have strengthened the individual as an energetic and productive member
of the group. The individual who "asserts himself" is one
to whom the social environment is especially reinforcing.
The environment which has characterized Western democratic
thought has had this effect. The point of view is particularly important in opposition to despotic control and can,
in fact, be understood only in relation to such control.
The first step in the countercontrol of a powerful agency
is to strengthen the controllee. If the governing agency
cannot be made to understand the value of the individual to
the agency itself, the individual himself must be made to
understand his own value. The effectiveness of the technique is evident in the fact that despotic governments have
eventually been countercontrolled by individuals acting in
concert to build a world which they find more reinforcing,
and in the fact that governing agencies which recognize the
importance of the individual have frequently become powerful.

The use of such concepts as individual freedom, initiative, and responsibility has, therefore, been well reinforced. When we turn to what science has to offer, however,
we do not find very comforting support for the traditional
Western point of view. The hypothesis that man is not free
is essential to the application of scientific method to the
study of human behavior. The free inner man who is held
responsible for the behavior of the external biological organism is only a prescientific substitute for the kinds of
causes which are discovered in the course of a scientific
analysis. All these alternative causes lie *outside* the
individual.[1] The biological substratum itself is determined

---

[1][Earlier in his book (pp. 115-116), Skinner speaks of these
"outside causes" in the following way: "The distinction between voluntary and involuntary behavior bears upon our

by prior events in a genetic process. Other important events are found in the nonsocial environment and in the culture of the individual in the broadest possible sense. These are the things which make the individual behave as he does. For them he is not responsible, and for them it is useless to praise or blame him. It does not matter that the individual may take it upon himself to control the variables of which his own behavior is a function or, in a broader sense, to engage in the design of his own culture. He does this only because he is the product of a culture which generates self-control or cultural design as a mode of behavior. The environment determines the individual even when he alters the environment.

This prior importance of the environment has slowly come to be recognized by those who are concerned with changing the lot of mankind. It is more effective to change the culture than the individual because any effect upon the individual as such will be lost at his death. Since cultures survive for much longer periods, any effect upon them is more reinforcing. There is a similar distinction between clinical medicine, which is concerned with the health of the individual, and the science of medicine, which is concerned with improving medical practices which will eventually affect the health of billions of individuals. Presumably, the emphasis on culture will grow as the relevance of the social environment to the behavior of the individual becomes clearer. We may therefore find it necessary to change from a philosophy which emphasizes the individual to one which emphasizes the culture or the group. But cultures also change and perish, and we must not forget

─────────────

[1](cont.) changing concept of personal responsibility. We do not hold people responsible for their reflexes—for example, for coughing in church. We hold them responsible for their operant behavior—for example, for whispering in church or remaining in church while coughing. But there are variables which are responsible for whispering as well as for coughing, and these may be just as inexorable. When we recognize this, we are likely to drop the notion of responsibility altogether and with it the doctrine of free will as an inner causal agent. This may make a great difference in our practices. The doctrine of personal responsibility is associated with certain techniques of controlling behavior—techniques which generate 'a sense of responsibility' or point out 'an obligation to society.' These techniques are relatively ill-adapted to their purpose." Ed.]

that they are created by individual action and survive only through the behavior of individuals.

Science does not set the group or the state above the individual or vice versa. All such interpretations derive from an unfortunate figure of speech, borrowed from certain prominent instances of control. In analyzing the determination of human conduct we choose as a starting point a conspicuous link in a longer causal chain. When an individual conspicuously manipulates the variables of which the behavior of another individual is a function, we say that the first individual controls the second, but we do not ask who or what controls the first. When a government conspicuously controls its citizens, we consider this fact without identifying the events which control the government. When the individual is strengthened as a measure of countercontrol, we may, as in democratic philosophies, think of him as a starting point. Actually, however, we are not justified in assigning to anyone or anything the role of prime mover. Although it is necessary that science confine itself to selected segments in a continuous series of events, it is to the whole series that any interpretation must eventually apply.

Even so, the conception of the individual which emerges from a scientific analysis is distasteful to most of those who have been strongly affected by democratic philosophies. As we saw in Chapter I, it has always been the unfortunate task of science to dispossess cherished beliefs regarding the place of man in the universe. It is easy to understand why men so frequently flatter themselves—why they characterize the world in ways which reinforce them by providing escape from the consequences of criticism or other forms of punishment. But although flattery temporarily strengthens behavior, it is questionable whether it has any ultimate survival value. If science does not confirm the assumptions of freedom, initiative, and responsibility in the behavior of the individual, these assumptions will not ultimately be effective either as motivating devices or as goals in the design of culture. We may not give them up easily, and we may, in fact, find it difficult to control ourselves or others until alternative principles have been developed. But the change will probably be made. It does not follow that newer concepts will necessarily be less acceptable. We may console ourselves with the reflection that science is, after all, a cumulative progress in knowledge which is due to man alone, and that the highest human dignity may be to accept the facts of human behavior regardless of their momentary implications.

A PREVENTIVE SYSTEM OF CRIMINAL LAW

Barbara Wootton

Before I embark on a discussion of the function of the criminal courts perhaps a word may be said about the atmosphere in which this function is performed. It is, in the higher courts at least, an atmosphere of archaic majesty and ritual. Moreover the members of the Bar, whether on or off the Bench, constitute a sodality that is, surely, unique among English professions; nor is there anything in their training which might widen their social horizons or enlarge their social observations. In consequence, there is perhaps no place in English life where the divisions of our society are more obtrusive: nowhere where one is more conscious of the division into "them" and "us." Of the effect of this each must judge for himself. Many of those who gave evidence before the Streatfeild Committee[1] expressed the view (though the Committee itself maintained a sceptical attitude) that the formality of the superior courts, along with the period of waiting before trial and the risk of incurring a substantial sentence, had a salutary effect upon offenders. There may indeed be cases where this is so. But my own opinion is that an opposite effect is more often likely: that the formal and unfamiliar language, the wigs and robes, the remoteness of the judge from the lives and temptations of many defendants detract from, rather than add to, the effectiveness of British justice.

Be that as it may, of the twin functions of the courts in identifying and dealing with (here I deliberately choose what I hope is a wholly neutral word) offenders, the first

From Barbara Wootton, *Crime and the Criminal Law* (London: Stevens and Sons, 1963), pp. 32–57. Copyright 1963 by The Baroness Wootton of Abinger. Reprinted with permission. Baroness Wootton is a sociologist and lay magistrate in England and is the author of *Social Science and Social Pathology* (London: Allen and Unwin, 1959).

[1]Interdepartmental Committee on the Business of the Criminal Courts, *Report* (H.M.S.O.) 1961, Cmnd. 1289, para. 93.

raises fewer controversies than the second. But even here certain of the customary procedures seem incongruous in a scientific age.

For instance, the legal process of examination, cross-examination and re-examination can hardly be rated highly as an instrument for ascertaining the facts of past history. At least no scientist would expect to extract the truth from opposite distortions, although it is perhaps not unknown for scientific controversies to resolve themselves—I nearly said degenerate—to this level. The accusatorial method is, however, so deeply rooted in our history that it would be idle to embark on any comparison of its merits with those of its inquisitorial rival. I will therefore only call attention in passing to the present Lord Chancellor's observation (though in a totally different context) that "where the task of a body is to ascertain what has happened, there is not, as far as I can see, any escape from an inquisitorial procedure"[2]—with its implication that in the courts the ascertainment of the facts cannot be the primary concern. That the place of historical truth in the legal process is indeed only secondary is no doubt acceptable legal doctrine—otherwise it would scarcely be possible for a distinguished lawyer to express his admiration of the success of another distinguished lawyer in obtaining an "almost impossible" verdict, as Lord Hailsham once did to the late Lord Birkett.[3] Nevertheless it is hard to see how the discovery of the truth and the protection of the innocent from unjust conviction can be regarded as alternative objectives: the more accurately the relevant facts are established the less the probability that a wrongful conviction will result. When, however, the facts are in doubt the price that must be paid for safeguarding the innocent is the risk that the guilty will go free; and the greater the doubt the higher this price will be.

Even within its own terms of reference, however, the process of trial might, perhaps, benefit from a little modernisation. No one can fail to be struck by the contrast between the high degree of sophistication attained by forensic science in the detection of crime, and the prescientific character of the criminal process itself—between the skill and zeal with which modern scientific methods are seized upon in order to bring an offender to justice, and the neglect of such methods in what happens

---

[2] House of Lords Debates, May 8, 1963, col. 712.

[3] House of Lords Debates, February 8, 1962, col. 342.

when he gets there. Consider for a moment some of the familiar aspects of a criminal trial. In order to arrive at
a verdict it is necessary to disentangle the truth about
past events from conflicting, incomplete, distorted and often deliberately falsified accounts. At the best of times
and in the best of hands this is bound to be an extremely
difficult matter. Many psychological experiments have demonstrated the unreliability of the ordinary person's recollection of previous happenings, even in circumstances in
which every effort is made to achieve accuracy and in which
there can be no motive for falsification. Yet in our criminal courts in the vast majority of cases, including those
of the utmost gravity, this task devolves upon completely
inexperienced juries or upon untrained magistrates; and in
the case of juries, upon whom the heaviest responsibility
rests, the sacred secrecy of the jury room precludes any
investigation into the methods by which, or the efficiency
with which, they discharge their task. Nor do these ama-
teurs even enjoy the help of modern technical devices.
Without benefit of tape-recorder or transcription, juries
are not even furnished with elementary facilities for taking notes. The facts upon which their verdict should be
based are recorded only in their memory of the witnesses'
memory of the original events: or in their memory of the
judge's summing-up of the witnesses' memory of the original
events. Indeed in the use of modern recording instruments
our courts are almost unbelievably antiquated. To this day
in London magistrates' courts evidence is written down by
the clerk in longhand—a procedure which I have never found
paralleled, although I have visited similar courts in the
United States, Canada, Australia, India, Japan and Ghana,
as well as in Europe.

     Some of these inadequacies are inevitable. Trials
cannot be held on the spot, and memories are bound to fade.
Trivial events which later prove to be of vital significance are bound to be overlooked at the time or imperfectly
recollected. But even so, something could I think be done
to improve the criminal process as a method of historical
investigation. Juries might be supplied with transcrip-
tions of the evidence—or better still with tape-recordings,
since it is not only what a witness says, but how he says
it, which is important; or, at the very least, a recording
should be available in the jury room of the judge's summing-
up, for this alone in an important case can be long enough
to impose a serious tax on memory: in the A6 trial it
lasted for ten hours. Admittedly such changes would add
to the cost of trials; but hardly in proportion to the risk
of convictions or acquittals not justified by the facts.

Memories, too, might be greener if the interval between the
commission of an offence and the trial of the person
charged were kept to a minimum. So far as the period between committal and trial is concerned, the Criminal Justice Administration Act of 1962, following on the recommendations of the Streatfeild Committee, should now make it
possible for the interval between committal and trial never
to exceed eight weeks, and normally to approximate to the
four-week period which is already usual at the Old Bailey
and such other courts as are in more or less continuous ses-
sion. These improvements, however, relate only to the
lapse of time between committal proceedings and subsequent
trial, and do nothing to mitigate the long delays which
sometimes occur before a prosecution is initiated. Even if
such delays are sometimes unavoidable in serious charges,
where evidence can often only be collected with difficulty
and over a considerable period of time, this does not explain the long interval that often elapses—in London at
any rate—particularly in motoring cases, between the commission of an offence and the resulting proceedings in the
magistrates' court. At the best of times evidence in traffic cases is apt to be singularly elusive; but the supposition that speeds and distances and traffic conditions in
a single incident on the road can be accurately recollected
six, seven or eight months later can only be described as
farcical.

Better recording and quicker trials would certainly do
something to improve the efficiency of fact-finding in the
criminal courts. Is it impertinent for a layman to suggest
that changes in the conventions of advocacy might do more?
In spite of the extreme conservatism of the legal profession, these conventions need not be regarded as wholly im-
mutable. Indeed they are subtly changing all the time.
The extravagant and often irrelevant oratory of an earlier
age, for instance, has today given way to a more sober
style, and the highly emotional approach of a generation or
two ago sounds very oddly in contemporary ears. So it is
not unreasonable to hope for further changes. In particular one could wish to see less readiness to pose unanswerable questions. Justice is not promoted by asking a witness, as I have heard a witness asked, why he did not see
the trafficator on a vehicle which he has already said he
did not see at all; nor by pressing a cyclist who was
thrown into the air by collision with a motorcycle to state
exactly on what part of his machine the impact occurred.
Too often, also, inferences from shaky premises become
clothed with an air of spurious certainty, as when elaborate

and convincing explanations are based on the behaviour of
a hypothetical person whose presence nobody can confidently
remember, but equally no one can categorically deny. By
the time that counsel has finished, this hypothetical figure has become so real that the court can almost picture
what he was wearing; and, most sinister of all, the witness
who first cast doubt upon his existence is now wholly convinced of his reality. Truth would be better served if
professional etiquette could be extended to require that
the distinction between the hypothetical and the agreed
(between "he could have been there" and "he was there")
must not be blurred. Witnesses, too, ought surely to be
more explicitly encouraged to admit the limitations of
their own memory or observation; and to appreciate that,
understandable as is their reluctance continually to repeat
"I do not know" or "I do not remember," there is nothing
discreditable in doing so. Particularly is this true in
the many cases in which the minutiae of time or space are
important. Judges, magistrates and lawyers might indeed do
well to study more closely the known facts of the psychology of perception, and to take to heart Professor Vernon's
warning that "experiments indicate that it is not possible
to perceive and attend to two events separately and inde-
pendently if these coincide too nearly in time or space.
Either one will cancel out the other or they will be combined in some way if this is at all possible."[4]

In other words, even within an accusatorial procedure,
more weight might be given on both sides to the ascertainment of fact. After all, in England at any rate, a criminal trial is not a free-for-all. The prosecutor at least
operates within many conventional restraints: he does not,
as in some other countries, clamour for the imposition of a
particular penalty; and he is often scrupulously fair in
exposing the weaknesses in his own case. Is it so certain
that the interests of justice or even the interests of defendants are served by the gross distortions of fact and
indeed the unmitigated nonsense which is often advanced by
defending counsel? For my part I could wish—and I suspect
that many experienced magistrates would say the same—that
the whole question of the conventions of defence advocacy,
and even more of the efficiency of present criminal procedure as a means of arriving at the truth, might be examined
by the Bar. The moment for such suggestions seems moreover
to be opportune, for the profession appears to be in a

---

[4]Vernon, M. D., *The Psychology of Perception* (Penguin
Books) 1962, p. 171.

remarkably receptive mood. Within two days of each other, first the Attorney-General is reported to have reminded the Bar Council that "the public could have no confidence in any profession unless it were alert frequently to review its practices and to see that they corresponded to the requirements of the modern age,"[5] and, second, the Lord Chancellor is said to have suggested at the judges' Mansion House dinner that the wind of change must be felt in the corridors of the courts "if we, in the law, are to keep abreast of the times."[6]

Proposals for the modernisation of the methods by which the criminal courts arrive at their verdicts do not, however, raise any question as to the object of the whole exercise. Much more fundamental are the issues which arise after conviction, when many a judge or magistrate must from time to time have asked himself just what it is that he is trying to achieve. Is he trying to punish the wicked, or to prevent the recurrence of forbidden acts? The former is certainly the traditional answer and is still deeply entrenched both in the legal profession and in the minds of much of the public at large; and it has lately been reasserted in uncompromising terms by a former Lord Chief Justice. At a meeting of magistrates earlier this year Lord Goddard is reported to have said that the duty of the criminal law was to punish—and that reformation of the prisoner was not the courts' business.[7] Those who take this view doubtless comfort themselves with the belief that the two objectives are nearly identical: that the punishment of the wicked is also the best way to prevent the occurrence of prohibited acts. Yet the continual failure of a mainly punitive system to diminish the volume of crime strongly suggests that such comfort is illusory; and it will indeed be a principal theme of these lectures that the choice between the punitive and the preventive[8] concept of the criminal process is a real one; and that, according as that choice is made, radical differences must follow in the

---

[5]*The Times*, July 16, 1963.

[6]*The Times*, July 18, 1963.

[7]*The Observer*, May 5, 1963.

[8]I use this word throughout to describe a system the primary purpose of which is to prevent the occurrence of offences, whether committed by persons already convicted or by other people. The relative importance of these two ("special" and "general") aspects of prevention is discussed in Chap. 4 below. See pp. 97–102.

courts' approach to their task. I shall, moreover, argue
that in recent years a perceptible shift has occurred away
from the first and towards the second of these two conceptions of the function of the criminal law: and that this
movement is greatly to be welcomed and might with advantage
be both more openly acknowledged and also accelerated.

 First, however, let us examine the implications of the
traditional view. Presumably the wickedness which renders
a criminal liable to punishment must be inherent either in
the actions which he has committed or in the state of mind
in which he has committed them. Can we then in the modern
world identify a class of inherently wicked actions? Lord
Devlin, who has returned more than once to this theme,
holds that we still can, by drawing a sharp distinction between what he calls the criminal and the quasi-criminal law.
The distinguishing mark of the latter, in his view, is that
a breach of it does not mean that the offender has done anything morally wrong. "Real" crimes, on the other hand, he
describes as "sins with legal definitions"; and he adds
that "It is a pity that this distinction, which I believe
the ordinary man readily recognises, is not acknowledged in
the administration of justice." "The sense of obligation
which leads the citizen to obey a law that is good in itself is," he says, "different in quality from that which
leads to obedience to a regulation designed to secure a
good end." Nor does his Lordship see any reason "why the
quasi-criminal should be treated with any more ignominy
than a man who has incurred a penalty for failing to return
a library book in time."[9] And in a personal communication
he has further defined the "real" criminal law as any part
of the criminal law, new or old, which the good citizen
does not break without a sense of guilt.

 Nevertheless this attempt to revive the lawyer's distinction between *mala in se* and *mala prohibita*—things
which are bad in themselves and things which are merely prohibited—cannot, I think, succeed. In the first place the
statement that a real crime is one about which the good
citizen would feel guilty is surely circular. For how is
the good citizen to be defined in this context unless as
one who feels guilty about committing the crimes that Lord
Devlin classifies as "real"? And in the second place the
badness even of those actions which would most generally be
regarded as *mala in se* is inherent, not in the physical
acts themselves, but in the circumstances in which they are

---

[9]Devlin, Sir Patrick (now Lord), *Law and Morals* (University
of Birmingham) 1961, pp. 3, 7, 8, 9.

performed. Indeed it is hard to think of any examples of
actions which could, in a strictly physical sense, be said
to be bad in themselves. The physical act of stealing
merely involves moving a piece of matter from one place to
another: what gives it its immoral character is the framework of property rights in which it occurs. Only the violation of these rights transforms an inherently harmless
movement into the iniquitous act of stealing. Nor can bodily assaults be unequivocally classified as *mala in se*; for
actions which in other circumstances would amount to grievous bodily harm may be not only legal, but highly beneficial, when performed by competent surgeons; and there are
those who see no wrong in killing in the form of judicial
hanging or in war.

One is indeed tempted to suspect that actions classified as *mala in se* are really only *mala antiqua*—actions,
that is to say, which have been recognised as criminal for
a very long time; and that the tendency to dismiss sundry
modern offences as "merely quasi-crimes" is simply a mark
of not having caught up with the realities of the contemporary world. The criminal calendar is always the expression
of a particular social and moral climate, and from one generation to another it is modified by two sets of influences.
On the one hand ideas about what is thought to be right or
wrong are themselves subject to change; and on the other
hand new technical developments constantly create new opportunities for anti-social actions which the criminal code
must be extended to include. To a thorough-going Marxist
these two types of change would not, presumably, be regarded as mutually independent: to the Marxist it is technical
innovations which cause moral judgments to be revised. But
for present purposes it does not greatly matter whether the
one is, or is not, the cause of the other. In either case
the technical and the moral are distinguishable. The fact
that there is nothing in the Ten Commandments about the in-
iquity of driving a motor-vehicle under the influence of
drink cannot be read as evidence that the ancient Israelites
regarded this offence more leniently than the contemporary
British. On the other hand the divergent attitudes of our
own criminal law and that of most European countries to homosexual practices has no obvious relation to technical development, and is clearly the expression of differing moral
judgments, or at the least to different conceptions of the
proper relation between morality and the criminal law.

One has only to glance, too, at the maximum penalties
which the law attaches to various offences to realise how
profoundly attitudes change in course of time. Life imprisonment, for example, is not only the obligatory sentence

for non-capital murder and the maximum permissible for manslaughter. It may also be imposed for blasphemy or for the
destruction of registers of births or baptisms. Again, the
crime of abducting an heiress carries a potential sentence
of fourteen years, while that for the abduction of a child
under fourteen years is only half as long. For administering a drug to a female with a view to carnal knowledge a
maximum of two years is provided, but for damage to cattle
you are liable to fourteen years' imprisonment. For using
unlawful oaths the maximum is seven years, but for keeping
a child in a brothel it is a mere six months. Such sentences strike us today as quite fantastic; but they cannot
have seemed fantastic to those who devised them.

For the origins of the supposed dichotomy between real
crimes and quasi-crimes we must undoubtedly look to theology, as Lord Devlin's use of the term "sins with legal definitions" itself implies. The links between law and religion are both strong and ancient. Indeed, as Lord
Radcliffe has lately reminded us, it has taken centuries
for "English judges to realise that the tenets and injunc-
tions of the Christian religion were not part of the common
law of England"[10]; and even today such realisation does not
seem to be complete. As recently as 1961, in the "Ladies
Directory" case, the defendant Shaw, you may remember, was
convicted of conspiring to corrupt public morals, as well
as of offences against the Sexual Offences Act of 1956 and
the Obscene Publications Act of 1959, on account of his
publication of a directory in which the ladies of the town
advertised their services, sometimes, it would seem, in
considerable detail. In rejecting Shaw's appeal to the
House of Lords on the charge of conspiracy, Lord Simonds
delivered himself of the opinion that without doubt "there
remains in the courts a residual power to . . . conserve
not only the safety but also the moral welfare of the
state"; and Lord Hodson, concurring, added that "even if
Christianity be not part of the law of England, yet the
common law has its roots in Christianity."[11]

In the secular climate of the present age, however,
the appeal to religious doctrine is unconvincing, and unlikely to be generally acceptable. Instead we must recog-
nise a range of actions, the badness of which is inherent
not in themselves, but in the circumstances in which they

---

[10]Radcliffe, Lord, *The Law and Its Compass* (Faber) 1961,
p. 12.

[11]*Shaw* v. *Director of Public Prosecutions* [1961] 2 W.L.R.
897.

are performed, and which stretches in a continuous scale from wilful murder at one end to failure to observe a no-parking rule or to return on time a library book (which someone else may be urgently wanting) at the other. (Incidentally a certain poignancy is given to Lord Devlin's choice of this last example by a subsequent newspaper report that a book borrower in Frankfurt who omitted, in spite of repeated requests, to return a book which he had borrowed two years previously was brought before a local magistrate actually—though apparently by mistake—in handcuffs.[12]) But however great the range from the heinous to the trivial, the important point is that the gradation is continuous; and in the complexities of modern society a vast range of actions, in themselves apparently morally neutral, must be regarded as in varying degrees anti-social, and therefore in their contemporary settings as no less objectionable than actions whose criminal status is of greater antiquity. The good citizen will doubtless experience different degrees of guilt according as he may have stabbed his wife, engaged in homosexual intercourse, omitted to return his library book or failed to prevent one of his employees from watering the milk sold by his firm. Technically these are all crimes; whether or not they are also sins is a purely theological matter with which the law has no concern. If the function of the criminal law is to punish the wicked, then everything which the law forbids must in the circumstances in which it is forbidden be regarded as in its appropriate measure wicked.

Although this is, I think, the inevitable conclusion of any argument which finds wickedness inherent in particular classes of action, it seems to be unpalatable to Lord Devlin and others who conceive the function of the criminal law in punitive terms. It opens the door too wide. Still the door can be closed again by resort to the alternative theory that the wickedness of an action is inherent not in the action itself, but in the state of mind of the person who performs it. To punish people merely for what they have done, it is argued, would be unjust, for the forbidden act might have been an accident for which the person who did it cannot be held to blame. Hence the requirement, to which traditionally the law attaches so much importance, that a crime is not, so to speak, a crime in the absence of *mens rea*.

Today, however, over a wide front even this requirement has in fact been abandoned. Today many, indeed almost

---

[12]*The Times*, November 11, 1961.

certainly the majority, of the cases dealt with by the
criminal courts are cases of strict liability in which
proof of a guilty mind is no longer necessary for conviction.   A new dichotomy is thus created, and one which in
this instance exists not merely in the minds of the judges
but is actually enshrined in the law itself—that is to say,
the dichotomy between those offences in which the guilty
mind is, and those in which it is not, an essential ingredient.   In large measure, no doubt, this classification co-
incides with Lord Devlin's division into real and quasi-
crimes; but whether or not this coincidence is exact must
be a question of personal judgment.   To drive a car when
your driving ability is impaired through drink or drugs is
an offence of strict liability: it is no defence to say
that you had no idea that the drink would affect you as it
did, or to produce evidence that you were such a seasoned
drinker that any such result was, objectively, not to be
expected.   These might be mitigating circumstances after
conviction, but are no bar to the conviction itself.   Yet
some at least of those who distinguish between real and
quasi-crimes would put drunken driving in the former category, even though it involves no question of *mens rea*.   In
the passage that I quoted earlier Lord Devlin, it will be
remembered, was careful to include new as well as old offences in his category of "real" crimes; but generally
speaking it is the *mala antiqua* which are held to be both
mala in se and contingent upon *mens rea*.

Nothing has dealt so devastating a blow at the punitive conception of the criminal process as the proliferation of offences of strict liability; and the alarm has
forthwith been raised.   Thus Dr. J.Ll.J. Edwards has expressed the fear that there is a real danger that the "widespread practice of imposing criminal liability independent
of any moral fault" will result in the criminal law being
regarded with contempt.   "The process of basing criminal
liability upon a theory of absolute prohibition," he writes,
"may well have the opposite effect to that intended and
lead to a weakening of respect for the law."[13]   Nor, in his
view, is it an adequate answer to say that absolute liability can be tolerated because of the comparative unimpor-
tance of the offences to which it is applied and because,
as a rule, only a monetary penalty is involved; for, in the
first place, there are a number of important exceptions to
this rule (drunken driving for example); and, secondly, as

---

[13]Edwards, J.Ll.J., *Mens Rea in Statutory Offences* (Macmillan) 1955, p. 247.

Dr. Edwards himself points out, in certain cases the penalty imposed by the court may be the least part of the punishment. A merchant's conviction for a minor trading offence may have a disastrous effect upon his business.

Such dislike of strict liability is not by any means confined to academic lawyers. In the courts, too, various devices have been used to smuggle *mens rea* back into offences from which, on the face of it, it would appear to be excluded. To the lawyer's ingenious mind the invention of such devices naturally presents no difficulty. Criminal liability, for instance, can attach only to voluntary acts. If a driver is struck unconscious with an epileptic seizure, it can be argued that he is not responsible for any consequences because his driving thereafter is involuntary: indeed he has been said not to be driving at all. If on the other hand he falls asleep, this defence will not serve since sleep is a condition that comes on gradually, and a driver has an opportunity and a duty to stop before it overpowers him. Alternatively, recourse can be had to the circular argument that anyone who commits a forbidden act must have intended to commit it and must, therefore, have formed a guilty intention. As Lord Devlin puts it, the word "knowingly" or "wilfully" can be read into acts in which it is not present; although as his Lordship points out this subterfuge is open to the criticism that it fails to distinguish between the physical act itself and the circumstances in which this becomes a crime.[14]   All that the accused may have intended was to perform an action (such as firing a gun or driving a car) which is not in itself criminal. Again, in yet other cases such as those in which it is forbidden to permit or to allow something to be done the concept of negligence can do duty as a watered down version of *mens rea*: for how can anyone be blamed for permitting something about which he could not have known?

All these devices, it cannot be too strongly emphasised, are necessitated by the need to preserve the essentially punitive function of the criminal law. For it is not, as Dr. Edwards fears, the criminal law which will be brought into contempt by the multiplication of offences of strict liability, so much as this particular conception of the law's function. If that function is conceived less in terms of punishment than as a mechanism of prevention these fears become irrelevant. Such a conception, however, apparently sticks in the throat of even the most progressive

---

[14]Devlin, Lord, *Samples of Law Making* (O.U.P.) 1962, pp. 71-80.

lawyers. Even Professor Hart, in his Hobhouse lecture on
Punishment and the Elimination of Responsibility,[15] seems
to be incurably obsessed with the notion of punishment,
which haunts his text as well as figuring in his title.
Although rejecting many traditional theories, such as that
punishment should be "retributive" or "denunciatory," he
nevertheless seems wholly unable to envisage a system in
which sentence is not automatically equated with "punishment." Thus he writes of "values quite distinct from those
of retributive punishment which the system of responsibility does maintain, and which remain of great importance even
if our aims in *punishing* are the forward-looking aims of
social protection"; and again "even if we *punish* men not as
wicked but as nuisances . . ." while he makes many refer-
ences to the principle that liability to punishment must
depend on a voluntary act. Perhaps it requires the naïveté
of an amateur to suggest that the forward-looking aims of
social protection might, on occasion, have absolutely no
connection with punishment.

If, however, the primary function of the courts is
conceived as the prevention of forbidden acts, there is
little cause to be disturbed by the multiplication of offences of strict liability. If the law says that certain
things are not to be done, it is illogical to confine this
prohibition to occasions on which they are done from malice
aforethought; for at least the material consequences of an
action, and the reasons for prohibiting it, are the same
whether it is the result of sinister malicious plotting, of
negligence or of sheer accident. A man is equally dead and
his relatives equally bereaved whether he was stabbed or
run over by a drunken motorist or by an incompetent one;
and the inconvenience caused by the loss of your bicycle is
unaffected by the question whether or not the youth who removed it had the intention of putting it back, if in fact
he had not done so at the time of his arrest. It is true,
of course, as Professor Hart has argued,[16] that the material consequences of an action by no means exhaust its effects. "If one person hits another, the person struck does
not think of the other as *just* a cause of pain to him. . . .
If the blow was light but deliberate, it has a significance
for the person struck quite different from an accidental
much heavier blow." To ignore this difference, he argues,
is to outrage "distinctions which not only underlie morali-

---

[15]Hart, H.L.A., *Punishment and the Elimination of Responsibility* (Athlone Press) 1962, pp. 27, 28. Italics mine.

[16]*Op. cit.*, pp. 29, 30.

ty, but pervade the whole of our social life." That these
distinctions are widely appreciated and keenly felt no one
would deny. Often perhaps they derive their force from a
purely punitive or retributive attitude; but alternatively
they may be held to be relevant to an assessment of the
social damage that results from a criminal act. Just as a
heavy blow does more damage than a light one, so also perhaps does a blow which involves psychological injury do
more damage than one in which the hurt is purely physical.

The conclusion to which this argument leads is, I
think, not that the presence or absence of the guilty mind
is unimportant, but that *mens rea* has, so to speak—and
this is the crux of the matter—*got into the wrong place*.
Traditionally, the requirement of the guilty mind is written into the actual definition of a crime. No guilty intention, no crime, is the rule. Obviously this makes sense
if the law's concern is with wickedness: where there is no
guilty intention, there can be no wickedness. But it is
equally obvious, on the other hand, that an action does not
become innocuous merely because whoever performed it meant
no harm. If the object of the criminal law is to prevent
the occurrence of socially damaging actions, it would be
absurd to turn a blind eye to those which were due to care-
lessness, negligence or even accident. The question of
motivation is *in the first instance* irrelevant.

But only in the first instance. At a later stage,
that is to say, after what is now known as a conviction,
the presence or absence of guilty intention is all-impor-
tant for its effect on the appropriate measures to be taken
to prevent a recurrence of the forbidden act. The prevention of accidental deaths presents different problems from
those involved in the prevention of wilful murders. The
results of the actions of the careless, the mistaken, the
wicked and the merely unfortunate may be indistinguishable
from one another, but each case calls for a different treatment. Tradition, however, is very strong, and the notion
that these differences are relevant only after the fact has
been established that the accused committed the forbidden
act seems still to be deeply abhorrent to the legal mind.
Thus Lord Devlin, discussing the possibility that judges
might have taken the line that all "unintentional" criminals might be dealt with simply by the imposition of a nom-
inal penalty, regards this as the "negation of law." "It
would,"[17] he says, "confuse the function of mercy which the
judge is dispensing when imposing the penalty with the

---

[17]Devlin, Lord, *Samples of Law Making* (O.U.P.) 1962, p. 73.

functions of justice. It would have been to deny to the
citizen due process of law because it would have been to
say to him, in effect: 'Although we cannot think that Par-
liament intended you to be punished in this case because
you have really done nothing wrong, come to us, ask for mercy, and we shall grant mercy.' . . . In all criminal matters the citizen is entitled to the protection of the law
. . . and the mitigation of penalty should not be adopted
as the prime method of dealing with accidental offenders."

Within its own implied terms of reference the logic is
unexceptionable. If the purpose of the law is to dispense
punishment tempered with mercy, then to use mercy as a consolation for unjust punishment is certainly to give a stone
for bread. But these are not the implied terms of reference of strict liability. In the case of offences of
strict liability the presumption is not that those who have
committed forbidden actions must be punished, but that appropriate steps must be taken to prevent the occurrence of
such actions.

Here, as often in other contexts also, the principles
involved are admirably illustrated by the many driving offences in which conviction does not involve proof of *mens
rea*. If, for instance, the criterion of gravity is the
amount of social damage which a crime causes, many of these
offences must be judged extremely grave. In 1961 299 persons were convicted on charges of causing death by dangerous driving, that is to say more than five times as many as
were convicted of murder (including those found guilty but
insane) and 85 per cent more than the total of convictions
for all other forms of homicide (namely murder, manslaughter and infanticide) put together. It is, moreover, a pe-
culiarity of many driving offences that the offender seldom
intends the actual damage which he causes. He may be to
blame in that he takes a risk which he knows may result in
injury to other people or to their property, but such injury is neither an inevitable nor an intended consequence of
the commission of the offence: which is not true of, for
example, burglary. Dangerous or careless driving ranges in
a continuous series from the almost wholly accidental,
through the incompetent and the negligent to the positively
and grossly culpable; and it is quite exceptionally difficult in many of these cases to establish just to what point
along this scale any particular instance should be assigned.
In consequence the gravity of any offence tends to be esti-
mated by its consequences rather than by the state of mind
of the perpetrator—which is less usual (although attempted
murder or grievous bodily harm may turn into murder, if the
victim dies) in the case of other crimes. In my experience

it is exceptional (though not unknown) for a driving charge to be made unless an accident actually occurs, and the nature of the charge is apt to be determined by the severity of the accident. I recall, for example, a case in which a car driver knocked down an elderly man on a pedestrian crossing, and a month later the victim died in hospital after an operation, his death being, one must suppose, in spite, rather than because, of this. Thereupon the charge, which had originally been booked by the police as careless, not even dangerous, driving was upgraded to causing death by dangerous driving.

For all these reasons it is recognised that if offences in this category are to be dealt with by the criminal courts at all, this can only be on a basis of strict liability. This particular category of offences thus illustrates all too vividly the fact that in the modern world in one way or another, as much and more damage is done by negligence, or by indifference to the welfare or safety of others, as by deliberate wickedness. In technically simpler societies this is less likely to be so, for the points of exposure to the follies of others are less numerous, and the daily chances of being run over, or burnt or infected or drowned because someone has left undone something that he ought to have done are less ominous. These new complexities were never envisaged by the founders of our legal traditions, and it is hardly to be wondered at if the law itself is not yet fully adapted to them. Yet it is by no means certain that the last chapter in the long and chequered history of the concept of guilt, which is so deeply rooted in our traditions, has yet been written. Time was when inanimate objects—the rock that fell on you, the tree that attracted the lightning that killed you—were held to share the blame for the disasters in which they were instrumental; and it was properly regarded as a great step forward when the capacity to acquire a guilty mind was deemed to be one of the distinctive capacities of human beings.[18] But now, perhaps, the time has come for the concept of legal guilt to be dissolved into a wider concept of responsibility or at least accountability, in which there is room for negligence as well as purposeful wrong doing; and for the significance of a conviction to be reinterpreted merely as evidence that a prohibited act has been committed, questions of motivation being relevant only in so far as they bear upon the probability of such acts being repeated.

---

[18]There could be an argument here, into which I do not propose to enter, as to whether this capacity is not shared by some of the higher animals.

I am not, of course, arguing that all crimes should immediately be transferred into the strict liability category. To do so would in some cases involve formidable problems of definition—as, for instance, in that of larceny. But I do suggest that the contemporary extension of strict liability is not the nightmare that it is often made out to be, that it does not promise the decline and fall of the criminal law, and that it is, on the contrary, a sensible and indeed inevitable measure of adaptation to the requirements of the modern world; and above all I suggest that its supposedly nightmarish quality disappears once it is accepted that the primary objective of the criminal courts is preventive rather than punitive. Certainly we need to pay heed to Mr. Nigel Walker's reminder[19] that "under our present law it is possible for a person to do great harm in circumstances which suggest that there is a risk of his repeating it, and yet to secure an acquittal." In two types of case, in both of which such harm can result, the concept of the guilty mind has become both irrelevant and obstructive. In this lecture I have been chiefly concerned with the first of these categories—that of cases of negligence. The second category—that of mental abnormality—will be the theme of that which follows.[20]

---

[19]Walker, N., "Queen Victoria Was Right," *New Society*, June 27, 1963.

[20][In her chapter on mentally abnormal offenders, Baroness Wootton outlines the way in which the mental condition of an offender can be relevant under a preventive system: "To discard the notion of responsibility does not mean that the mental condition of an offender ceases to have any importance, or that psychiatric considerations become irrelevant. The difference is that they become relevant, not to the question of determining the measure of his culpability, but to the choice of the treatment most likely to be effective in discouraging him from offending again" (p. 77). When a preventive, rather than a punitive, outlook is adopted "one of the most important consequences must be to obscure the present rigid distinction between the penal and the medical institution" (p. 79). Ed.]

CRIMINAL JUSTICE, LEGAL VALUES,
AND THE REHABILITATIVE IDEAL

Francis A. Allen

Although one is sometimes inclined to despair of any
constructive changes in the administration of criminal justice, a glance at the history of the past half-century reveals a succession of the most significant developments.
Thus, the last fifty years have seen the widespread acceptance of three legal inventions of great importance: the
juvenile court, systems of probation and of parole. During
the same period, under the inspiration of continental research and writing, scientific criminology became an established field of instruction and inquiry in American universities and in other research agencies. At the same time,
psychiatry made its remarkable contributions to the theory
of human behavior and, more specifically, of that form of
human behavior described as criminal. These developments
have been accompanied by nothing less than a revolution in
public conceptions of the nature of crime and the criminal,
and in public attitudes toward the proper treatment of the
convicted offender.[1]

This history with its complex developments of thought,
institutional behavior, and public attitudes must be approached gingerly; for in dealing with it we are in peril
of committing the sin of oversimplification. Nevertheless,
despite the presence of contradictions and paradox, it
seems possible to detect one common element in much of this
thought and activity which goes far to characterize the

Reprinted with permission from the *Journal of Criminal Law,
Criminology, and Police Science* 50 (1959), pp. 226-232.
Copyright © 1959 by Northwestern University School of Law.
The author is Professor of Law at the University of Michi-
gan.

[1]These developments have been surveyed in Allen, *Law and
the Future: Criminal Law and Administration*, 51 Nw. L. Rev.
207, 207-208 (1956). See also Harno, *Some Significant Developments in Criminal Law and Procedure in the Last Century*, 42 J. Crim. L., C. and P.S. 427 (1951).

history we are considering. This common element or theme I shall describe, for want of a better phrase, as the rise of the rehabilitative ideal.

The rehabilitative ideal is itself a complex of ideas which, perhaps, defies completely precise statement. The essential points, however, can be articulated. It is assumed, first, that human behavior is the product of antecedent causes. These causes can be identified as part of the physical universe, and it is the obligation of the scientist to discover and to describe them with all possible exactitude. Knowledge of the antecedents of human behavior makes possible an approach to the scientific control of human behavior. Finally, and of primary significance for the purposes at hand, it is assumed that measures employed to treat the convicted offender should serve a therapeutic function, that such measures should be designed to effect changes in the behavior of the convicted person in the interests of his own happiness, health, and satisfaction and in the interest of social defense.

Although these ideas are capable of rather simple statement, they have provided the arena for some of the modern world's most acrimonious controversy. And the disagreements among those who adhere in general to these propositions have been hardly less intense than those prompted by the dissenters. This is true, in part, because these ideas possess a delusive simplicity. No idea is more pervaded with ambiguity than the notion of reform or rehabilitation. Assuming, for example, that we have the techniques to accomplish our ends of rehabilitation, are we striving to produce in the convicted offender something called "adjustment" to his social environment or is our objective something different from or more than this? By what scale of values do we determine the ends of therapy?[2]

These are intriguing questions, well worth extended consideration. But it is not my purpose to pursue them in this paper. Rather, I am concerned with describing some of the dilemmas and conflicts of values that have resulted from efforts to impose the rehabilitative ideal on the system of criminal justice. I know of no area in which a more effective demonstration can be made of the necessity for greater mutual understanding between the law and the behavioral disciplines.

----

[2] "We see that it is not easy to determine what we consider to be the sickness and what we consider to be the cure." Fromm, *Psychoanalysis and Religion* (1950) 73. See also the author's development of these points at 67–77.

There is, of course, nothing new in the notion of reform or rehabilitation of the offender as one objective of
the penal process.   This idea is given important emphasis,
for example, in the thought of the medieval churchmen.   The
church's position, as described by Sir Francis Palgrave,
was that punishment was not to be "thundered in vengeance
for the satisfaction of the state, but imposed for the good
of the offender: in order to afford the means of amendment
and to lead the transgressor to repentance, and to mercy."[3]
Even Jeremy Bentham, whose views modern criminology has often scorned and more often ignored, is found saying: "It is
a great merit in a punishment to contribute to the *reformation of the offender*, not only through fear of being punished again, but by a change in his character and habits."[4]
But this is far from saying that the modern expression of
the rehabilitative ideal is not to be sharply distinguished
from earlier expressions.   The most important differences,
I believe, are two.   First, the modern statement of the rehabilitative ideal is accompanied by, and largely stems
from, the development of scientific disciplines concerned
with human behavior, a development not remotely approxi-
mated in earlier periods when notions of reform of the offender were advanced.   Second, and of equal importance for
the purposes at hand, in no other period has the rehabilitative ideal so completely dominated theoretical and schol-
arly inquiry, to such an extent that in some quarters it is
almost assumed that matters of treatment and reform of the
offender are the only questions worthy of serious attention
in the whole field of criminal justice and corrections.

---

[3]Quoted in Dalzell, *Benefit of Clergy and Related Matters*
(1955) 13.

[4]Bentham, *The Theory of Legislation* (Ogden, C. K., ed.,
1931) 338-339.   (Italics in the original.)   But Bentham
added: "But when [the writers] come to speak about the
means of preventing offenses, of rendering men better, of
perfecting morals, their imagination grows warm, their
hopes excited; one would suppose they were about to produce
the great secret, and that the human race was going to receive a new form.   It is because we have a more magnificent
idea of objects in proportion as they are less familiar,
and because the imagination has a loftier flight amid vague
projects which have never been subjected to the limits of
analysis."   Id. at 359.

THE NARROWING OF SCIENTIFIC INTERESTS

This narrowing of interests prompted by the rise of the rehabilitative ideal during the past half-century should put us on our guard. No social institutions as complex as those involved in the administration of criminal justice serve a single function or purpose. Social institutions are multi-valued and multi-purposed. Values and purposes are likely on occasion to prove inconsistent and to produce internal conflict and tension. A theoretical orientation that evinces concern for only one or a limited number of purposes served by the institution must inevitably prove partial and unsatisfactory. In certain situations it may prove positively dangerous. This stress on the unfortunate consequences of the rise of the rehabilitative ideal need not involve failure to recognize the substantial benefits that have also accompanied its emergence. Its emphasis on the fundamental problems of human behavior, its numerous contributions to the decency of the criminal-law processes are of vital importance. But the limitations and dangers of modern trends of thought need clearly to be identified in the interest, among others, of the rehabilitative ideal, itself.

My first proposition is that the rise of the rehabilitative ideal has dictated what questions are to be investigated, with the result that many matters of equal or even greater importance have been ignored or cursorily examined. This tendency can be abundantly illustrated. Thus, the concentration of interest on the nature and needs of the criminal has resulted in a remarkable absence of interest in the nature of crime. This is, indeed, surprising, for on reflection it must be apparent that the question of what is a crime is logically the prior issue: how crime is defined determines in large measure who the criminal is who becomes eligible for treatment and therapy.[5] A related observation was made some years ago by Professor Karl Llewellyn, who has done as much as any man to develop sensible interdisciplinary inquiry involving law and the behavioral disciplines:[6] "When I was younger I used to hear smuggish assertions among my sociological friends, such as: 'I take

---

[5]Cf. Hart, *The Aims of the Criminal Law*, 23 Law and Cont. Prob. 401 (1958).

[6]See Llewellyn and Hoebel, *The Cheyenne Way* (1941). See also *Crime, Law and Social Science: A Symposium*, 34 Colum. L. Rev. 277 (1934).

the sociological, *not* the legal, approach to crime'; and I
suspect an inquiring reporter could still hear much the
same (perhaps with 'psychiatric' often substituted for 'sociological')—though it is surely somewhat obvious that
when you take 'the legal' out, you also take out 'crime'".[7]
This disinterest in the definition of criminal behavior has
afflicted the lawyers quite as much as the behavioral scientists. Even the criminal law scholar has tended, until
recently, to assume that problems of procedure and treatment are the things that "really matter".[8] Only the issue
of criminal responsibility as affected by mental disorder
has attracted the consistent attention of the non-lawyer,
and the literature reflecting this interest is not remarkable for its cogency or its wisdom. In general, the behavioral sciences have left other issues relevant to crime
definition largely in default. There are a few exceptions.
Dr. Hermann Mannheim, of the London School of Economics,
has manifested intelligent interest in these matters.[9] The
late Professor Edwin Sutherland's studies of "white-collar
crime"[10] may also be mentioned, although, in my judgment,
Professor Sutherland's efforts in this field are among the
least perceptive and satisfactory of his many valuable contributions.[11]

The absence of wide-spread interest in these areas is
not to be explained by any lack of challenging questions.
Thus, what may be said of the relationships between legislative efforts to subject certain sorts of human behavior
to penal regulation and the persistence of police corruption and abuse of power?[12] Studies of public attitudes

---

[7]*Law and the Social Sciences—Especially Sociology*, 62 Harv.
L. Rev. 1286, 1287 (1949).

[8]Allen, *op. cit. supra*, note 1, at 207-210.

[9]See, especially, his *Criminal Justice and Social Recon-
struction* (1946).

[10]*White-Collar Crime* (1949). See also Clinard, *The Black
Market* (1952).

[11]Cf. Caldwell, *A Re-examination of the Concept of White-
Collar Crime*, 22 Fed. Prob. 30 (March, 1958).

[12]An interesting question of this kind is now being debated
in England centering on the proposals for enhanced penalties for prostitution offenses made in the recently-issued
Wolfenden Report. See Fairfield, *Notes on Prostitution*, 9
Brit. J. Delin. 164, 173 (1959). See also Allen, *The*

toward other sorts of criminal legislation might provide valuable clues as to whether given regulatory objectives are more likely to be attained by the provision of criminal penalties or by other kinds of legal sanctions. It ought to be re-emphasized that the question, what sorts of behavior should be declared criminal, is one to which the behavioral sciences might contribute vital insights. This they have largely failed to do, and we are the poorer for it.

Another example of the narrowing of interests that has accompanied the rise of the rehabilitative ideal is the lack of concern with the idea of deterrence—indeed the hostility evinced by many modern criminologists toward it. This, again, is a most surprising development.[13] It must surely be apparent that the criminal law has a general preventive function to perform in the interests of public order and of security of life, limb, and possessions. Indeed, there is reason to assert that the influence of criminal sanctions on the millions who never engage in serious criminality is of greater social importance than their impact on the hundreds of thousands who do. Certainly, the assumption of those who make our laws is that the denouncing of conduct as criminal and providing the means for the enforcement of the legislative prohibitions will generally have a tendency to prevent or minimize such behavior. Just what the precise mechanisms of deterrence are is not well understood. Perhaps it results, on occasion, from the naked threat of punishment. Perhaps, more frequently, it derives from a more subtle process wherein the mores and moral sense of the community are recruited to advance the attainment of the criminal law's objectives.[14] The point is that we know very little about these vital matters, and the resources of the behavioral sciences have rarely been employed to contribute knowledge and insight in their investigation. Not only have the criminologists displayed little interest in these matters, some have suggested that the whole idea of general prevention is invalid or worse. Thus, speaking of the deterrent theory of punishment, the authors of a leading textbook in criminology assert: "This is simply a

---

[12](cont.) *Borderland of the Criminal Law: Problems of "Socializing" Criminal Justice*, 32 Soc. Ser. Rev. 107, 110-111 (1958).

[13]But see Andenaes, *General Prevention—Illusion or Reality?* 43 J. Crim. L., C. and P.S. 176 (1952).

[14]This seems to be the assertion of Garafalo. See his *Criminology* (Millar trans. 1914) 241-242.

derived rationalization of revenge. Though social revenge
is the actual psychological basis of punishment today, the
apologists for the punitive regime are likely to bring forward in their defense the more sophisticated, but equally
futile, contention that punishment deters from [sic]
crime."[15] We are thus confronted by a situation in which
the dominance of the rehabilitative ideal not only diverts
attention from many serious issues, but leads to a denial
that these issues even exist.

DEBASEMENT OF THE REHABILITATIVE IDEAL

Now permit me to turn to another sort of difficulty
that has accompanied the rise of the rehabilitative ideal
in the areas of corrections and criminal justice. It is a
familiar observation that an idea once propagated and introduced into the active affairs of life undergoes changes.
The real significance of an idea as it evolves in actual
practice may be quite different from that intended by those
who conceived it and gave it initial support. An idea
tends to lead a life of its own; and modern history is full
of the unintended consequences of seminal ideas. The application of the rehabilitative ideal to the institutions of
criminal justice presents a striking example of such a development. My second proposition, then, is that the rehabilitative ideal has been debased in practice and that the
consequences resulting from this debasement are serious and,
at times, dangerous.

This proposition may be supported, first, by the observation that, under the dominance of the rehabilitative
ideal, the language of therapy is frequently employed, wit-
tingly or unwittingly, to disguise the true state of affairs that prevails in our custodial institutions and at
other points in the correctional process. Certain measures,
like the sexual psychopath laws, have been advanced and
supported as therapeutic in nature when, in fact, such a
characterization seems highly dubious.[16] Too often the
vocabulary of therapy has been exploited to serve a public-
relations function. Recently, I visited an institution devoted to the diagnosis and treatment of disturbed children.

---

[15]Barnes and Teeters, *New Horizons in Criminology* (2nd ed.
1954) 337. The context in which these statements appear
also deserves attention.

[16]See note 25, *infra.*

The institution had been established with high hopes and, for once, with the enthusiastic support of the state legislature. Nevertheless, fifty minutes of an hour's lecture, delivered by a supervising psychiatrist before we toured the building, were devoted to custodial problems. This fixation on problems of custody was reflected in the institutional arrangements which included, under a properly euphemistic label, a cell for solitary confinement.[17] Even more disturbing was the tendency of the staff to justify these custodial measures in therapeutic terms. Perhaps on occasion the requirements of institutional security and treatment coincide. But the inducements to self-deception in such situations are strong and all too apparent. In short, the language of therapy has frequently provided a formidable obstacle to a realistic analysis of the conditions that confront us. And realism in considering these problems is the one quality that we require above all others.[18]

There is a second sort of unintended consequence that has resulted from the application of the rehabilitative ideal to the practical administration of criminal justice. Surprisingly enough, the rehabilitative ideal has often led to increased severity of penal measures. This tendency may be seen in the operation of the juvenile court. Although frequently condemned by the popular press as a device of leniency, the juvenile court, is authorized to intervene punitively in many situations in which the conduct, were it committed by an adult, would be wholly ignored by the law or would subject the adult to the mildest of sanctions. The tendency of proposals for wholly indeterminate sentences, a clearly identifiable fruit of the rehabilitative ideal,[19] is unmistakably in the direction of lengthened periods of imprisonment. A large variety of statutes authorizing what is called "civil" commitment of persons, but

---

[17]As I recall, it was referred to as the "quiet room". In another institution the boy was required to stand before a wall while a seventy pound fire hose was played on his back. This procedure went under the name of "hydrotherapy."

[18]Cf. Wechsler, *Law, Morals and Psychiatry*, 18 Colum. L. School News 2, 4 (March 4, 1959): "The danger rather is that coercive regimes we would not sanction in the name of punishment or of correction will be sanctified in the name of therapy without providing the resources for a therapeutic operation."

[19]Cf. Tappan, *Sentencing under the Model Penal Code*, 23 Law and Cont. Prob. 538, 530 (1958).

which, except for the reduced protections afforded the parties proceeded against, are essentially criminal in nature,
provide for absolutely indeterminate periods of confinement.
Experience has demonstrated that, in practice, there is a
strong tendency for the rehabilitative ideal to serve purposes that are essentially incapacitative rather than therapeutic in character.[20]

THE REHABILITATIVE IDEAL AND INDIVIDUAL LIBERTY

The reference to the tendency of the rehabilitative
ideal to encourage increasingly long periods of incarceration brings me to my final proposition. It is that the
rise of the rehabilitative ideal has often been accompanied
by attitudes and measures that conflict, sometimes seriously, with the values of individual liberty and volition. As
I have already observed, the role of the behavioral sciences in the administration of criminal justice and in the
areas of public policy lying on the borderland of the criminal law is one of obvious importance. But I suggest that,
if the function of criminal justice is considered in its
proper dimensions, it will be discovered that the most fundamental problems in these areas are not those of psychiatry, sociology, social case work, or social psychology. On
the contrary, the most fundamental problems are those of political philosophy and political science. The administration of the criminal law presents to any community the most
extreme issues of the proper relations of the individual
citizen to state power. We are concerned here with the per-
ennial issue of political authority: Under what circumstances is the state justified in bringing its force to bear on
the individual human being? These issues, of course, are
not confined to the criminal law, but it is in the area of
penal regulation that they are most dramatically manifested.
The criminal law, then, is located somewhere near the center of the political problem, as the history of the twentieth century abundantly reveals. It is no accident, after
all, that the agencies of criminal justice and law enforcement are those first seized by an emerging totalitarian regime.[21] In short, a study of criminal justice is most

---

[20]Cf. Hall, Jerome, *General Principles of Criminal Law*
(1947) 551. And see Sellin, *The Protective Code: A Swedish
Proposal* (1957) 9.

[21]This development in the case of Germany may be gleaned
from Crankshaw, *Gestapo* (1956).

fundamentally a study in the exercise of political power. No such study can properly avoid the problem of the abuse of power.

The obligation of containing power within the limits suggested by a community's political values has been considerably complicated by the rise of the rehabilitative ideal. For the problem today is one of regulating the exercise of power by men of good will, whose motivations are to help not to injure, and whose ambitions are quite different from those of the political adventurer so familiar to history. There is a tendency for such persons to claim immunity from the usual forms of restraint and to insist that professionalism and a devotion to science provide sufficient protections against unwarranted invasion of individual right. This attitude is subjected to mordant criticism by Aldous Huxley in his recent book, "Brave New World Revisited." Mr. Huxley observes: "There seems to be a touching belief among certain Ph.D's in sociology that Ph.D's in sociology will never be corrupted by power. Like Sir Galahad's, their strength is the strength of ten because their heart is pure —and their heart is pure because they are scientists and have taken six thousand hours of social studies."[22]   I suspect that Mr. Huxley would be willing to extend his point to include professional groups other than the sociologists. There is one proposition which, if generally understood, would contribute more to clear thinking on these matters than any other. It is not a new insight. Seventy years ago the Italian criminologist Garafalo asserted: "The mere deprivation of liberty, however benign the administration of the place of confinement, is undeniably punishment."[23]   This proposition may be rephrased as follows: Measures which subject individuals to the substantial and involuntary deprivation of their liberty are essentially punitive in character, and this reality is not altered by the facts that the motivations that prompt incarceration are to provide therapy or otherwise contribute to the person's well-being or reform. As such, these measures must be closely scrutinized to insure that power is being applied consistently with those values of the community that justify interferences with liberty for only the most clear and compelling reasons.

But the point I am making requires more specific and concrete application to be entirely meaningful. It should be pointed out, first, that the values of individual liberty

---

[22]Huxley, *Brave New World Revisited* (1958) 34-35.

[23]*Op. cit. supra*, note 14, at 256.

may be imperiled by claims to knowledge and therapeutic
technique that we, in fact, do not possess and by failure
candidly to concede what we do not know. At times, practitioners of the behavioral sciences have been guilty of
these faults. At other times, such errors have supplied
the assumptions on which legislators, lawyers and lay people generally have proceeded. Ignorance, in itself, is not
disgraceful so long as it is unavoidable. But when we rush
to measures affecting human liberty and human dignity on
the assumption that we know what we do not know or can do
what we cannot do, then the problem of ignorance takes on a
more sinister hue.[24] An illustration of these dangers is
provided by the sexual psychopath laws, to which I return;
for they epitomize admirably some of the worst tendencies
of modern practice. These statutes authorize the indefinite incarceration of persons believed to be potentially
dangerous in their sexual behavior. But can such persons
be accurately identified without substantial danger of
placing persons under restraint who, in fact, provide no
serious danger to the community? Having once confined them,
is there any body of knowledge that tells us how to treat
and cure them? If so, as a practical matter, are facilities and therapy available for these purposes in the state
institutions provided for the confinement of such persons?[25]
Questions almost as serious can be raised as to a whole
range of other measures. The laws providing for commitment
of persons displaying the classic symptoms of psychosis and
advanced mental disorder have proved a seductive analogy
for other proposals. But does our knowledge of human behavior really justify the extension of these measures to provide for the indefinite commitment of persons otherwise afflicted? We who represent the disciplines that in some
measure are concerned with the control of human behavior
are required to act under weighty responsibilities. It is
no paradox to assert that the real utility of scientific
technique in the fields under discussion depends on an accurate realization of the limits of scientific knowledge.

---

[24]I have developed these points in Allen, *op. cit. supra,*
note 12, at 113–115.

[25]Many competent observers have asserted that none of these
inquiries can properly be answered in the affirmative. See,
e.g., Sutherland, *The Sexual Psychopath Laws,* 40 J. Crim.
L., C. and P.S. 543 (1950); Hacker and Frym, *The Sexual Psychopath Act in Practice: A Critical Discussion,* 43 Calif. L.
Rev. 766 (1955). See also Tappen, *The Habitual Sex Offender* (Report of the New Jersey Commission) (1950).

There are other ways in which the modern tendencies of thought accompanying the rise of the rehabilitative ideal have imperiled the basic political values. The most important of these is the encouragement of procedural laxness and irregularity. It is my impression that there is greater awareness of these dangers today than at some other times in the past, for which, if true, we perhaps have Mr. Hitler to thank. Our increased knowledge of the functioning of totalitarian regimes makes it more difficult to assert that the insistence on decent and orderly procedure represents simply a lawyer's quibble or devotion to outworn ritual. Nevertheless, in our courts of so-called "socialized justice" one may still observe, on occasion, a tendency to assume that, since the purpose of the proceeding is to "help" rather than to "punish", some lack of concern in establishing the charges against the person before the court may be justified. This position is self-defeating and otherwise indefensible. A child brought before the court has a right to demand, not only the benevolent concern of the tribunal, but justice. And one may rightly wonder as to the value of therapy purchased at the expense of justice. The essential point is that the issues of treatment and therapy be kept clearly distinct from the question of whether the person committed the acts which authorize the intervention of state power in the first instance.[26] This is a principle often violated. Thus, in some courts the judge is supplied a report on the offender by the psychiatric clinic before the judgment of guilt or acquittal is announced. Such reports, while they may be relevant to the defendant's need for therapy or confinement, ordinarily are wholly irrelevant to the issue of his guilt of the particular offense charged. Yet it asks too much of human nature to assume that the judge is never influenced on the issue of guilt or innocence by a strongly adverse psychiatric report.

Let me give one final illustration of the problems that have accompanied the rise of the rehabilitative ideal.

---

[26] A considerable literature has developed on these issues. See, e.g., Allen, *The Borderland of the Criminal Law: Problems of "Socializing" Criminal Justice*, 32 Soc. Ser. Rev. 107 (1958); Diana, *The Rights of Juvenile Delinquents: An Appraisal of Juvenile Court Proceedings*, 44 J. Crim. L., C. and P.S. 561 (1957); Paulsen, *Fairness to the Juvenile Offender*, 41 Minn. L. Rev. 547 (1957); Waite, *How Far Can Court Procedures Be Socialized without Impairing Individual Rights?* 12 J. Crim. L. and C. 430 (1921).

Some time ago we encountered a man in his eighties incar-
cerated in a state institution. He had been confined for
some thirty years under a statute calling for the automatic
commitment of defendants acquitted on grounds of insanity
in criminal trials. It was generally agreed by the institution's personnel that he was not then psychotic and probably had never been psychotic. The fact seemed to be that
he had killed his wife while drunk. An elderly sister of
the old man was able and willing to provide him with a home,
and he was understandably eager to leave the institution.
When we asked the director of the institution why the old
man was not released, he gave two significant answers. In
the first place, he said, the statute requires me to find
that this inmate is no longer a danger to the community;
this I cannot do, for he may kill again. And of course the
director was right. However unlikely commission of homicide by such a man in his eighties might appear, the director could not be certain. But, as far as that goes, he
also could not be certain about himself or about you or me.
The second answer was equally interesting. The old man, he
said, is better off here. To understand the full significance of this reply it is necessary to know something about
the place of confinement. Although called a hospital, it
was in fact a prison, and not at all a progressive prison.
Nothing worthy of the name of therapy was provided and very
little by way of recreational facilities.

   This case points several morals. It illustrates,
first, a failure of the law to deal adequately with the new
requirements being placed upon it. The statute, as a condition to the release of the inmate, required the director
of the institution virtually to warrant the future good behavior of the inmate, and, in so doing, made unrealistic
and impossible demands on expert judgment. This might be
remedied by the formulation of release criteria more conso-
nant with actuality. Provisions for conditional release to
test the inmate's reaction to the free community would considerably reduce the strain on administrative decisionmaking. But there is more here. Perhaps the case reflects
that arrogance and insensitivity to human values to which
men who have no reason to doubt their own motives appear
peculiarly susceptible.[27]

---

[27]One further recent and remarkable example is provided by
the case, In re Maddox, 351 Mich. 358, 88 N.W. 2d 470
(1958). Professor Wechsler, *op cit. supra*, note 18, at 4,
describes the facts and holding as follows: "Only the other
day, the Supreme Court of Michigan ordered the release of

CONCLUSION

In these remarks I have attempted to describe certain
of the continuing problems and difficulties associated with
what I have called the rise of the rehabilitative ideal.
In so doing, I have not sought to cast doubt on the substantial benefits associated with that movement. It has exposed some of the most intractable problems of our time to
the solvent properties of human intelligence. Moreover,
the devotion to the ideal of empirical investigation provides the movement with a self-correcting mechanism of
great importance, and justifies hopes for constructive future development.

Nevertheless, no intellectual movement produces only
unmixed blessings. It has been suggested in these remarks
that the ascendency of the rehabilitative ideal has, as one
of its unfortunate consequences, diverted attention from
other questions of great criminological importance. This
has operated unfavorably to the full development of criminological science. Not only is this true, but the failure
of many students and practitioners in the relevant areas to
concern themselves with the full context of criminal justice has produced measures dangerous to basic political
values and has, on occasion, encouraged the debasement of
the rehabilitative ideal to produce results, unsupportable
whether measured by the objectives of therapy or of corrections. The worst manifestations of these tendencies are
undoubtedly deplored as sincerely by competent therapists
as by other persons. But the occurrences are neither so
infrequent nor so trivial that they can be safely ignored.

---

[27](cont.) a prisoner in their State prison at Jackson, who
had been transferred from the Ionia State Hospital to which
he was committed as a psychopath. The ground of transfer,
which was defended seriously by a State psychiatrist, was
that the prisoner was 'adamant' in refusing to admit sexual
deviation that was the basis of his commitment; and thus,
in the psychiatrist's view, resistant to therapy! The
Court's answer was, of course, that he had not been tried
for an offense."

THE MYTH OF MENTAL ILLNESS

Thomas S. Szasz

I

At the core of virtually all contemporary psychiatric
theories and practices lies the concept of mental illness.
A critical examination of this concept is therefore indis-
pensable for understanding the ideas, institutions, and interventions of psychiatrists.

My aim in this essay is to ask if there is such a
thing as mental illness, and to argue that there is not.
Of course, mental illness is not a thing or physical object;
hence it can exist only in the same sort of way as do other
theoretical concepts. Yet, to those who believe in them,
familiar theories are likely to appear, sooner or later, as
"objective truths" or "facts." During certain historical
periods, explanatory concepts such as deities, witches, and
instincts appeared not only as theories but as *self-evident
causes* of a vast number of events. Today mental illness is
widely regarded in a similar fashion, that is, as the cause
of innumerable diverse happenings.

As an antidote to the complacent use of the notion of
mental illness—as a self-evident phenomenon, theory, or
cause—let us ask: What is meant when it is asserted that
someone is mentally ill? In this essay I shall describe
the main uses of the concept of mental illness, and I shall
argue that this notion has outlived whatever cognitive usefulness it might have had and that it now functions as a
myth.

From Thomas S. Szasz, *Ideology and Insanity: Essays on the
Psychiatric Dehumanization of Man* (Garden City, N.Y.:
Doubleday Anchor, 1970), pp. 12-24. Copyright 1970 by
Thomas S. Szasz. Reprinted with permission of the author.
Dr. Szasz is Professor of Psychiatry at the State Univer-
sity of New York Upstate Medical Center in Syracuse, New
York. He is the author of numerous books and articles, in-
cluding *The Myth of Mental Illness* (New York: Harper and
Row, 1961) and *Law, Liberty, and Psychiatry* (New York: Mac-
millan, 1963).

II

The notion of mental illness derives its main support from such phenomena as syphilis of the brain or delirious conditions—intoxications, for instance—in which persons may manifest certain disorders of thinking and behavior. Correctly speaking, however, these are diseases of the brain, not of the mind. According to one school of thought, *all* so-called mental illness is of this type. The assumption is made that some neurological defect, perhaps a very subtle one, will ultimately be found to explain all the disorders of thinking and behavior. Many contemporary physicians, psychiatrists, and other scientists hold this view, which implies that people's troubles cannot be caused by conflicting personal needs, opinions, social aspirations, values, and so forth. These difficulties—which I think we may simply call *problems in living*—are thus attributed to physiochemical processes that in due time will be discovered (and no doubt corrected) by medical research.

Mental illnesses are thus regarded as basically similar to other diseases. The only difference, in this view, between mental and bodily disease is that the former, affecting the brain, manifests itself by means of mental symptoms; whereas the latter, affecting other organ systems—for example, the skin, liver, and so on—manifests itself by means of symptoms referable to those parts of the body.

In my opinion, this view is based on two fundamental errors. In the first place, a disease of the brain, analogous to a disease of the skin or bone, is a neurological defect, not a problem in living. For example, a *defect* in a person's visual field may be explained by correlating it with certain lesions in the nervous system. On the other hand, a person's *belief*—whether it be in Christianity, in Communism, or in the idea that his internal organs are rotting and that his body is already dead—cannot be explained by a defect or disease of the nervous system. Explanations of this sort of occurrence—assuming that one is interested in the belief itself and does not regard it simply as a symptom or expression of something else that is more interesting—must be sought along different lines.

The second error is epistemological. It consists of interpreting communications about ourselves and the world around us as symptoms of neurological functioning. This is an error not in observation or reasoning, but rather in the organization and expression of knowledge. In the present case, the error lies in making a dualism between mental and physical symptoms, a dualism that is a habit of speech and not the result of known observations. Let us see if this is so.

.   In medical practice, when we speak of physical disturbances we mean either signs (for example, fever) or symptoms
(for example, pain). We speak of mental symptoms, on the
other hand, when we refer to a patient's communications
about himself, others, and the world about him. The patient might assert that he is Napoleon or that he is being
persecuted by the Communists. These would be considered
mental symptoms only if the observer believed that the patient was *not* Napoleon or that he was *not* being persecuted
by the Communists. This makes it apparent that the statement "X is a mental symptom" involves rendering a judgment
that entails a covert comparison between the patient's
ideas, concepts, or beliefs and those of the observer and
the society in which they live. The notion of mental symptom is therefore inextricably tied to the social, and particularly the ethical, context in which it is made, just as
the notion of bodily symptom is tied to an anatomical and
genetic context.[1]

To sum up: For those who regard mental symptoms as
signs of brain disease, the concept of mental illness is
unnecessary and misleading. If they mean that people so
labeled suffer from diseases of the brain, it would seem
better, for the sake of clarity, to say that and not something else.

III

The term "mental illness" is also widely used to describe something quite different from a disease of the
brain. Many people today take it for granted that living
is an arduous affair. Its hardship for modern man derives,
moreover, not so much from a struggle for biological survival as from the stresses and strains inherent in the social
intercourse of complex human personalities. In this context, the notion of mental illness is used to identify or
describe some feature of an individual's so-called personality. Mental illness—as a deformity of the personality,
so to speak—is then regarded as the cause of human disharmony. It is implicit in this view that social intercourse
between people is regarded as something inherently harmonious, its disturbance being due solely to the presence of
"mental illness" in many people. Clearly, this is faulty

---

[1] See Szasz, T. S.: *Pain and Pleasure: A Study of Bodily
Feelings* (New York: Basic Books, 1957), especially pp. 70-
81; "The problem of psychiatric nosology," *Amer. J. Psychiatry*, 114:405-13 (Nov.), 1957.

reasoning, for it makes the abstraction "mental illness" into a cause of, even though this abstraction was originally created to serve only as a shorthand expression for, certain types of human behavior. It now becomes necessary to ask: What kinds of behavior are regarded as indicative of mental illness, and by whom?

The concept of illness, whether bodily or mental, implies deviation from some clearly defined norm. In the case of physical illness, the norm is the structural and functional integrity of the human body. Thus, although the desirability of physical health, as such, is an ethical value, what health is can be stated in anatomical and physiological terms. What is the norm, deviation from which is regarded as mental illness? This question cannot be easily answered. But whatever this norm may be, we can be certain of only one thing: namely, that it must be stated in terms of psychosocial, ethical, and legal concepts. For example, notions such as "excessive repression" and "acting out an unconscious impulse" illustrate the use of psychological concepts for judging so-called mental health and illness. The idea that chronic hostility, vengefulness, or divorce are indicative of mental illness is an illustration of the use of ethical norms (that is, the desirability of love, kindness, and a stable marriage relationship). Finally, the widespread psychiatric opinion that only a mentally ill person would commit homicide illustrates the use of a legal concept as a norm of mental health. In short, when one speaks of mental illness, the norm from which deviation is measured is a *psychosocial and ethical* standard. Yet, the remedy is sought in terms of *medical* measures that —it is hoped and assumed—are free from wide differences of ethical value. The definition of the disorder and the terms in which its remedy are sought are therefore at serious odds with one another. The practical significance of this covert conflict between the alleged nature of the defect and the actual remedy can hardly be exaggerated.

Having identified the norms used for measuring deviations in cases of mental illness, we shall now turn to the question, Who defines the norms and hence the deviation? Two basic answers may be offered: First, it may be the person himself—that is, the patient—who decides that he deviates from a norm; for example, an artist may believe that he suffers from a work inhibition; and he may implement this conclusion by seeking help *for himself* from a psychotherapist. Second, it may be someone other than the "patient" who decides that the latter is deviant—for example, relatives, physicians, legal authorities, society generally; a psychiatrist may then be hired by persons other than the "patient" to do something *to him* in order to correct the deviation.

These considerations underscore the importance of asking the question, Whose agent is the psychiatrist? and of giving a candid answer to it. The psychiatrist (or non-medical mental health worker) may be the agent of the patient, the relatives, the school, the military services, a business organization, a court of law, and so forth. In speaking of the psychiatrist as the agent of these persons or organizations, it is not implied that his moral values, or his ideas and aims concerning the proper nature of remedial action, must coincide exactly with those of his employer. For example, a patient in individual psychotherapy may believe that his salvation lies in a new marriage; his psychotherapist need not share this hypothesis. As the patient's agent, however, he must not resort to social or legal force to prevent the patient from putting his beliefs into action. If his *contract* is with the patient, the psychiatrist (psychotherapist) may disagree with him or stop his treatment, but he cannot engage others to obstruct the patient's aspirations.[2] Similarly, if a psychiatrist is retained by a court to determine the sanity of an offender, he need not fully share the legal authorities' values and intentions in regard to the criminal, nor the means deemed appropriate for dealing with him; such a psychiatrist cannot testify, however, that the accused is not insane, but that the legislators are—for passing the law that decrees the offender's actions illegal.[3] This sort of opinion could be voiced, of course—but not in a courtroom, and not by a psychiatrist who is there to assist the court in performing its daily work.

To recapitulate: In contemporary social usage, the finding of mental illness is made by establishing a deviance in behavior from certain psychosocial, ethical, or legal norms. The judgment may be made, as in medicine, by the patient, the physician (psychiatrist), or others. Remedial action, finally, tends to be sought in a therapeutic —or covertly medical—framework. This creates a situation in which it is claimed that psychosocial, ethical, and legal deviations can be corrected by medical action. Since

---

[2] See Szasz, T. S.: *The Ethics of Psychoanalysis: The Theory and Method of Autonomous Psychotherapy* (New York: Basic Books, 1965).

[3] See Szasz, T. S.: *Law, Liberty, and Psychiatry: An Inquiry into the Social Uses of Mental Health Practices* (New York: Macmillan, 1963).

medical interventions are designed to remedy only medical problems, it is logically absurd to expect that they will help solve problems whose very existence has been defined and established on non-medical grounds.

IV

Anything that people *do*—in contrast to things that *happen* to them[4]—takes place in a context of value. Hence, no human activity is devoid of moral implications. When the values underlying certain activities are widely shared, those who participate in their pursuit often lose sight of them altogether. The discipline of medicine—both as a pure science (for example, research) and as an applied science or technology (for example, therapy)—contains many ethical considerations and judgments. Unfortunately, these are often denied, minimized, or obscured, for the ideal of the medical profession as well as of the people whom it serves is to have an ostensibly value-free system of medical care. This sentimental notion is expressed by such things as the doctor's willingness to treat patients regardless of their religious or political beliefs. But such claims only serve to obscure the fact that ethical considerations encompass a vast range of human affairs. Making medical practice neutral with respect to some specific issues of moral value (such as race or sex) need not mean, and indeed does not mean, that it can be kept free from others (such as control over pregnancy or regulation of sex relations). Thus, birth control, abortion, homosexuality, suicide, and euthanasia continue to pose major problems in medical ethics.

Psychiatry is much more intimately related to problems of ethics than is medicine in general. I use the word "psychiatry" here to refer to the contemporary discipline concerned with problems in living, and not with diseases of the brain, which belong to neurology. Difficulties in human relations can be analyzed, interpreted, and given meaning only within specific social and ethical contexts. Accordingly, the psychiatrist's socioethical orientations will influence his ideas on what is wrong with the patient, on what deserves comment or interpretation, in which directions change might be desirable, and so forth. Even in medicine proper, these factors play a role, as illustrated by

---

[4]Peters, R. S.: *The Concept of Motivation* (London: Routledge & Kegan Paul, 1958), especially pp. 12-15.

the divergent orientations that physicians, depending on their religious affiliations, have toward such things as birth control and therapeutic abortion.   Can anyone really believe that a psychotherapist's ideas on religion, politics, and related issues play no role in his practical work?   If, on the other hand, they do matter, what are we to infer from it?   Does it not seem reasonable that perhaps we ought to have different psychiatric therapies—each recognized for the ethical positions that it embodies—for, say, Catholics and Jews, religious persons and atheists, democrats and Communists, white supremacists and Negroes, and so on?   Indeed, if we look at the way psychiatry is actually practiced today, especially in the United States, we find that the psychiatric interventions people seek and receive depend more on their socioeconomic status and moral beliefs than on the "mental illnesses" from which they ostensibly suffer.[5]   This fact should occasion no greater surprise than that practicing Catholics rarely frequent birth-control clinics, or that Christian Scientists rarely consult psychoanalysts.

V

The position outlined above, according to which contemporary psychotherapists deal with problems in living, not with mental illnesses and their cures, stands in sharp opposition to the currently prevalent position, according to which psychiatrists treat mental diseases, which are just as "real" and "objective" as bodily diseases.   I submit that the holders of the latter view have no evidence whatever to justify their claim, which is actually a kind of psychiatric propaganda: their aim is to create in the popular mind a confident belief that mental illness is some sort of disease entity, like an infection or a malignancy. If this were true, one could *catch* or *get* a mental illness, one might *have* or *harbor* it, one might *transmit* it to others, and finally one could *get rid* of it.   Not only is there not a shred of evidence to support this idea, but, on the contrary, all the evidence is the other way and supports the view that what people now call mental illnesses are, for the most part, *communications* expressing unacceptable ideas, often framed in an unusual idiom.

[5]Hollingshead, A. B., and Redlich, F. C.: *Social Class and Mental Illness* (New York: Wiley, 1958).

This is not the place to consider in detail the similarities and differences between bodily and mental illnesses. It should suffice to emphasize that whereas the term "bodily illness" refers to physiochemical occurrences that are not affected by being made public, the term "mental illness" refers to sociopsychological events that are crucially affected by being made public. The psychiatrist thus cannot, and does not, stand apart from the person he observes, as the pathologist can and often does. The psychiatrist is committed to some picture of what he considers reality, and to what he thinks society considers reality, and he observes and judges the patient's behavior in the light of these beliefs. The very notion of "mental symptom" or "mental illness" thus implies a covert comparison, and often conflict, between observer and observed, psychiatrist and patient. Though obvious, this fact needs to be re-emphasized, if one wishes, as I do here, to counter the prevailing tendency to deny the moral aspects of psychiatry and to substitute for them allegedly value-free medical concepts and interventions.

Psychotherapy is thus widely practiced as though it entailed nothing other than restoring the patient from a state of mental sickness to one of mental health. While it is generally accepted that mental illness has something to do with man's social or interpersonal relations, it is paradoxically maintained that problems of values—that is, of ethics—do not arise in this process. Freud himself went so far as to assert: "I consider ethics to be taken for granted. Actually I have never done a mean thing."[6] This is an astounding thing to say, especially for someone who had studied man as a social being as deeply as Freud had. I mention it here to show how the notion of "illness"—in the case of psychoanalysis, "psychopathology," or "mental illness"—was used by Freud, and by most of his followers, as a means of classifying certain types of human behavior as falling within the scope of medicine, and hence, by fiat, outside that of ethics. Nevertheless, the stubborn fact remains that, in a sense, much of psychotherapy revolves around nothing other than the elucidation and weighing of goals and values—many of which may be mutually contradictory—and the means whereby they might best be harmonized, realized, or relinquished.

Because the range of human values and of the methods by which they may be attained is so vast, and because many

---

[6]Quoted in Jones, E.: *The Life and Work of Sigmund Freud* (New York: Basic Books, 1957), Vol. III, p. 247.

such ends and means are persistently unacknowledged, conflicts among values are the main source of conflicts in
human relations. Indeed, to say that human relations at
all levels—from mother to child, through husband and wife,
to nation and nation—are fraught with stress, strain, and
disharmony is, once again, to make the obvious explicit.
Yet, what may be obvious may be also poorly understood.
This, I think, is the case here. For it seems to me that
in our scientific theories of behavior we have failed to
accept the simple fact that human relations are inherently
fraught with difficulties, and to make them even relatively
harmonious requires much patience and hard work. I submit
that the idea of mental illness is now being put to work to
obscure certain difficulties that at present may be inherent—not that they need to be unmodifiable—in the social
intercourse of persons. If this is true, the concept functions as a disguise: instead of calling attention to conflicting human needs, aspirations, and values, the concept
of mental illness provides an amoral and impersonal "thing"
—an "illness"—as an explanation for problems in living.
We may recall in this connection that not so long ago it
was devils and witches that were held responsible for man's
problems in living. The belief in mental illness, as something other than man's trouble in getting along with his
fellow man, is the proper heir to the belief in demonology
and witchcraft. Mental illness thus exists or is "real" in
exactly the same sense in which witches existed or were
"real."

VI

While I maintain that mental illnesses do not exist,
I obviously do not imply or mean that the social and psychological occurrences to which this label is attached also
do not exist. Like the personal and social troubles that
people had in the Middle Ages, contemporary human problems
are real enough. It is the labels we give them that concern me, and, having labeled them, what we do about them.
The demonologic concept of problems in living gave rise to
therapy along theological lines. Today, a belief in mental
illness implies—nay, requires—therapy along medical or
psychotherapeutic lines.

I do not here propose to offer a new conception of
"psychiatric illness" or a new form of "therapy." My aim
is more modest and yet also more ambitious. It is to suggest that the phenomena now called mental illnesses be
looked at afresh and more simply, that they be removed from

the category of illnesses, and that they be regarded as the expressions of man's struggle with *the problem of how he should live*. This problem is obviously a vast one, its enormity reflecting not only man's inability to cope with his environment, but even more his increasing self-reflectiveness.

By problems in living, then, I refer to that explosive chain reaction that began with man's fall from divine grace by partaking of the fruit of the tree of knowledge. Man's awareness of himself and of the world about him seems to be a steadily expanding one, bringing in its wake an ever larger *burden of understanding*.[7] This burden is to be expected and must not be misinterpreted. Our only rational means for easing it is more understanding, and appropriate action based on such understanding. The main alternative lies in acting as though the burden were not what in fact we perceive it to be, and taking refuge in an outmoded theological view of man. In such a view, man does not fashion his life and much of his world about him, but merely lives out his fate in a world created by superior beings. This may logically lead to pleading non-responsibility in the face of seemingly unfathomable problems and insurmountable difficulties. Yet, if man fails to take increasing responsibility for his actions, individually as well as collectively, it seems unlikely that some higher power or being would assume this task and carry this burden for him. Moreover, this seems hardly a propitious time in human history for obscuring the issue of man's responsibility for his actions by hiding it behind the skirt of an all-explaining conception of mental illness.

VII

I have tried to show that the notion of mental illness has outlived whatever usefulness it may have had and that it now functions as a myth. As such, it is a true heir to religious myths in general, and to the belief in witchcraft in particular. It was the function of these belief-systems to act as social tranquilizers, fostering hope that mastery of certain problems may be achieved by means of substitutive, symbolic-magical, operations. The concept of mental illness thus serves mainly to obscure the everyday fact

---

[7] In this connection, see Langer, S. K.: *Philosophy in a New Key* [1942] (New York: Mentor Books, 1953), especially Chaps. 5 and 10.

that life for most people is a continuous struggle, not for biological survival, but for a "place in the sun," "peace of mind," or some other meaning or value. Once the needs of preserving the body, and perhaps the race, are satisfied, man faces the problem of personal significance: What should he do with himself? For what should he live? Sustained adherence to the myth of mental illness allows people to avoid facing this problem, believing that mental health, conceived as the absence of mental illness, automatically insures the making of right and safe choices in the conduct of life. But the facts are all the other way. It is the making of wise choices in life that people regard, retrospectively, as evidence of good mental health!

When I assert that mental illness is a myth, I am not saying that personal unhappiness and socially deviant behavior do not exist; what I am saying is that we categorize them as diseases at our own peril.

The expression "mental illness" is a metaphor that we have come to mistake for a fact. We call people physically ill when their body-functioning violates certain anatomical and physiological norms; similarly, we call people mentally ill when their personal conduct violates certain ethical, political, and social norms. This explains why many historical figures, from Jesus to Castro, and from Job to Hitler, have been diagnosed as suffering from this or that psychiatric malady.

Finally, the myth of mental illness encourages us to believe in its logical corollary: that social intercourse would be harmonious, satisfying, and the secure basis of a good life were it not for the disrupting influences of mental illness, or psychopathology. However, universal human happiness, in this form at least, is but another example of a wishful fantasy. I believe that human happiness, or well-being, is possible—not just for a select few, but on a scale hitherto unimaginable. But this can be achieved only if many men, not just a few, are willing and able to confront frankly, and tackle courageously, their ethical, personal, and social conflicts. This means having the courage and integrity to forego waging battles on false fronts, finding solutions for substitute problems—for instance, fighting the battle of stomach acid and chronic fatigue instead of facing up to a marital conflict.

Our adversaries are not demons, witches, fate, or mental illness. We have no enemy that we can fight, exorcise, or dispel by "cure." What we do have are problems in living—whether these be biologic, economic, political, or sociopsychological. In this essay I was concerned only with problems belonging in the last-mentioned category, and within this group mainly with those pertaining to moral values. The field to which modern psychiatry addresses itself is vast, and I made no effort to encompass it all. My argument was limited to the proposition that mental illness is a myth, whose function it is to disguise and thus render more palatable the bitter pill of moral conflicts in human relations.

CRIMINAL PUNISHMENT AND PSYCHIATRIC FALLACIES

Jeffrie G. Murphy

> Experience should teach us to be most on our guard to protect liberty when the government's purposes are beneficent. Men born to freedom are naturally alert to repel invasions of their liberty by evil-minded rulers. The greatest dangers to liberty lurk in insidious encroachment by men of zeal, well meaning but without understanding.—Louis D. Brandeis

Nowhere is this general tendency expressed by Brandeis more prominent than in the area of criminal law. In spite of the reasoned warnings of some writers, we are greeted by a continuous stream of books and articles from psychiatrists and psychoanalysts (and their judicial followers) with one common theme: Criminal punishment is an unscientific survival of barbarism and must be replaced by a system of individual and social therapy.[1] To believe otherwise is to be unscientific and (if the distinction is recognized) immoral.

Reprinted with permission of the publisher from *Law and Society Review*, Volume 4, Number 1, August, 1969.

[1]Standard sources for such a view are Alexander and Staub (1956), and Abrahamsen (1960). This theme is also to be found throughout most of the books produced by winners of the Isaac Ray Award. The most detailed and persuasive case against this position has been made by Szasz (1963). See also Wertham (1955).

The most recent attempt to argue this position comes from the pen of Dr. Karl Menninger. In his Isaac Ray Award book, *The Crime of Punishment* (New York: The Viking Press, 1968), Dr. Menninger launches (in the name of scientific psychiatry) a radical attack on the institution of criminal punishment as it operates in the context of the Anglo-American legal system. He does not wish merely to change parts of the existing system (e.g., the insanity defense) but wants, as an ideal, the elimination of that system entirely. The idea is then to replace this system with a more "scientific" system of social control. With sentencing largely in the control of psychiatrists and other health workers, and increased use of preventive detention, the new system would not be subject to the inefficiencies in controlling crime that characterize our present judicial adversary system.

> The juridical system seems to the doctor to be an unscientific jumble based on clumsy and often self-defeating precedents. Psychiatrists cannot understand why the legal profession continues to lend its support to such a system after the scientific discoveries of the past century have become common knowledge. That this knowledge is coolly ignored and flouted by the system is not so much an affront to the scientists as it is a denial of what was once mystery and is now common sense. . . .

> Being against punishment is not a sentimental conviction. It is a logical conclusion drawn from scientific experience.

> The criminal court should cease with the findings of guilt and innocence, and the "procedure thereafter should be guided by a professional treatment tribunal composed, say, of a psychiatrist, a psychologist, a sociologist or cultural anthropologist, an educator, and a judge with long experience in criminal trials and with special interest in the protection of the rights of those charged with crime."[2]

---

[2] It is significant that the judge is listed last, and that it is not specified whether or not he is to have a decisive veto power with respect to a violation of the prisoner's rights. The judge must simply be "interested" in these rights. The quoted portion of the extract is from Glueck (1936).

Why not a large number of *community safety centers* or crime prevention centers? Such a center would be concerned far more with the prevention of crime than with the arrest and mop-up. Offenders or supposed offenders upon capture would be conveyed immediately to the proper center for identification and examination, and then, if indicated, transferred to a central court and/or diagnostic center. Later—if the judge so desires—a program for continuing correction and/or parole could be assigned, again to the officers of the local center. [pp. 91-92; 204; 139; 268][3]

It is my view that Menninger's position is totally and systematically wrong—that its defense is fabricated solely upon confusions and fallacies (e.g., that moral conclusions can be drawn from scientific premises). And thus, in this brief essay, I should like to expose these confusions and fallacies. This task is important for three main reasons. First, though his book is in many ways erroneous, Dr. Menninger is a popular and widely influential practitioner in his field; and thus it is important to show that he is wrong and to point out the implications of his positions.[4] Second, if my reading constitutes a fair sample, his views are representative of what is a common position among psychiatrists, psychoanalysts, and social scientists in general. Third, and perhaps most important, his views are not merely incorrect, but are of a kind that is socially and politically dangerous.

---

[3] It is important to note that Menninger's recommendations range over *supposed* offenders. Nowhere does he suggest that the operations of these centers (including their detention powers) are to be restricted to those who have been convicted of some legal wrong.

[4] Menninger is often called in for expert testimony at legislative hearings on criminal law reform, for he is taken to be a chief spokesman for a liberal and humane jurisprudence. Such a reputation accounts, I gather, for his selection for a feature interview in the issue of "Psychology Today" devoted to law and psychology (February 1969). Views like Menninger's are surely in part behind the pressure for sexual psychopath laws and other laws for the preventive detention of those (e.g., drug addicts, homosexuals, and drunks) who are judged to present a "potential danger" to the community.

Enough by way of introduction. I should now like to pass to a consideration of the argument itself and the character of the confusions and fallacies it exhibits. These are of three main kinds: moral, legal, and (ironically) scientific.

VALUES, COMPETING VALUES, AND JUSTICE

When we speak of moral values we can mean either of two very different things. First, we can mean those moral beliefs which, as a matter of fact, people or groups of people have. The term "mores" is sometimes used for values in this sense. Second, we can mean those values which ought to be promoted—regardless of whether or not they are in fact promoted or believed valuable. This is the sphere, not of mores, but of ethics or morality proper. And quite clearly the two spheres are different. No one, for example, really believes that it was morally right for the Nazis to persecute the Jews (or that they ought to have done it) just because they believed it was right. One holding such a view would be committed to the proposition that the Nazis were subject to no moral criticism for what they did, and this is absurd. Being wrong about morality may, under some circumstances, excuse; but it can never justify. For example, we may absolve from moral blame the Jehovah's Witness who lets her child die for lack of a transfusion without thereby agreeing that the action performed was really right and ought to be recommended to others.

Now it should be fairly clear that it is only values in the first sense (mores) which can be regarded as discoverable by empirical science. Beliefs about values are not themselves values; they are facts. And thus, like all facts, they are open to the expert analysis of the behavioral scientists. But we must not be deceived into thinking that this expert authority about beliefs or mores extends to pronouncements about what really ought to be done. The scientist, like any other rational and informed man, may certainly be competent in moral discussion; but (and this is crucial) he is not *professionally* competent. Though his studies may give him access to facts relevant in moral argument, they do not give him special insight into moral conclusions. To put the point in another and perhaps even more obvious way: Scientists are professionally competent to tell us the most efficient means for the technical attainment of our goals; but they are not competent *qua* scientists to set those goals or to morally assess the means. Efficiency is not to be identified with morality.

These points are often forgotten when important decisions of social policy are being made. Menninger ignores them entirely:

> The very word *justice* irritates scientists. No surgeon expects to be asked if an operation for cancer is just or not. No doctor will be reproached on the grounds that the dose of penicillin he has prescribed is less or more than *justice* would stipulate. Behavioral scientists regard it as equally absurd to invoke the question of justice in deciding what to do with a woman who cannot resist her propensity to shoplift, or with a man who cannot repress an impulse to assault somebody. This sort of behavior has to be controlled; it has to be discouraged; it has to be *stopped*. This (to the scientist) is a matter of public safety and amicable coexistence, not of justice. . . .
>
> Being against punishment is not a sentimental conviction. It is a logical conclusion drawn from scientific experience. [pp. 17; 204]

It is almost impossible to believe that Menninger intends that we take these remarks seriously. How in the world is "being against" anything logically derivable from scientific premises? (I would love to see such an argument formalized.) And what moral are we supposed to draw from the remarks about the surgeon? It is, of course, true that no surgeon expects to be asked if an operation is just. But neither does he expect to be asked if an operation is hexagonal, approaches middle C, or tastes good. Are we thus to conclude that hexagonality, middle C, and good taste are meaningless concepts?

Of course, Menninger's thesis may be restricted solely to moral values, and the argument may be that their inaccessibility to scientific procedures renders them meaningless. But there is not a single reason to hold such a view (to hold that "meaningful" means "scientifically useful"); and, in fact, I do not think that Menninger himself really holds such a view—even if he does espouse it in theory. To say that a concept is meaningless and to really believe this are two different things. For example: Does Menninger really believe that, if police broke into his home and detained him for months without trial because some psychiatrist thought he was dangerous, he would be talking nonsense if he described his treatment as unjust? I seriously doubt it.

What is really going on in the quoted passage is, I think, the following: Menninger has noted that science, as a social institution,[5] has incarnate in it certain mores. And it is Menninger's view that these mores ought to be elevated to a more influential place in our moral decisions than they now occupy. But this is itself a piece of moral advice—a judgment of value priority and not of fact—and so it is open to the same kinds of standards we use in evaluating any moral recommendation. No matter how much Menninger propagandizes for the scientific status of his recommendations, the fact remains that they are recommendations and not findings. Thus with respect to them he has no professional competence. We must, therefore, evaluate his proposals in the light of all those considerations which are relevant from the moral point of view.

What are these considerations? To avoid starting a treatise in moral philosophy, I shall state rather dogmatically that there are two main kinds of considerations relevant to moral evaluation: considerations of utility; and considerations of justice. Utilitarian considerations are concerned with promoting the greatest amount of happiness and well-being in the world as possible. Considerations of justice function as checks on social utility, weighing against promoting happiness if in so doing some people must be treated unfairly in the process. These considerations compete and often have to be weighed against each other. But it is just this competitive nature of basic moral values that Menninger fails to appreciate. In effect, he opts for considerations of utility (e.g., health and public safety) to the exclusion of considerations of justice. And he does this with a vengeance:

> Eliminating one offender who happens to get caught *weakens* public security by creating a false sense of diminished danger through a definite remedial measure. Actually, it does not remedy anything, and it bypasses completely the real and unsolved problem of how to *identify, detect, and detain potentially dangerous citizens.* [p. 108]

The argument here seems to be that since health is the predominant value in psychiatry, its social analogue (public

---

[5]For an elaboration of the institutional character of science, and of psychiatry in particular, see the material by Szasz in Schoeck and Wiggins (1962).

safety) ought to be the predominant political value. What
is being suggested is that we deprive people of their liberty as a kind of preventive medicine, and this is clearly
to choose social utility over one of the mainstays of criminal justice: procedural due process.

Our system of criminal due process involves such guarantees as the following: (1) No man is to be deprived of
his liberty for what he is or what he might do, but only because he has in fact violated some legal prohibition. This
is the traditional requirement for an overt act. (2) A man
is to be presumed innocent. This means that the state must
prove its case beyond a reasonable doubt to a jury of the
defendant's peers and that the defendant may exploit the
adversary system to its full to make such proof impossible.
(3) A man is to be responsible only for what he has done as
an individual. He is not to be held guilty because others
like him often commit crimes.[6]   (4) A man is not to be
forced to testify against himself, to help the state in its
attempt to deprive him of his liberty.

Such guarantees would have no place in a purely therapeutic or preventive context, and Menninger quite correctly
argues that the procedures they involve are not the best
way to arrive at truth and thus that they interfere with
the efficiency of securing public safety (pp. 53 ff.). But
of course they do; *that is their very function*! They aim,
not at the discovery of truth, but at the protection of the
defendant in his otherwise unequal battle with the state.
And our employment of these procedures tests the sincerity
of our commitment to what is often claimed as the basic moral value in our system of criminal justice—namely, the belief that it is better to free some guilty persons than to
convict some innocent ones.

We can begin to understand the tensions inherent in
the criminal process only if we realize how the values of
justice and due process compete with the utilitarian value
of public safety.[7]   If we were only interested in public

---

[6]It is often not noticed that provisions for preventive detention (especially if they rest on statistical evidence)
tend to involve *collective* rather than individual criteria
for guilt. It is judged that Jones is to be detained because he is a member of some class (e.g., vagrants) which
manifests a high crime rate. This point is totally missed
in the otherwise excellent article on preventive detention
by Dershowitz in the "New York Review" (13 March 1969).

[7]An important recent book, Packer (1968), illuminates the
tension inherent in our system of criminal punishment by
contrasting the "crime control model" with the "due process
model."

safety, we would let the police coerce confessions, deny
any excuses for wrongdoing, and even punish some innocent
people to keep everyone else careful. One only has to call
to mind Nazi Germany, Soviet Russia, and present-day South
Africa and Greece for a picture of the logical outcome of a
society which places order and public safety over all values of justice. (Almost unbelievably, from a man famous for
his liberal and benevolent humanism, Menninger looks with
wistful longing at the security provided by the legal systems of Greece and China!) [p. 277]

Being involuntarily deprived of our liberty (even by a
benevolent Dr. Menninger who calls it therapy rather than
punishment) is an evil most of us would like to avoid—particularly if we have done nothing wrong, but only appear to
have "dangerous tendencies." Thus we should be quite stu-
pid to take steps that would involve giving up the guarantees which help us avoid this evil. Menninger, of course,
does not explicitly say that he is against due process (who
would?); but if he is not against it, then his set of proposals involves a fundamental paradox. For if his proposed
system is to retain all present guarantees to preserve fairly the freedom of each individual, why suppose that it will
be any more efficient than present practices? To make it
more efficient, some due process will necessarily have to
be sacrificed.

THE SCIENTIFIC EXAMINATION OF DETERRENCE THEORY

It is absurd to characterize public safety as the *real*
problem of criminal law (as though other issues, like due
process, are illusions), but surely such safety is admittedly one of the important values that any system of criminal
law must seek to promote. And so it is worth inquiring if
it is even true that, as a matter of fact, our present system of criminal punishment fails to work in providing for
our security. Here we are dealing with an empirical scientific issue, and one would think that Menninger would be
on safe ground. But he is not. He tells us that we must
replace punishment with therapy because the only possible
defense for punishment is deterrence theory; and this theory is known to be false.[8] But he is quite wrong here.

---

[8]Menninger dismisses entirely the arguments of those who
have advocated a retributive theory of punishment. For example, he fails to consider the possible alteration in our
concept of a human being (and how we *treat* human beings) if
we cease to regard people as agents of dignity and responsibility who are capable of being blameworthy for what they

Deterrence theory is not known to be false, and Menninger fails to show that it is false. His whole case is one of ridicule supported by no evidence whatsoever. Here is all that he says to support his attack on deterrence theory:

> ["Brushes" with the law] are dreary, repetitious crises in the dismal, dreary life of one of the miserable ones. They are signals of distress, signals of failure, signals of crises which society sees primarily in terms of *its* annoyance, *its* irritation, *its* injury. They are the spasms and struggles and convulsions of a submarginal human being trying to make it in our complex society with inadequate equipment and inadequate preparations.

> [We have described] a man who seemed to have spent his life going from one difficulty into another, into the jail and out of it, only to get back in again, like one caught in a revolving door. It ended in death. The grinding mills of the law did nothing for Crow; they cost Kansas City a lot of money, mostly wasted. It gave a score of people something to do, mostly useless. One might wonder what could have been done early in this chap's life to have protected his victims better. [pp. 19; 21-22]

It is almost impossible to know what Menninger expects us to conclude from these passages, for they appear to involve at least two gross confusions. First, as a psychiatrist, Menninger has perhaps seen a limited number of criminals who really are compulsive and thus are nondeterrable. And the existence of such people certainly points up a distinct failure within our system of criminal punishment. But they will indict the system *as a whole* only if they can be regarded as representative of criminality in general. But this is just the conclusion we may not draw on the basis of so limited a sample. What about the college student who smokes marijuana, or the Martin Luther King who engages in civil disobedience, or the university professor who omits some lecture fees on his tax return? These are all legally criminals, but are their actions "the spasms and

---

[8](cont.) do. To see that one can offer a retributive theory which is something more than disguised vengeance, consult Morris (1968).

struggles and convulsions of a submarginal human being"?
Note what Menninger says:

> "Ah," the reader will say, "perhaps what you say
> is true in those violent rape and murder cases,
> but take everyday bank robbing and check forging
> and stealing—you cannot tell me that these peo-
> ple are not out for the money!"
>
> I would not deny that money is desired and ob-
> tained, but I would also say that the *taking* of
> money from the victim by these devices means some-
> thing special, and something quite different from
> what you think it does. [p. 183]

Here we enter the world of apparent fantasy. The actions of our pot smoker, our civil disobedient, and our tax
evader are all symbolic of something unconscious. But,
even if this is true, just how is it relevant? It will, presumably, be relevant only if it is the case that these unconscious motives can be said to compel the agent in such a
way that he is not responsible and thus not a proper object
for punishment. But, having ridiculed the notions of fault
and responsibility, and having modestly declared the inability of the psychiatrist in a courtroom ever to say with any
certainty that an action of a particular man was compulsive
(and thus nonresponsible) because of mental disorder (pp.
312 ff.), Menninger can hardly go forth and present a perfectly general theory of determinism for all human action.
A general theory of determinism, if it rests on no induc-
tive basis of established particular cases, is a metaphysical theory and not a scientific conclusion. And if, as a
metaphysical theory, it requires that we stop distinguishing the actions of a Martin Luther King from those of a
Daniel M'Naghten, then it is a useless bit of stipulation.
    The second confusion in Menninger's rejection of deter-
rence theory is related to the first. It is the failure to
distinguish special from general deterrence.[9]   He thus
makes a quite misleading use of the facts of recidivism.
Recidivism surely shows that criminal punishment does not
deter many of the particular people who are caught up in
the criminal process. But this fact is quite irrelevant to
the claim that having a deterrence system has the general
effect of keeping many members of society from ever engaging in criminal conduct and thus making themselves eligible

---

[9]For more on this distinction, see Packer (1968).

for the process. It is not difficult to believe, for example, that one major reason why more of us do not smoke marijuana or submit fraudulent tax returns is that we are deterred by the criminal penalties. To scientifically refute deterrence theory, and thus provide a basis for replacing our entire system of punishment with something else, it would have to be shown that substantial numbers of those who do not now commit crimes would continue to be law-abiding if all criminal sanctions were abolished. But we have no evidence at all on this complex counterfactual. And, in the absence of any such evidence, it is irresponsible to ridicule and reject deterrence theory in the name of science.

LAW AND PSYCHIATRY

The psychiatrist, Menninger argues, should be removed from the courtroom entirely (p. 138). I have some sympathy with these sentiments, but not for the reasons Menninger offers. His suggestion (a not unfamiliar one) is that at the most psychiatric testimony is relevant to establishing the *mens rea* of the offense—that is, the mental element which establishes the degree of personal responsibility or blameworthiness for what was done. But, with much invective and ridicule, Menninger says that we should drop inquiries into mens rea entirely. We should simply inquire if the offense was committed, regardless of the mental state with which it was committed. If we determine that the prisoner (patient?) did commit the offense, he should be turned over to a team of psychiatrists and other experts. They would then inquire into his mental state in order to determine how long to detain him for society's protection and his own rehabilitation (pp. 113 ff., 139).

Though this proposal has a plausible ring to it, it is in fact almost impossible to give it a coherent interpretation. How, for example, can one convict for the offense alone when a mens rea is typically a material (i.e., defining) element of the offense itself? Was the offense murder or manslaughter? The question cannot be answered without an inquiry into mens rea—i.e., did the actor have malice aforethought? The revisions and complexities that elimination of mens rea would introduce into our legal system are vast. If he is aware of such problems, Menninger totally ignores them.[10]

---

[10] Some psychiatrists try to meet this worry by advocating a *bifurcated trial* (something along the lines of the Cali-

Suppose, however, we did eliminate mens rea at the trial and then had our fellow convicted for the offense of (say) "causally bringing about the death of another human being." And now he is turned over to psychiatrists. The kinds of problems that might arise become obvious. Suppose he caused the death by nonculpable accident (that is, he did not even have what we would now call the mens rea of negligence). Further suppose that, upon examination, he was found to be "potentially dangerous." Should he be locked up for a period of enforced therapy (perhaps for life) even though he had committed no wrong at all? Or consider trivial offenders. Should a man who compulsively cashes bad checks be sent to a mental institution for an indeterminate period because he is hopeless? The questions are not medical or scientific. They are questions of *moral* and *political decision*, and we should be foolish to entrust our responsibility for them to a team of "experts." Criminal judges, whatever their weaknesses, are at least bound by the rules of our community. They may not, as may psychiatrists, act on their own personal conceptions of what is good for or dangerous to the community.

An actual example is illustrative here: The closest existing analogue to what Menninger advocates is to be found in the American juvenile courts. Here it has been traditional to suspend guarantees of due process because the state was presumably acting in the benevolent interest of the juvenile rather than as a punishing agent. (It is really astounding how we can deceive ourselves merely by changing the name of what we do.) A reading of the opinion of Justice Fortas in the 1967 Gault case (where some due process is finally guaranteed to juveniles) should give us pause before we hand over any other area of human liberty to benevolent experts.[11] Menninger is right in his premise that

---

[10](cont.) fornia practice). There is to be a guilt trial and a sanity trial. At the former, considerations of mens rea will be relevant and allowed. All questions of sanity, however, will be reserved for the second trial; and thus it is only at this second trial that psychiatric testimony will be allowed. This system, however, will fail for the following reason: If a man is insane, he might be incapable of having the mens rea required for the commission of the offense. It would thus deny him due process to exclude psychiatric testimony from the first trial. See People v. Wells.

[11]See also the horror stories of arbitrary mental commitment cited by Szasz (1963). Szasz has raised profound questions and deserves a serious answer. Menninger simply pro-

science and due process do not mix well. The moral to be
drawn, however, is the following: Beware of psychiatrists
bearing gifts.

Near the end of his argument, after dismissing the notions of blameworthiness and responsibility, Menninger suggests that instead of punishing people we might impose *penalties* on them:

> If a burglar takes my property, I would like to
> have it returned or paid for by him if possible,
> and the state ought to be reimbursed for its
> costs, too. This could be forcibly required to
> come from the burglar. This would be equitable;
> it would be just, and it would not be "punitive."
> [p. 203]

Just how "punitive" this would be depends, I suppose,
on just how rich the burglar is and on just what happens to
him for nonpayment. But this is not the objection I want
to pursue. What interests me is the suggestion that criminal law ought to move toward becoming a part of tort law—
the law of damages for harms done not involving breach of
contract. Does Menninger find damages attractive for any
other reason than that they are not *called* "punishment"?
After all, in tort law conditions of blameworthiness and
responsibility are relevant. We do not normally make a man
pay damages in the absence of any fault on his part. We
rather, as the phrase goes, let the loss lie where it falls.
If I am not negligent, then normally (though not always) I
am not liable for damages. What if Menninger's burglar was
a man who believed the property was his own, or who was
sleepwalking, or caused damage in an epileptic seizure, or
took it to use for his self-defense? Judgments of liability for damages might well differ in all these cases. And
so even this move toward tort will not allow us to avoid
something like the criminal law's mens rea.

---

[11] (cont.) poses to eliminate such abuses by training police
and mental health workers with the proper *therapeutic attitudes* (pp. 260; 271). But this misses the point entirely;
benevolence is not justice, and therapeutic attitudes are
not necessarily due process attitudes. Menninger might also recall Lord Acton's reminder about the corruptive nature
of power. Or does he perhaps think that psychiatrists are
immune from such corruption? Nice, benevolent people are
perhaps preferable to mean, stubborn ones, but it does not
follow from this that the former should be allowed to coerce and confine the latter.

CONCLUSION

Dr. Menninger is a decent and generous man, and I do not mean to charge that he intentionally advocates injustice. He has simply fallen victim to the trap which often leads benevolent men to pursue an unjust course: the single-minded pursuit of one social goal to the exclusion of all others. In addressing himself to the limited goals of public safety and rehabilitation, he does highlight some terrible abuses and inadequacies that exist within our present system of criminal punishment. What we do not get from him, however, is a persuasive case against that system itself.

I would not pose as a man devoted to our system of criminal punishment. It contains much hypocrisy and moral pretension and is, at best, a necessary evil. However, in spite of its admitted shortcomings, it does appear to do at least a tolerable job of balancing public safety against the often competing values of liberty and due process. And thus there is a presumption in its favor. By this I mean nothing more than that the burden of proof lies on the man who would replace it to provide careful arguments which are conceptually clear, empirically well-founded, and morally cogent. It is just this burden which Dr. Menninger has failed totally to bear.

CASES

People v. Wells (1949) Cal. 2d 33: 330; P. 2d. 202: 53.
In re Gault (1967) U.S. 387: 1.

REFERENCES

Abrahamsen, D. (1960) *The Psychology of Crime*. New York: Columbia Univ. Press.

Alexander, F. and H. Staub (1956) *The Criminal, the Judge and the Public: A Psychological Analysis*. Glencoe: Free Press.

Glueck, S. (1936) *Crime and Justice*. Boston: Little, Brown.

Morris, H. (1968) "Persons and punishment." *Monist* 52 (October): 475-501.

Packer, H. L. (1968) *The Limits of the Criminal Sanction*. Stanford: Stanford Univ. Press.

Schoeck, H. and J. W. Wiggins (1962) [eds.] *Psychiatry and Responsibility*. Princeton: Van Nostrand.

Szasz, T. S. (1963) *Law, Liberty, and Psychiatry*. New York: Macmillan.

Wertham, F. (1955) "Psychoauthoritarianism and the law." *Univ. of Chicago Law Rev.* 22 (Winter): 336-338.

PREVENTIVE DETENTION AND PSYCHIATRY

Jeffrie G. Murphy

> They that can give up essential liberty to obtain
> a little temporary safety, deserve neither liber-
> ty nor safety.—*Benjamin Franklin*

It is no surprise that our society contains people who
support the idea of preventive detention. What is surprising is that this support cuts across the usual political
ideologies and allegiances. Dr. Karl Menninger, a benevolent humanist, and Attorney General Mitchell, a law-and-
order hard-liner, have both recently come out in support of
the idea of preventive detention as a partial solution to
the crime problem—Menninger in his *The Crime of Punishment*
(Viking, 1968) and Mitchell in proposed criminal legislation for the District of Columbia.[1]

Preventive detention, generally speaking, consists in
locking people up for what they *might* do, rather than for
what they have in fact done. It is generally taught that
our legal system does not in theory countenance such proceedings. But, of course, it does countenance and even encourage them in fact—though generally under some euphemistic description. Obvious examples are status crimes (like
vagrancy), refusal of bail for those accused—though not
convicted—of crime, involuntary commitment for the "insane," and wide judicial discretion in matters of parole
and length of sentence. Such discretion might allow a
judge to extend a man's sentence (for either punishment or
therapy) if he believes the man is still prone to crime.
The old retributive idea that a man, having paid the
price, may regain his liberty is being replaced with the

Reprinted with permission of the publisher from *Dissent*,
September-October, 1970, pp. 448-450 and 460.

[1]For a discussion of Menninger's views, see my article
"Criminal Punishment and Psychiatric Fallacies," In *Law
and Society Review*, August 1969, pp. 111-122. Menninger
would no doubt be an opponent of any preventive detention
that would not provide for therapy.

idea that liberty depends on something more—on his "rehabilitation."

Both the attractiveness and danger of these proposals
lie in their scientific and even benevolent facade—especially if detention is coupled with therapy. Who could object to rehabilitation? It seems more sensible than traditional punishment. And even those too toughminded to
object to vengeance *simpliciter* must admit that mere vengeance does not work. The people we put in prisons because
they have harmed us get out, harm us again, and return to
prison—a seemingly useless waste of time and resources.
So, for once, it seems that the interests of benevolent men,
prone to forgive the criminal, and harsh men, whose only
concern is to prevent crime, coincide. Once we have determined that a man is dangerous, why wait until he actually
does harm? Why not *prevent* the harm by detaining him in
advance? Objections we might feel to this can be dispelled
if preventive detention is coupled with therapy and rehabilitation. Punishing a man for what he might do is admittedly bad; but, we are to be led to believe, rehabilitating a
man for what he might do is not. We can help the man and
society at the same time.

This rosy picture is too good to be true. Let me outline the most important, and in my judgment fatal, objections to preventive detention—whether punitive or therapeutic.

1. PREDICTION AND PRINCIPLE

One morally ineffectual way in which people sometimes
seek to oppose preventive detention is to rest their case
against it solely on the difficulty of prediction. This
allows them to avoid the troublesome appeal to moral values. Professor Alan Dershowitz of the Harvard Law School,
for example, has argued that no important issues of principle are involved in preventive detention. The important
objection, in his judgment, is practical—the difficulty of
accurate prediction and the institutional pressures that
make a prediction of dangerousness much more likely than a
prediction of non-dangerousness.

> When we establish rules for convicting the guilty,
> we do not require certainty; we only require that
> guilt be proved "beyond a reasonable doubt". . . .
> What difference is there between imprisoning a man
> for past crimes on the basis of "statistical like-
> lihood" and detaining him to prevent future crimes

on the same kind of less-than-certain information? The important difference here may not be
one of principle; it may be, as Justice Holmes
said all legal issues are, one of degree.

The most serious danger inherent in any
system of preventive detention is that it always
seems to be working well, even when it is performing dismally; this is so because it is the
nature of any system of preventive detention to
display its meager successes in preventing crime
while hiding its errors. One such area . . . is
the confinement of the mentally ill on the basis
of psychiatric prediction of injurious conduct.
. . . The psychiatrist almost never learns about
his erroneous predictions of violence. But he
almost always learns about his erroneous predictions of non-violence—often from newspaper head-
lines announcing the crime. The fact that the
errors of underestimating the possibilities of
violence are more visible than errors of over-
estimating inclines the psychiatrist—whether
consciously or unconsciously—to err on the side
of confining rather than of releasing. His *modus
operandi* becomes: When in doubt, don't let him
out.[2]

Dershowitz's practical case is important. But surely
he is wrong on the question of principle. First, it is
important to see that the case for preventive detention is
based on a kind of evidence that would be *constitutionally
inadmissible in a criminal trial*. One may not, in a trial,
introduce statistical evidence against the defendant—
evidence that he is a member of a social group (say, vagrants) which manifests a high crime rate. Evidence at a
criminal trial is, to be sure, less than certain, but this
does not make it statistical evidence. To allow statistical evidence would represent a shift from an individualized
conception of guilt to a collective or group criterion.
This would seem a kind of guilt by association and would
involve a moral regression of utmost gravity. It would
represent a way of circumventing a basic rule of procedural

---

[2]"On Preventive Detention," *New York Review*, March 13, 1969,
pp. 22-27.

due process and would surely, therefore, raise a vital issue of principle.[3]

Second, it is important to see that competing models of human nature are involved here. Traditionally, the criminal law has regarded men as agents of freedom and dignity—agents who, up to the very last minute, are capable of having changes of heart, of deciding *not* to perform a certain evil action in the face of even a very high probability that they will perform it. This is why the criminal law does not punish for merely intending, planning, and preparing for a crime. It also explains, in part, why the criminal law punishes less severely for attempts than for completed crimes. Preventive detention, of course, rests upon a totally different model: locate a man in a sociological framework and deal with him accordingly—deal with him, as you would with an object, solely in terms of prediction and control. As in so many other areas of contemporary life, an elevation of the importance of technology (especially that of the social sciences) results in the demotion of the importance of humanity, freedom, and dignity as these concepts have been traditionally understood.

2. THERAPY AND PUNISHMENT

If preventive detention is coupled with therapy, objections to the program tend to be blunted. But they should not be. We should delude ourselves neither about the efficacy of therapy nor about its benevolence and justice. Attempts at criminal rehabilitation have not been markedly successful. They represent the promises of psychology rather than a fulfillment. Also, it is dangerously simple-minded to assume the moral preferability of a therapy system to a punishing system. For the central and often ignored point is that common to both criminal punishment and

---

[3]This circumvention would be purely linguistic. That is, we would not *call* the preventive detention hearing a trial. We could then claim that the constitutional bar on statistical evidence did not here apply since the proceedings did not constitute a criminal trial. But we would, of course, be doing substantively exactly the same thing to the defendant. This may sound outlandish, but intelligent men have been taken in by even less: Consider, by way of example, how the injustices of the juvenile court system were masked by benevolent rhetoric—rhetoric finally exploded by the Supreme Court's 1967 Gault decision.

preventive rehabilitation is the *involuntary deprivation of liberty*. It is at least *prima facie* wrong to do to a man what he does not want done to him, to confine him against his will, no matter whether you call what you do to him punishment or therapy, or whether you call where you put him a prison or a hospital. If therapy is so benevolent and glorious, and rehabilitation so desirable, how can we account for the fact that people resist it as much as (sometimes more than) punishment? When we are to be punished, we at least know what we are bargaining for. Not so when we believe that someone is going to attempt to restructure our personality against our will.

Now I am not, let me insist, an opponent of therapy or rehabilitation. Quite the contrary. It is a moral disgrace that neither our prisons nor our state mental hospitals provide decent opportunities for meaningful therapy—little more than monthly talks with a psychiatrist or a few electric shock treatments. What I do oppose is the *involuntary* deprivation of liberty for the purpose of therapy, for the attempt at rehabilitation *against the will* of the man to be rehabilitated. Punitive detention is at least honest. It is oppressive and cruel, and everyone knows it. Thus, we are alert to guard our liberty against it. Therapeutic detention, however, masks practically identical treatment with the slogans of benevolence. But Big Brother is Big Brother—even if he wears a Jesus costume.

3. IDEOLOGY AND REHABILITATION

Another important and seldom noted problem is the extent to which political preference and ideology may affect our application of a notion like "needs rehabilitation."[4] Consider, for example, the psychiatric concept of the *psychopathic* or *sociopathic* personality. Psychopaths are said to "lack a moral sense" and to "show no normal care and concern for the interests of others." But just imagine the political danger of setting up persons with the authority

---

[4]Thomas Szasz makes a similar point about the concept "mentally ill" in his *The Myth of Mental Illness* (Harper, 1961). Not being a trained psychiatrist, I am not competent to pronounce on his claim that *all* so-called "mental illness" may be so analyzed. Surely at least some cases may be, and this in itself is enough to raise substantial political worries.

to deprive people of their liberty on such nebulous grounds.
How would Martin Luther King have fared at the hands of
Southern state psychiatrists? How would the Black Panthers
fare at the hands of some Northern state psychiatrists?
Psychiatrists, especially state psychiatrists, are not immune from the tendency to project their own fears and hos-
tilities onto the man they are evaluating.[5] What hope
would any of us have under a system of preventive detention
based on such criteria as "probably dangerous" or "lacks a
moral sense"? This is not to say, of course, that all the
people declared dangerous by judges and psychiatrists are
in fact quite safe. Some of them are indeed frighteningly
dangerous. But surely free men must have the courage to
brave this sort of danger (the danger of waiting until the
people actually commit a criminal act before detaining them)
—at least if we consider the *1984* alternative.

Finally, we should take an honest look at what sometimes counts as rehabilitation in our state hospitals and
prisons. We should not kid ourselves into believing that
those pronounced rehabilitated have necessarily developed
morally sensitive and highly principled characters. Quite
the contrary may be the case. They may have simply learned
to identify with the aggressor and adapt to repression, to
have learned the dubious virtues of civility and conformity,
to have learned to do what others want them to do rather
than what their own characters dictate. Some inmates will
not so compromise, but they of course then pay the price of
staying longer (in either prison or hospital) than their
more pliable fellows.

> It may be that I can harm myself by speaking
> frankly and directly, but I do not care about
> that at all. Of course I want to get out of
> prison, badly, but I shall get out some day.
> I am more concerned with what I am going to be
> after I get out. I know that by following the
> course which I have charted I will find my sal-
> vation. If I had followed the path laid down
> for me by the officials, I'd undoubtedly have

---

[5]*State* psychiatrists are particularly to be feared for the
obvious reason that they act, not as the agent of the defendant, but as a paid arm of the established political
structure. Surely some of them will (as would some of us
in similar roles) be corrupted away from objectivity. Indeed, labels like "lacks a moral sense" invite such corruption.

long since been out of prison—but I'd be less of
a man. I'd be weaker and less certain of where
I want to go, what I want to do, and how to go
about it.[6]

Here is a man holding on to his personal integrity
against heavy odds, odds which are probably even greater
in state mental hospitals than in state prisons.

The protagonist of Anthony Burgess's novel *A Clockwork
Orange* acts on violent impulses. Diagnosed a criminal psychopath, he is subjected to Ludovico's Technique—a refined
Pavlovian technique that conditions in him utter revulsion
to any form of violence. It also results, alas, in his being rendered incapable of appreciating the music of Beetho-
ven—the one experience in his previous life that had any
meaning or character. There is a lesson here.

[6]Eldridge Cleaver, *Soul on Ice* (Delta, 1968), p. 17.

CRIME, CLUTCHABILITY, AND INDIVIDUATED TREATMENT

Joel Feinberg

That justice consists in treating similar cases in
similar ways and dissimilar cases in dissimilar ways is one
of the oldest philosophical truisms. Those who are accused
of committing serious crimes are all similar in at least
that respect, and as a consequence they are treated in
similar ways—tried, acquitted or convicted, released or
punished (usually) by incarceration in a prison. Yet there
are many differences between these persons that might well

From Joel Feinberg, *Doing and Deserving* (Princeton, N.J.:
Princeton University Press, 1970), pp. 252-271. Copyright
© 1970 by Princeton University Press. Reprinted with permission of Princeton University Press. Joel Feinberg is
Professor of Philosophy at Rockefeller University and is
the author of numerous articles in moral and legal philosophy.

be the basis for dissimilar treatment. The difference that
has received most attention recently is that some of them
are psychologically normal and others mentally ill; but
this, of course, is not the only relevant difference between
them, or even necessarily the most prominent or important.
Still, it is a useful focus for a moralist's attention
since it serves well to highlight a problem: persons who
are *both* similar and dissimilar in morally relevant respects should be treated in ways that are both similar and
dissimilar, but such treatment would require institutional
proliferation of a magnitude to constitute itself a major
threat to justice and liberty.

It is not always clear what we are talking about, or
whether we are making any sense at all, when we talk about
mental illness, and it is even less clear why we should regard mental illness as a bar to moral blame or criminal
punishment. Part of this confusion stems from the generic
notions of health and sickness themselves; part is peculiar
to the notion of mental disease; and part stems from linger-
ing uncertainties about the point of blame and punishment.

I

Central to the concept of disease in general is the
idea of the impairment of a vital function, that is, a
function of some organ or faculty upon which the important
or proper functioning of the whole organism depends.[1] To
ascribe a function to a component part of an organic system[2]

---

[1]Disease thus differs from local disorders in that its impairments of part-functions lead to a generalized breakdown
of the whole organism. One's body as a whole can continue
to function more or less efficiently with a cut finger or a
broken arm, but not when it is in high fever, nausea, ver-
tigo, or extreme debility.

[2]Only living organisms are ever called healthy or sick,
though complex machines are often enough honored by these
terms through courtesy of metaphor. Machines, of course,
are different in many ways from living things. For the
most part, only the latter are capable of growth and repro-
duction, for example. But machines and living bodies are
perfectly similar in one important respect: both are *organic systems*, that is, complexes composed of component parts
related in such a way that the macroscopic functioning of
the whole depends on the microscopic functioning of the
parts, and to some extent, at least, vice versa.

—a liver or a carburetor—is to say that, in virtue of its morphological structure and its place in the general economy of components, it behaves in a certain way and, further, that the macroscopic functioning of the whole system causally depends upon its behaving in this way. It may seem, then, that ascription of functions to component parts or subsystems is a wholly factual matter consisting of, first, a description of a part's effects and, second, a causal judgment that these effects are necessary conditions for the occurrence of some more comprehensive effects. But the illusion of value-neutrality vanishes when we come to ascribe a function to the organic system itself.[3] We do not turn to the medical profession to learn the function of a man.

It follows that even statements ascribing functions to component organs will not be entirely value-neutral, for the macroscopic functions for which their effects are necessary conditions will contain value specifications in *their* descriptions. Thus Carl Hempel interprets the statement that the heartbeat in vertebrates has the function of circulating the blood to mean that "the heartbeat *has the effect* of circulating the blood, and this ensures the satisfaction of certain conditions (supply of nutriment and removal of waste) that are necessary for the *proper working* of the organism."[4] (In another formulation Hempel refers to conditions "necessary for the system's remaining in adequate, or effective, or proper, working order.")[5] Now there is in fact very little disagreement among us over what constitutes the proper working order of the human *body*. We all

---

[3]With a machine or artifact the illusion may persist: the "true function" of a knife or an automobile may be the purpose for which it was designed, or perhaps the task for which it is best suited by its nature. Even a plant or tree might be claimed to have as its "true" or "proper" function the performing of some service for us—yielding fruit or shade. But it becomes quite implausible to interpret judgments about the proper function of an animal—especially a human animal—as pure matters of technological or biological fact.

[4]"The Logic of Functional Analysis," in *Symposium on Sociological Theory*, ed. Llewellyn Gross (New York: Harper & Row, 1959); reprinted in *Purpose in Nature*, ed. John V. Canfield (Englewood Cliffs: Prentice-Hall, 1966). The quote is on page 98 of the latter volume. Italics have been added.

[5]*Ibid.*, 99.

would agree that a body with paralyzed limbs was no more in "good working order" than a car with flat tires; and, in general, our culture identifies bodily health with vigor and vitality. But we can imagine a society of mystics or ascetics who find vitality a kind of nervous distraction (much as we regard hyperthyroid activity)—a frustrating barrier to contemplation and mystic experience and a source of material needs that make constant and unreasonable demands for gratification. Such a group might regard bodily vitality as a sickness and certain kinds of vapidity and feebleness as exemplary health. Our disagreement with these people clearly would not be a purely medical matter.[6]

II

If mental illness shares the generic character of sickness, it must then consist in the disabling impairment of some vital mental function, such as reasoning, remembering, feeling, or imagining. The most conspicuous mental illnesses are those that involve impairment of the cognitive faculties and consequent chronic irrationality of one kind or another. Most forms of "proper functioning" are quite impossible for a person whose memory has totally failed, or who is incapable of drawing inferences or of distinguishing fact from fantasy. There is general agreement among us that the sorts of incapacities directly consequent upon these functional failures constitute "being out of proper working order" and, therefore, being sick.

Much more difficult questions are posed by the mental dysfunctions that are noncognitive. Persons are now com-

---

[6] Cf. the following "medical" statement in which a controversial value judgment is hardly disguised at all: "Hormone therapy is based on the theory that the female change of life should be treated as a preventable disease. 'Menopause,' says Dr. Joseph W. Goldzieher . . . 'is one of nature's mistakes.'" *Newsweek*, April 3, 1967, 55.

Steffi Lewis has argued that, if ninety percent of humanity came, through evolution, to be able to digest cellulose, and if, further, this capacity became importantly useful (perhaps through critical shortages of other foods), the remaining ten percent (who are physiologically exactly the same as us, their ancestors) would quite properly be said to be deformed, or sick, or lacking in "basic" human equipment. What is "healty," then, is relative to our resources, technical capacities, and purposes.

monly called mentally ill when their affective or emotional or volitional faculties are awry, even when there is no attendant cognitive dysfunction. If one's "superego" is a mental faculty, and it fails to instruct or restrain, is its possessor mentally ill? Surely, there is one obvious sense in which no person can function "properly" if he has no conscience. And one might argue that any person who commits batteries, rapes, and murders is not in "good working order" and that certain moral norms, therefore, must be included among the criteria of proper functioning. If failure to act in accordance with the norms of a rational morality is the necessary consequence of some misfunction of mental faculty, such as failure of memory, deformity of conscience, caprice of will, hollowness of affect, perhaps even persistent deviant desires, then such immoral acts are, by definition, "sick." And, indeed, how can any organic system be out of proper working order unless there is some component that is misfiring? If an automobile won't run or runs only with great difficulty, it cannot possibly be that all its parts and component systems are in good working order. By this mode of argument, inclusion of noncognitive faculties among the "components" whose part-failure can cause overall malfunction leads us to the brink of the theory that *all* patently immoral behavior is sick and, therefore, excused.[7] And yet, despite this unwelcome apparent

---

[7]One can avoid tumbling into the Erewhonian chasm by denying that a *person* is an organic system, or by denying that moral norms belong among the norms of "proper functioning," or by denying the analogy between the relation that connects at least some of the "noncognitive faculties" and personal functioning, on the one hand, and that which connects organs and bodily functioning, on the other. One way out, however, seems closed by recent developments in psychotherapy. It is no longer open to us to say that sick criminals are those who are treatable by medical means while normal criminals are those not so treatable, for it is no longer clear just what a "medical means" is. As Lady Wootton points out: "We have thus reached the position in which an important branch of medical practice consists simply of talk, even if this is a rather special form of talk. . . . When the medical profession has enlarged its toolbox to make room for words alongside of its traditional bottles, drugs, and forceps—at this stage the definition of medical methods becomes infinitely elastic: and there is no longer any logical reason why the medical treatment of crime should not be interpreted as covering all known

consequence, there is good reason, as I shall try to show, to acknowledge mental illnesses that do not affect reasoning.

III

Let us imagine that there is a small gland whose secretions into the bloodstream help regulate emotional states. When various cells in this gland become cancerous, the character of its secretions is subtly altered, so that a person falls out of emotional equilibrium easily and tends to overreact emotionally to commonplace stimuli. At a certain stage the person is subject to powerful moods of melancholy alternating with consuming inner rages. Soon his consciousness is pervaded by these feelings, and his experience chronically colored by them. Anything done or said to him and anything he can turn his attention to in reverie make him angry. He finds himself, to his own dismay, rehearsing assaults and murders in his imagination. He is subject to paroxysms of resentment and hate. Such a person, we should all agree, is one unhappy fellow.

We should also agree, I think, that he is sick. Because one of his component parts (in this case a physical organ) is not performing its regulative function, it is impossible for the organism as a whole to "function properly." In our imaginary case, there is no other conspicuous impairment of bodily function—no fever, nausea, debility, or pain. If we classify diseases by their causes, this is a physical disease; but if we classify by the type of impairment caused, it is a mental disease, since its symptoms (on the macroscopic level) are primarily emotional. It is the victim's mental life that is disordered.

Let us change the example, so that the symptoms are the same but cannot be accounted for by any physical dysfunction. Now our victim's moods and rages are a mental illness in the strongest sense, namely, the impairment of mental function from no discoverable physical cause. Note that there need not be any cognitive impairment. The victim may still be capable of consecutive reasoning and valid inferences; he may suffer no perceptual aberrations; and although he may enjoy entertaining paranoid fantasies, he does not really believe them.

---

[7](cont.) methods of dealing with antisocial persons. . . ." *Social Science and Social Pathology* (London: Allen & Unwin, 1959), 243.

The chances are good that our unhappy fellow will sooner or later commit a crime of violence. It could come in a sudden explosion of wrath, but that is not the case that interests me. Suppose instead that he broods for days over an affront, considers measures of vengeance, and entertains fantasies in which he inflicts the sharpest agonies on his enemy. Gradually fantasy merges into plan and plan into action. Still he does not *want* to take action; he knows it is wrong and knows it would endanger himself. For many days he constrains himself; but then his angry mood flares up again, and his hateful desire regains its frightening strength. On the day of his crime he could have stopped himself yet again. There was no irresistible compulsion to commit the crime then and there; and if there had been a "policeman at his elbow," he surely would not have done it then and there. But the crime was "in the cards," and it almost certainly would have happened sooner or later.

It is difficult to know exactly what moral judgment to pass on our unhappy criminal. Given that his rational faculties were unaffected by his sick moods and desires, perhaps we should have expected him to be cognizant of his problem and to have made special compensatory efforts to cope with it. On the other hand, the very strength and unprofitable character of the desires themselves may seem to us, in a calm and reflective hour, to have been an unreasonable burden for him to carry (even though they lacked "compulsive force" at the moment of the crime), thereby entitling him to our special consideration. In any case, insofar as we think of the desires themselves as the product of an illness, rather than a natural expression of his character, we must think of him in a way different from that in which we consider other kinds of criminals. If he had not suffered the illness, he would not even have had the desire to commit the crime. In that sense, at least, his motivating desire was sick. But it is not the intrinsic character of the desire that is importantly relevant to our responses to the criminal, but rather the condition that underlies it.

Consider the man with a purely physical illness that sends him to bed with a high fever. Microorganisms have invaded his body, and its temperature has risen to create an inhospitable environment for them. In effect the patient's body has become a battlefield, and the struggle incapacitates him until the tide of battle turns and the heat goes down. The fever in this case *is* the disease, the state of organic incapacity or overall impairment. It can also be taken as a *symptom* of the particular impairments of part-function that underlie the breakdown of the whole organism. If the patient is very thirsty, his craving for water can be taken in turn as a *symptom of the fever*.

Fever is a symptom of underlying subfunctional impairment (such as infection) in a stronger sense of "symptom" than that in which a desire for water is a symptom of fever. In the stronger sense, a symptom is an *infallible indication* (a sufficient condition) of the presence of something else; in the weak sense, a symptom is a mere sign, or clue, or *ground for suspicion*. The mentally ill man's morbid desire to kill is a symptom of his illness in roughly the way the physically ill man's craving for water is a symptom of his fever. One can lust to kill without being ill, just as one can be thirsty without having a fever.[8] On the other hand, the chronically gloomy moods and inner rages are, like the fever, in themselves sickness, that is, states of being in which a person cannot function properly; and, further, they are symptoms (in the strong sense) of some underlying part-functional impairment.

If our suspicions of underlying illness, based on the occurrence of the hateful (or thirsty) desire are confirmed, then what we took to be a sign of possible illness is now seen to be an actual symptom in still a third sense. The desire is a *necessary consequence* of the pathological condition: given fever, it is necessary that there be dryness, and, given morbid inner rages of the appropriate type, it is necessary that there be murderous desires. A genuinely sick desire, then, is one which is a symptom in this strong third sense. It is the expression of a pathological condition which is not only necessary but even sufficient for its occurrence, a condition in turn which presupposes underlying part-functional impairment.

IV

Our sick criminal has committed a proscribed act and is still a dangerous person. He has this much in common with persons of many other types. But consider also the

---

[8]Thus "odd tastes," such as those of the homosexual, the pedophiliac, the bestialist, or the exhibitionist, are not *necessarily* sick desires, even though they are usually consequences of mental illness and always "grounds for suspicion." There is nothing about an odd taste as such which exonerates when it leads to crime. What tends to excuse is a sick condition which may or may not be its cause.

contrasts! There is the respectable middle-aged bank tell-
er with no previous record who, after having weighed the
risks carefully and "rationally," commits embezzlement.
His is the type we have in mind when we speak of "gain" as
a motive and talk of punishment as a "pricing system" and
of the criminal as "paying his debt" and "wiping his moral
slate clean." Then there is the fallen sinner—the good
man who succumbs to temptation and is susceptible to remorse. Punishment may lead him directly to repentance,
since he will feel it to be the proper consequence of his
fault. Indeed, it may be the only way to escape the guilt
that burdens him. His is the type that led our ancestors
to speak of prisons as penitentiaries. The risk-taker and
sinner may be one and the same person, or they may be contrasting types. In any case, for rational self-interested
men with developed consciences not quite strong enough to
constrain them, punishment may provide (1) new self-
interested motives to obey the law and (2), after the fact
of disobedience, the necessary means of repentance.

Some interested crimes, of course, are not self-
interested. Some are done to advance or retard a cause, to
help a loved one, or to hurt an enemy, often at great cost
to the criminal's own interest. Insofar as these crimes
are not self-regarding, it might seem that the usual sorts
of price tags put on them by the criminal law are vain and
pointless. But this is not so. One may wish to commit a
crime solely for another's sake, with no thought of self-
advancement, yet refrain out of fear for one's own safety.
Nevertheless, the deterrent efficacy of punishment for such
crimes as a whole is probably a good deal less than for
crimes of gain. Similarly, although it is no doubt common
enough for persons to act against their own consciences for
benevolent, malevolent, or other nonselfish reasons, still
there is probably less genuine repentance for wholly other-
regarding crimes than for crimes of gain. The dedicated
zealot, the revolutionary, the Robin Hood bandit, the man
overcome by love or pity (or hate for that matter) are not
as likely to be repentant for their crimes as the ambitious
bourgeois embezzler.

For a much larger class of criminals, repentence is a
notion with no application whatever. I refer to those psychologically normal individuals who "had the misfortune of
adjusting themselves to a weaker part of the community,"[9]

---

[9]Franz Alexander and Hugo Staub, *The Criminal, the Judge,
and the Public*, rev. edn. (New York: Collier Books, 1962),
65.

the "normal criminal with a criminal superego." Most of these are young and provincial;[10] others are at war with society; some are committed professionals. Punishment per se is not likely to bring any of these to repentance, for none has sinned against his own ideals. Some may weigh risks in deciding when and how to commit crimes, but few weigh the risks of the criminal and noncriminal lives generally. Moreover, excessive prudence may lead to loss of status in criminal subcommunities. Thus methods and tools other than the price tag and the penitentiary seem called for as a response to those in this category: persuasion, reeducation, integration into the larger community, provision of a stake in it and a new source of pride. Intimidation "reforms" only the cowardly and dispirited from this group.

Finally, there are those criminals said to suffer from a "psychopathic character disorder," who commit one petty crime after another, are convicted, imprisoned, reassigned to hospitals, released, only to begin the familiar pattern of pointless self-damaging crime again. One could lock the psychopath up for good in solitary confinement, but permanent incarceration would violate his rights; or one could subject him to briefer but equally ferocious treatment. Yet there is no way of terrorizing him. He is incapable of anxiety or any powerful passion. He experiences nothing like inner compulsion; he has no care about the future, about his own good, or about other people's feelings. He is incapable of pangs of conscience; probably because of parental deprivation in childhood,[11] he has no superego at all. This condition can be called "mental illness" with propriety,[12] but it is probably incurable in an adult. Thus the psychopath is not fit to be free, and he is not

---

[10]These individuals may be virtually unaware of the moral standards of the larger middle-class community or consciously alienated from that community. They usually adhere faithfully enough to the requirements of their own subculture: they respond with violence to affronts to their manliness, they run in packs, they demonstrate their virtues through acts of reckless bravery or great antisocial impact.

[11]See William and Joan McCord, *The Psychopath* (Princeton: Van Nostrand, 1964), 85-87.

[12]This point is argued convincingly by Hervey Cleckley in his classic *The Mask of Sanity* (St. Louis: C. V. Mosley, 1941).

fit to be tied. Perhaps incorrigibles should be consigned
permanently to "places of safety" that are neither hospitals nor prisons but are pleasant and only minimally restrictive. Such places would be no more unpleasant for the
psychopath than the outside world; they would be hellish
only for the poor attendants and supervisors.

V

Traditionally Western penal systems, no doubt under
the direct influence of Christianity, have been designed
primarily for the fallen sinner, the moral agent who has
succumbed to temptation but is at least potentially capable
of remorse. The better self in such persons, as Hegel put
it, has a right to its punishment and is honored by it.
Eventually there was superimposed on this model of *prisoner
as penitent* that of *prisoner as debtor*—a properly self-
interested individualist who has freely assumed a risk, has
lost, and now must pay the price. This superimposition of
images has never come into clear focus, but now the situation is more complicated than ever. For still other prisoners are righteous self-sacrificers; others are like prisoners of war in a war that never ends; others must be treated
as patients; and the psychopaths must simply be detained as
humanely as possible.[13]
The problem for our society is to match the generic
mode of treatment to the criminal. It is very likely that
punishment in a strict sense is not a suitable means of
dealing with many types of criminal, perhaps only the peni-
tents and risk-takers. For most of the others, it is pointless or self-defeating. What distinguishes punishment from
alternative modes of response is that it is a form of deliberately hard treatment that expresses blame and condemnation. It is a forceful and emphatic way of impressing upon
the wrongdoer the public judgment that he has done wrong
and that society resents him for it. Punishment is a hard
fate for the criminal and also a symbolic way of telling him

---

[13]Still others are insane in the sense of "totally deranged"
and do not know what they are doing; others are children—
or are like children—and must be instructed for the first
time about what is permitted in the larger community. And
the situation is still more complicated because this list
of general categories is not exhaustive; the categories are
not all mutually exclusive, and each contains a motley of
subtypes.

that he has deserved his hard fate, that he has it coming, that it serves him right. When we punish, as Samuel Butler's visitor to Erewhon put it, "we add contumely to our self-protection," and we rub it in. It is true, of course, that punishment may have extra-punitive effects: *by* punishing we may sometimes reform, deter, cure, intimidate, instruct, or detain. But *in*[14] punishing we (necessarily) condemn and inflict pain that is meant to be ignominious and shameful.[15] It would be a mistake, however, to infer (as Lady Wootton apparently does)[16] that we must choose *either* punishment *or* preventive treatment and that the choice of punishment can only be made on the grounds that blaming the blameworthy and punishing the wicked are ends in themselves. To draw such a conclusion would be to underestimate grossly the beneficial side effects of punishment for certain types of criminal. For the "fallen sinner," like Dostoevski's Raskolnikov, it may be *the* prescribed course of rehabilitative treatment. It may also be the most effective intimidation for the rational risk-taker. But for the others it is usually vain.

Sound policy would therefore seem to require a wide variety of types of institutions for treating criminals and great administrative flexibility in procedures for selecting among them. But here is the catch. Flexibility presupposes discretion and liberty to experiment. These in turn presuppose freedom from rigid statutory impediments. But such freedom is a form of power over human beings, and relatively unanswerable power at that. Whatever the defects of the traditional system that preserved the linkage between crime and punishment, it at least offered the protections of due process to the criminal from first arrest to final release. If we break that link, do we not also sever the connection between crime and responsible legal procedures? There is already some evidence of the erosion of due process in the plight of those who have been deprived

----

[14]Cf. J. L. Austin's distinction between "illocution" and "perlocution" in *How To Do Things With Words* (Cambridge: Harvard University Press, 1962), 94ff.

[15]Lady Wootton adopts this usage in her *Crime and the Criminal Law*, where she distinguishes between "punitive" and "preventive" treatment. It is a useful tautology, I think, that punishment must be punitive. See also my "The Expressive Function of Punishment," in *Doing and Deserving*, 95-118.

[16]*Ibid.*, Chs. 2, 3.

of legally effective means to avoid or eventually to end compulsory therapeutic confinement. The problem posed by justice, then, is: how can we achieve flexibility in our responses to crime without giving up the protection of individual rights long associated with our criminal law?

Common to some recent attempts to deal with the problem is the idea of what might be called a "clutch line": the criminal trial becomes a mere preliminary hearing to establish whether the state has the right to get a defendant in its clutches. If convicted, the accused is properly under the state's control. He can no longer decide his own fate, and it is up to the authorities to decide what kind of treatment, if any, to impose upon him. Defending the accused's rights through adversary proceedings is held to be an especially important matter before the clutch line is crossed. Hardly any reformers advocate suspension of the requirement that there be a criminal act before there can be criminal liability. Even zealous moralists and psychiatrists have not suggested that courts should have the power to convict people simply on the ground that they have character flaws or neurotic symptoms that make them "dangerous persons." Being a dangerous person has been a crime only in the most oppressive tyrannies. Except when they consider the vexatious question of civil commitment, most writers are still satisfied with the maxim that "every dog is entitled to his first bite." This approach creates risks—one recent dog's first bite was the assassination of a president—but most are content to pay this price for the greater benefits of due process and freedom from arbitrary interference.

Before anyone can properly fall into the state's clutches and forfeit his right to determine his future by his own choice, then, he must do something prohibited by law.[17] Lady Wootton would make this the *only* requirement for conviction, reserving inquiries into the defendant's mental states for a time after the clutch line has been crossed. Presumably, those who committed their "crimes" by accident, or mistake, or under duress, would be released at a subsequent hearing, unless it turned out that they had suspicious symptoms or dangerous tendencies (such as accident-proneness), in which case they would be "sentenced" to an appropriate measure of counseling, therapy, or punishment—whichever would be likely to be most effective.

---

[17]Or omit something required by law. I take this to be the legal requirement of *actus reus* (or *corpus delicti*).

Professor Hart[18] takes issue with this chilling proposal on the grounds that it would allow persons to fall into the state's clutches even when they had no "fair opportunity" to obey the law and that most of us would be deprived to some extent of the "chance to predict and plan and determine our own future." He concedes that we run some risk of further harm from acquitted offenders but argues that this is preferable to the loss of protection against meddling authorities. Hart does endorse, however, what he calls a modified version of Lady Wootton's proposal. He would require for conviction both a prohibited act (*actus reas*) and most of the "mental conditions" included under the term *mens rea*. He would require the prosecution to prove that the accused acted knowingly or purposely (or recklessly or negligently, as the case may be) in bringing about a certain result. If this is what is meant by *mens rea*, then Hart would make *mens rea* a material element of every crime. But he would stop there. He would not include sanity as one of the elements to be proved by the prosecution, nor would he allow insanity to be an affirmative defense. In short, he agrees with Lady Wootton that no inquiry into the defendant's *mental health* should be permitted before the clutch line is passed. "Not guilty by reason of insanity" would no longer be a possible verdict.

There seem to be at least four reasons for this proposal: (1) the difficulty of evaluating evidence about how capable a person was at some past time of conforming to the law when no external constraints are at issue; (2) the inappropriateness of the courtroom as a forum for deciding questions of medical diagnosis; (3) the great practical difficulty of formulating unconfusing instructions for juries who must be primarily concerned with guilt or innocence and for expert witnesses who prefer their own terminological categories; and (4), perhaps most important, the argument that some mentally ill persons are socially dangerous persons[19] and should not, therefore, be allowed to escape the

---

[18]H.L.A. Hart, *The Morality of the Criminal Law* (Jerusalem: Magnes Press, 1965), Lecture 1; reprinted in *Punishment and Responsibility* (Oxford: Clarendon Press, 1968), Ch. 8.

[19]Professor Norvall Morris quite properly took exception to an earlier stronger version of this statement. He pointed out to me that very likely only a small percentage of socially dangerous people are mentally ill, and that even a smaller percentage of mentally ill people are socially dangerous. The overlap between the two classes has been grossly exaggerated.

state's clutches just because they lack the "capacity for guilt," especially since they have already had their "first bite."

The main source of opposition to the proposal is probably the general obsession with blameworthiness. It is widely believed that no one should be pronounced guilty of a crime unless he deserves the odium expressed by that verdict. Mentally ill persons deserve sympathy rather than stigmatization (so the argument goes); therefore, they should not be pronounced guilty. But, in the first place, it is not even true of all sane defendants that guilt implies blameworthiness;[20] and, secondly, to Hart's proposal might be added the recommendation that the entire proceeding prior to crossing the clutch line be reconceived so that all suggestion of disgrace and censure is removed from it. Perhaps the words "guilty" and "innocent" might be expunged altogether, and defendants be found "clutchable as charged" or "unclutchable," on the model of the civil law, where they are found "liable" or "not liable" for damages and where no mention is made of guilt. Determining whether the defendant is properly clutchable, then, would require proof beyond a reasonable doubt of all the material elements of the crime. Inquiry into the question of whether he intentionally did an act which is in fact forbidden, and was not compelled or tricked into doing it, would be undertaken for the purpose of establishing not how blameworthy he is, but only whether he had a "fair opportunity" to conform his conduct to the law.

The primary weakness of Hart's proposal consists in its failure to recognize that a defendant's mental health may have some bearing on the question of *mens rea*, so that it may be impossible to exclude the former while considering the latter. The defense may well introduce evidence of cognitive derangement to cast doubt on the prosecution's proof that the defendant knew what he was doing when he committed the crime. Since the prosecution's failure to prove every element of the crime beyond a reasonable doubt results in acquittal in the sense of outright release, evidence of derangement could turn dangerous madmen loose on the community. But there is a way out for Hart. Mental illness *without cognitive impairment*, I believe, would not tend to overturn evidence of *mens rea*; only "insanity" in

---

[20] Some "guilty" persons—patriots, civil protesters, men of rocklike integrity—make the law look bad, rather than vice versa. The stigma of "criminal" looks good to them, like a badge of honor.

a strict and narrow sense (say, as determined by the Mc-
Naghten Rules) would do that. And if the defense established that degree of derangement, it would by the same
token have established the need for detainment for medical
treatment. Thus any evidence of mental disorder strong
enough to overturn guilt will be strong enough to establish
proper clutchability.[21] Hence no evidence of mental illness could be sufficient to defeat clutchability—the conclusion Hart embraces.

VI

The real problems for the Hart-Wootton proposal come
after the clutch line has been crossed. Procedures must be
devised to make possible the assignment of clutchables to
appropriately individualized modes of treatment and also
the effective protection at every stage of their right not
to be mistreated. Clutchability must involve at least temporary forfeiture of not only the right to liberty of movement but also the right to privacy. If the system is to
have any chance of working, the clutchable will be subjected to tests, interviews, and measurements. Many of the
inquiries that were banned at the first trial now become
centrally important; inquiries into his motives in committing the crime, his ulterior objectives, and his emotional
states, his cognitive capacities, his affective dispositions; his praise- or blameworthy traits of character, his
attitudes and beliefs. He should be examined by sociologists and moralists as well as psychologists, and little respect should be shown for the line between severe "character
disorder" and mental illness; for the totally depraved and

---

[21]Since the Criminal Lunatics Act of 1800, acquittal on the
ground of insanity both in England and in most American ju-
risdictions has not meant outright release, but rather commitment in a nonpenal institution. Thus the effect of the
insanity defense in our present system has not been to defeat clutchability. Joseph Goldstein and Jay Katz comment:
"Like defense of self, the defense of insanity, if successfully pleaded, results in 'acquittal.' But unlike the acquittal of self-defense which means liberty, the acquittal
of the insanity defense means deprivation of liberty for an
indefinite term in a 'mental institution'. . . . Thus the
insanity defense is not a defense, it is a device for trig-
gering indeterminate restraint." "Abolish the Insanity
Defense—Why Not," *Yale Law Journal*, 72 (1963), 858, 868.

incorrigibly vicious man of deeply rooted, lifelong bad habits of feeling and action is a not implausible nominee for mental illness himself, if we mean by illness the incapacity to "function properly" based on some failure of part-function. A vicious character, as Aristotle saw, can be very much like a fever making it difficult for its possessor to be in "proper control of himself"; and, as Bishop Butler saw, meanness and malevolence can themselves be states of pure misery.

I should think that such inquiries, if unimpeded, could yield evidence of high reliability, even in our present backward state of social scientific knowledge, that the convicted clutchable is either a clear case of one or another of the main categories of criminal—gambling consumer, fallen sinner, class enemy, mentally disturbed, or whatever —or else a marginal case, or otherwise one not easily classifiable. This evidence then would be presented at another hearing to a committee of post-clutch-line judges, perhaps composed of jurists, sociologists, psychologists, and lay jurymen in equal numbers, with the prisoner's lawyer present to challenge parts of it if he wishes, but not necessarily in accordance with the strict assignments of presumptions and burdens and other procedures characteristic of the adversary system. The prisoner himself would be interrogated by the committee; and, finally, a decision would be reached either to release him outright as no longer dangerous or to condemn him to penal servitude for a time-period with a fixed upper limit, or fine him, or parole him under supervision, or assign him to a mental hospital, or rehabilitory work camp, or some comfortable but permanent "place of safety." Wherever he goes, if the committee does its work well, he will find others of his own type; he may in the course of his career move from one kind of institution to another, but no institution will mix functions indiscriminately,[22] for the different kinds of required treatment can get in the way of one another; and what is good for one kind of clutchable may be poison for another.

But now how are we to protect the prisoner from falling permanently under the arbitrary power of some doctor or administrator who regards him as too dangerous ever to be

---

[22]The sketch here differs from the one offered by Lady Wootton, who would (in her words) "obscure the present rigid distinction between the penal and the medical institution" and send all clutchables to a kind of neutral "place of safety." *Crime and the Criminal Law*, 79.

released, whatever his own opinion of the matter may be? Obviously, we must keep as much protection of due process at every stage as is possible. Too much power over the fate of other human beings is as dangerous to the public security and to individual justice as crime itself and must everywhere be made to be responsible. If outside friends are not available to look after the prisoner's interests and press his claims, the state should have officers of its own to perform precisely this service. These officers should come from some administratively autonomous agency, like the Inspector General's Office in the Army. They should actively investigate the condition of every prisoner at regular intervals, and, like the Scandinavian ombundsman, they should be available continuously to receive complaints. Moreover, there should be elaborate procedures for *appeals* of decisions, not only court decisions but also those of assignment committees, or penal or therapeutic authorities. There should be mandatory reviews at regular intervals, and disagreements should be adjudicated by specialist, mixed-specialist, and nonspecialist juries.

The social cost of these checks and balances would no doubt be very high. The system of individuated treatment with protected rights would make us a more litigious society than ever, with hospital rooms and training camps and detainment centers turned into little courtrooms, and fates of persons decided more directly and more often by greater numbers of free citizens. This would in a sense make all of us more responsible generally for what happens to our social misfits, since all of us would have more occasion to participate in the decisionmaking that determines their fates. Constant litigation can become a burden and a bore, but that is the price we shall have to pay if we are to have effective social control and protected human liberty too.

APPENDIX ON PSYCHOSURGERY

Jeffrie G. Murphy

As in most other areas of human life, fads and fashions come and go with great rapidity on the part of those who advocate a therapeutic response to crime. Freudian psychoanalysis was superseded by the "harder" sciences of behavioral psychology and sociology; and, as this anthology goes to press, it appears that current therapeutic fascination will be found in the even "harder" science of neurophysiology. The book *Violence and the Brain*, by Vernon H. Mark and Frank R. Ervin, has recently caused a great stir with its suggestions that (a) a significant amount of criminal violence is caused by brain pathology and (b) the best way to "cure" such violence is through stereotactic brain surgery—a form of psychosurgery which, unlike the crude lobotomies of the past, electro-stimulates and/or destroys only a small number of brain cells and thus (so it is claimed) leaves normal human functioning intact.

Though the trappings are different (e.g., the talk is now of brain dysfunction rather than mental illness), this new fashion raises all the same kinds of issues that the reader has already encountered in coming to terms with the more traditional forms of the therapeutic approach: (1) Is there good evidence, produced through carefully controlled experiments and follow-up studies, that a significant amount of criminal violence is the result of brain dysfunction and that surgery does in fact eliminate the violence and leave normal functioning intact? (2) Is the concept of brain dysfunction a value-neutral medical concept or is it, as Thomas Szasz claimed was the case with the concept of mental illness, evaluatively defined for certain moral or political purposes—e.g., is a person being diagnosed as suffering from brain disease *solely* because he engages in disapproved acts of violence or is there a test for brain disease that is violence-independent? (Significantly and strangely, Mark and Ervin claim (a) that impulsively violent behavior is often caused by temporal lobe epilepsy and (b) that stereotactic surgery eliminates the violence but *not the epilepsy*!) (3) Even if it is agreed that the surgery works and that it leaves other functions intact, are

we going to require due process of law (a traditional criminal conviction) before administering the surgery to a person or will we employ "preventive" surgery?   (4) Even if we
limit the surgery to those convicted of criminal offenses,
will their informed consent be required or will the surgery
be involuntary?   (5) Who will ultimately hold the political
and legal power to make the important decisions affecting
liberty—psychiatrists and neurosurgeons?

Suggestions for further readings on psychosurgery,
both pro and con, are cited in the following bibliography.
Its best known advocates are Mark and Ervin; its best known
opponent is psychiatrist Peter Breggin, a man who will no
doubt come to be known as the Thomas Szasz of psychosurgery.

Bibliography

Legal Background

For an excellent collection of legal cases and materials on punishment and the rehabilitative ideal, the reader is advised to consult pages 63 to 200 of the casebook *Criminal Law and Its Processes, Cases and Materials,* Second Edition, compiled by Sanford H. Kadish and Monrad G. Paulsen (Boston: Little, Brown, 1969).

Books and Articles

The following bibliography makes no pretense of being complete. It contains only suggestions for further readings in English that are likely to be available in almost any university library. For a more detailed listing, consult the bibliography at the end of the Acton collection listed below.

Acton, H. B., ed. *The Philosophy of Punishment.* London: Macmillan, 1969. This collection contains most of the important articles on punishment that have appeared in the leading Anglo-American philosophical journals in recent years. It has an excellent introduction and an extensive bibliography.

Beccaria, C. B. *On Crimes and Punishments,* 1764. Indianapolis: Bobbs-Merrill, 1963.

Bonger, Willem. *Criminality and Economic Conditions.* Boston: Little, Brown, 1916.

Bonsanquet, Bernard. *The Philosophical Theory of the State.* London: Macmillan, 1923.

Bradley, F. H. *Collected Essays,* Volume I. Oxford: Oxford University Press, 1935.

Breggin, Peter. "The Return of Lobotomy and Psychosurgery," *Congressional Record*, February 24 and March 30, 1972.

Brett, Peter. *An Inquiry into Criminal Guilt.* Sydney: Law Book Company of Australia, 1963.

Chambliss, William J. "Types of Deviance and the Effectiveness of Legal Sanctions," *Wisconsin Law Review*, 1967.

Ewing, A. C. *The Morality of Punishment.* London: Kegan Paul, 1929.

Ezorsky, Gertrude. *Philosophical Perspectives on Punishment.* Albany: State University of New York Press.

Fingarette, Herbert. *The Meaning of Criminal Insanity.* Berkeley: University of California Press, 1972.

Fitzgerald, P. J. *Criminal Law and Punishment.* Oxford: The Clarendon Press, 1962.

Flugel, J. C. *Man, Morals and Society.* New York: International Universities Press, 1945.

Friends Service Committee. *Struggle for Justice.* New York: Hill and Wang, 1971.

Glover, Jonathan. *Responsibility.* New York: Humanities Press, 1970.

Goffman, Erving. *Asylums.* New York: Doubleday, 1961.

Goldstein, Abraham S. *The Insanity Defense.* New Haven, Conn.: Yale University Press, 1967.

Green, T. H. *Lectures on the Principles of Political Obligation*, 1882. Ann Arbor: University of Michigan Press, 1967.

Guttmacher, Manfred S., and Weihofen, Henry. *Psychiatry and the Law.* New York: Norton, 1952.

Haksar, Vinit. "The Responsibility of Psychopaths," *Philosophical Quarterly*, 1965.

Hall, Jerome. *General Principles of the Criminal Law.* Indianapolis: Bobbs-Merrill, 1947.

Halleck, Seymour L. *Psychiatry and the Dilemmas of Crime.* New York: Harper and Row, 1967.

_____. *The Politics of Therapy.* New York: Science House, 1971.

Hart, Harold H., ed. *Punishment: For and Against.* New York: Hart Publishing Company, 1971.

Hart, H.L.A. *Punishment and Responsibility: Essays in the Philosophy of Law.* Oxford: Oxford University Press, 1968. These essays, by the most influential legal philosopher of the twentieth century, would be a good starting place for the student who wishes to read further on the topic of punishment.

Hearings Before the Senate Subcommittee on Constitutional Rights of the Mentally Ill (the "Ervin Committee") 1961, 1963, 1969, and 1970. Washington: U.S. Government Printing Office.

Hegel, G.W.F. *The Philosophy of Right, 1821.* Oxford: Oxford University Press, 1942.

Hollingshead, A. B., and F. C. Redlick. *Social Class and Mental Illness.* New York: Wiley, 1958.

Honderich, Ted. *Punishment: The Supposed Justifications.* New York: Harcourt, Brace and World, 1969.

Ingraham, Barton L. and Gerald W. Smith. "The Use of Electronics in the Observation and Control of Human Behavior and Its Possible Use in Rehabilitation and Parole," *Issues in Criminology*, Vol. 7, No. 2, Fall, 1972, pp. 35-53 and 95-100.

Katz, Jay, *et al.*, eds. *Psychoanalysis, Psychiatry and the Law.* New York: Free Press, 1967.

Kittrie, Nicholas N. *The Right to Be Different: Deviance and Enforced Therapy.* Baltimore: Johns Hopkins Press, 1971.

Livermore, Joseph M., Carl P. Malmquist, and Paul E. Meehl. "On the Justifications for Civil Commitment," *University of Pennsylvania Law Review*, Vol. 117, 1968, p. 75.

Livermore, Joseph M. and Paul Meehl. "The Virtues of M'Naghten," *Minnesota Law Review*, Vol. 51, 1967, p. 789.

Lucas, J. R. "Or Else," *Proceedings of the Aristotelian Society*, 1968-69.

Mark, Vernon H., and Frank R. Ervin. *Violence and the Brain.* New York: Harper, 1970.

Mechanic, David. *Mental Health and Social Policy.* Englewood Cliffs, N.J.: Prentice-Hall, 1969.

Moberly, Walter. *The Ethics of Punishment.* Hamden, Conn.: Shoe String Press, 1968.

Morris, Herbert. Review of Thomas Szasz's work. *U.C.L.A. Law Review*, Vol. 18, No. 6, June, 1971, pp. 1164-1172.

Morris, Norval, and Gordon Hawkins. *The Honest Politician's Guide to Crime Control.* Chicago: University of Chicago Press, 1969.

Murphy, Jeffrie G. "Three Mistakes about Retributivism," *Analysis*, April, 1971.

_____. "Involuntary Acts and Criminal Liability," *Ethics*, July, 1971.

_____. "Moral Death: A Kantian Essay on Psychopathy," *Ethics*, July, 1972.

_____. "Kant's Theory of Criminal Punishment," *Proceedings of the Third International Kant Congress*, ed. Lewis W. Beck. Dordrecht: D. Reidel, 1972.

_____. "Marxism and Retribution," *Philosophy and Public Affairs*, Spring, 1973.

Scheff, Thomas J. *Being Mentally Ill: A Sociological Theory*. Chicago: Aldine, 1969.

Schur, Edwin M. *Our Criminal Society: The Social and Legal Sources of Crime in America*. Englewood Cliffs, N.J.: Prentice-Hall, 1969.

Shapiro, Michael H. "The Uses of Behavior Control Technologies," *Issues in Criminology*, Vol. 7, No. 2, Fall, 1972, pp. 55-93.

Strawson, P. F. "Freedom and Resentment," *Proceedings of the British Academy*, 1962.

Szasz, Thomas S. *Psychiatric Justice*. New York: Macmillan, 1965.

Tarde, Gabriel de. *Penal Philosophy*. Boston: Little, Brown, 1912.

Wasserstrom, Richard. "Strict Liability in the Criminal Law," *Stanford Law Review*, 1960.

_____. *Morality and the Law*. Belmont, Calif.: Wadsworth, 1971.

Wayne Law Review, March, 1973, Vol. 19, No. 3. Entire issue devoted to the issue "Dismantling the Criminal Law System: Decriminalization and Divestment."

Wexler, David B. Review of Mark and Ervin, *Violence and the Brain*. *Harvard Law Review*, Vol. 85, No. 7, May, 1972, pp. 1489-1498.

_____. "Therapeutic Justice," *Minnesota Law Review*, Vol. 57, No. 2, December, 1972, pp. 289-338.

_____. "Token and Taboo: Behavior Modification, Token Economies, and the Law," *California Law Review*, Vol. 61, No. 1, January, 1973, pp. 81-109.

Wexler, David B., and Scoville, Stanley E., eds. "The Administration of Psychiatric Justice: Theory and Practice in Arizona," special issue of the *Arizona Law Review*, Vol. 13, No. 1, 1971.

Winch, Peter. "Ethical Reward and Punishment," in *Ethics and Action*. London: Routledge and Kegan Paul, 1972.

Zimring, Franklin E. and Gordon J. Hawkins. *Deterrence*. Chicago: University of Chicago Press, 1972.

Basic Problems in Philosophy Series

A. I. Melden and Stanley Munsat
University of California, Irvine
General Editors

The Problem of Abortion
Joel Feinberg

Introduction   An Almost Absolute Value in History, *John T. Noonan, Jr.*   Abortion Decisions: Personal Morality, *Daniel Callahan*   Abortion and the Argument from Innocence, *Marvin Kohl*   Understanding the Abortion Argument, *Roger Wertheimer*   A Defense of Abortion and Infanticide, *Michael Tooley*   Abortion, Infanticide, and Respect for Persons, *S. I. Benn*   Abortion and the Sanctity of Human Life, *Baruch A. Brody*   A Defense of Abortion, *Judith Jarvis Thomson*   Abortion and the Law, *Baruch A. Brody*   Abortion Laws, *Daniel Callahan*   Williams v. State of New York   A Cause for "Wrongful Life": A Suggested Analysis, *Minnesota Law Review*   The 1973 Supreme Court Decisions on State Abortion Laws: Excerpts from Opinion in *Roe* v. *Wade*   Abortion: The New Ruling, *Hastings Center Report*   Bibliography

Ethical Relativism
John Ladd

Introduction   Custom Is King, *Herodotus*   Ethics and Law: Eternal Truths, *Friedrich Engels*   Folkways, *William Graham Sumner*   The Meaning of Right, *W. D. Ross*   Ethical Relativity? *Karl Duncker*   Cultural Relativism and Cultural Values, *Melville J. Herskovits*   Ethical Relativity: Sic et Non, *Clyde Kluckhohn*   Social Science and Ethical Relativism, *Paul W. Taylor*   The Issue of Relativism, *John Ladd*   The Universally Human and the Culturally Variable, *Robert Redfield*   Bibliography

Human Rights
A. I. Melden

Introduction   The Second Treatise of Civil Government, Chapters 2 and 5, *John Locke*   Anarchical Fallacies, *Jeremy Bentham*   Natural Rights, *Margaret MacDonald*   Are There Any Natural Rights?, *H.L.A. Hart*   Justice and Equality, *Gregory Vlastos*   Rights, Human Rights, and Racial Discrimination, *Richard Wasserstrom*   Persons and Punishment, *Herbert Morris*   Appendices   Bibliography

Egoism and Altruism
Ronald D. Milo

Introduction   Self-Love and Society, *Thomas Hobbes*   Upon the Love of Our Neighbor, *Joseph Butler*   Morality, Self-Love, and Benevolence, *David Hume*   Morality and the Duty of Love toward Other Men, *Immanuel Kant*   Hedonism and Egoism, *Moritz Schlick*   Egoism as a Theory of Human Motives, *C. D. Broad*   An Empirical Basis for Psychological Egoism, *Michael A. Slote*   Altruistic Behavior, *Justin Aronfreed*   The Possibility of Altruism, *Thomas Nagel*   Bibliography

Guilt and Shame
Herbert Morris

Introduction   Stavrogin's Confession, *Fyodor Dostoyevsky*   Differentiation of German Guilt, *Karl Jaspers*   Origin of the Sense of Guilt, *Sigmund Freud*   Guilt and Guilt Feelings, *Martin Buber*   Real Guilt and Neurotic Guilt, *Herbert Fingarette*   "Guilt," "Bad Conscience," and the Like, *Friedrich Neitzsche*   The Sense of Justice, *John Rawls*   Shame, *Gerhart Piers* and *Milton B. Singer*   Autonomy v. Shame and Doubt, *Erik H. Erikson*   The Nature of Shame, *Helen Merrell Lynd*   Bibliography

The Analytic-Synthetic Distinction
Stanley Munsat

Introduction   First Truths, *Gottfried Wilhelm von Leibniz*   Necessary and Contingent Truths, *Gottfried Wilhelm von Leibniz*   Of Proposition, *Thomas Hobbes*   Introduction to the Critique of Pure Reason, *Immanuel Kant*   Kant, *Arthur Papp*   Of Demonstration, and Necessary Truths, *John Stuart Mill*   Views of Some Writers on the Nature of Arithmetical

Propositions, *Gottlob Frege* What Is an Empirical Science?
Bertrand Russell Two Dogmas of Empiricism, *Willard Van Or-
man Quine* The Meaning of a Word, *John Austin* In Defense
of a Dogma, *H. P. Grice* and *P. F. Strawson* Bibliography

Civil Disobedience and Violence
Jeffrie G. Murphy

Introduction On Disobeying the Law, *Socrates* On the Duty
of Civil Disobedience, *Henry David Thoreau* Legal Obliga-
tion and the Duty of Fair Play, *John Rawls* Social Protest
and Civil Obedience, *Sydney Hook* The Vietnam War and the
Right of Resistance, *Jeffrie G. Murphy* Civil Disobedience:
Prerequisite for Democracy in Mass Society, *Christian Bay*
Non-violence, *Mohandas K. Gandhi* A Fallacy on Law and
Order: That Civil Disobedience Must Be Absolutely Nonvio-
lent, *Howard Zinn* On Not Prosecuting Civil Disobedience,
Ronald Dworkin Law and Authority, *Peter Kropotkin*
Bibliography

Punishment and Rehabilitation
Jeffrie G. Murphy

Introduction People v. Levy, *California District Court of
Appeals* Punishment, *Stanley I. Benn* The Right to Punish,
Immanuel Kant Persons and Punishment, *Herbert Morris*
Punishment and Utility, *Jeremy Bentham* Punishment as a
Practice, *John Rawls* Capital Punishment, *Karl Marx* Two
Models of the Criminal Process, *Herbert L. Packer* Crimi-
nal Psychodynamics: A Platform, *Benjamin Karpman* Therapy,
Not Punishment, *Karl Menninger* Punishment, *B. F. Skinner*
A Preventive System of Criminal Law, *Barbara Wootton* Crim-
inal Justice, Legal Values, and the Rehabilitative Ideal,
Francis A. Allen The Myth of Mental Illness, *Thomas S.
Szasz* Criminal Punishment and Psychiatric Fallacies, *Jef-
frie G. Murphy* Preventive Detention and Psychiatry,
Jeffrie G. Murphy Crime, Clutchability, and Individuated
Treatment, *Joel Feinberg* Appendix on Psychosurgery, *Jef-
frie G. Murphy* Bibliography

Immortality
Terence Penelhum

Introduction Immortality, *Peter Geach* Survival and the
Idea of "Another World," *H. H. Price* The Resurrection of

Christ and the Resurrection of Men, *St. Paul*   Immortality
of the Soul or Resurrection of the Dead?, *Oscar Cullmann*
from "Theology and Falsification," *John Hick*   The Resurrection: Objections and Answers, *St. Thomas Aquinas*   The
Problem of Life After Death, *H. H. Price*   The Question of
Survival, *Antony Flew*   Towards a Christian Theology of
Death, *John Hick*   Bibliography

Morality and the Law
Richard A. Wasserstrom

Introduction   On Liberty, *John Stuart Mill*   Morals and
the Criminal Law, *Lord Patrick Devlin*   Immorality and
Treason, *H.L.A. Hart*   Lord Devlin and the Enforcement of
Morals, *Ronald Dworkin*   Sins and Crimes, *A. R. Louch*
Morals Offenses and the Model Penal Code, *Louis B. Schwartz*
Paternalism, *Gerald Dworkin*   Four cases involving the en-
forcement of morality   Bibliography

War and Morality
Richard A. Wasserstrom

Introduction   The Moral Equivalent of War, *William James*
The Morality of Obliteration Bombing, *John C. Ford, S.J.*
War and Murder, *Elizabeth Anscombe*   Moral Judgment in Time
of War, *Michael Walzer*   Pacifism: A Philosophical Analysis,
Jan Narveson   On the Morality of War: A Preliminary In-
quiry, *Richard Wasserstrom*   Judgment and Opinion, The In-
ternational Tribunal, Nuremberg, Germany   Superior Orders,
Nuclear Warfare, and the Dictates of Conscience, *Guenter
Lewy*   Selected Bibliography